Rev. EDWIN WARRINER.

THE
WARRINER FAMILY
of
NEW ENGLAND ORIGIN

BEING A HISTORY AND GENEALOGY OF

William Warriner

PIONEER SETTLER OF SPRINGFIELD, MASS., AND
HIS DESCENDANTS EMBRACING
NINE GENERATIONS
FROM
1638 TO 1898

WITH AN APPENDIX CONTAINING GENEALOGICAL NOTES OF
OTHER PERSONS AND FAMILIES IN AMERICA
BEARING THE SAME NAME

BY

Rev. Edwin Warriner

Author of "Old Sands Street Church."

———

"Those only deserve to be remembered by posterity
Who treasure up the history of their ancestors."
—**Burke.**

HERITAGE BOOKS
2011

HERITAGE BOOKS

AN IMPRINT OF HERITAGE BOOKS, INC.

Books, CDs, and more—Worldwide

For our listing of thousands of titles see our website
at
www.HeritageBooks.com

A Facsimile Reprint
Published 2011 by
HERITAGE BOOKS, INC.
Publishing Division
100 Railroad Ave. #104
Westminster, Maryland 21157

Originally published:
Albany, New York
Joel Munsell's Sons, Publishers
1899

International Standard Book Numbers
Paperbound: 978-0-7884-1794-8
Clothbound: 978-0-7884-8630-2

PREFACE.

Veneration for ancestors ranks high among virtues in all ages and climes. The Penates or household gods which were cherished and transmitted from generation to generation by the ancient Romans, served a good purpose, as they called to mind the names and deeds of honored forefathers. With great reverence those images were handled and looked upon by the children, and while the fathers and mothers rehearsed the story of the noble lives of the heroic dead, the hearts of the youthful listeners swelled with virtuous and valorous resolves.

The simple fact that one has had a line of ancestors, or that he can repeat their names or tell their nationality, is not worth investigating or mentioning. From curiosity, or fashion, or a desire to join some order dependent on one's lineage, the work of ancestry hunting is sometimes overdone. Not long since a witless fellow was so very successful in his ancestral researches that, according to his own account, he traced his pedigree in America to the year 1359!

Some one has said: "The question is not how far we may trace the line of our ancestors, or whether they were Dutch-men, or Puritans, or Huguenots, or Cavaliers; but were they honest, brave and true? did they work or steal? were they settlers or fighting men? and when these questions begin to be answered we shall all be in favor of confining our researches to a limited number of generations.

Some of the foregoing questions, if applied to *our* ancestors find answer in this book:

The descendants of William Warriner have furnished soldiers for all the American wars, from the Colonial times to the present, and have been well represented among the pastors of several denominations, Congregational, Presbyterian, Episcopal, Baptist and Methodist. Thus the satisfaction which the author of this book has found and hopes to share with those who will read the results of his researches, springs chiefly from the sturdy, stalwart character of the New England sires, contributing high incentives to those who follow in their steps.

In the midst of his labor in preparing this work he has been conscious of a desire to perform a real service which not one in ten thousand would care to undertake. The thought that he might be remembered as a benefactor by the Warriners of future generations has ofttimes prevented his giving up in complete discouragement. Some of the difficulties have arisen from a surprising want of knowledge on the part of those from whom information was sought; and still more disheartening has been the strange indifference which a few have shown, even amounting to persistent failures to reply to letters asking for facts which they alone could supply.

But the helps have been far more than the hindrances. The great majority of the many hundred letters written have received prompt and helpful replies. Officers and clerks in charge of valuable records have shown uniform courtesy and kindness. A few relatives have contributed to the expense of traveling, etc., which the extended researches of the author have incurred. The following are some of the authorities which have been consulted with thoroughness, and from which many facts have been obtained:

Town Records of Springfield, Mass.
Town Records of Wilbraham, Mass.
Town Records of Enfield, Conn.
Town Records of Monson, Mass.
Town Records of West Springfield, Mass.
Town Records of Hadley, Mass.
Town Records of Brimfield, Mass.
Town Records of Vershire, Vt.
Old Colony Records.
New England Historical and Genealogical Regi ter, 44 volumes.
Savage's Genealogical Dictionary.
Durrie's Index.
Temple's History of Northfield.
Stiles' Ancient Windsor.
Register of Canterbury Cathedral.
Register of St. Dionis, Back Church, London.
Register of St. George's, Hanover Sq., County of Middlesex.
Register of St. James', Clerkenwell.
Register of Parish of Kensington, County Middlesex.
Visitations of London.
Visitations of Yorkshire (manuscript in British Museum).
Stebbins' Wilbraham Centennial.

Great pains have been taken to secure accuracy, but it would be quite impossible to avoid all errors in collecting such a multiplicity of dates and proper names from such a variety of sources; hence, in that respect especially, the author craves the kind indulgence of his friends.

Attention is called to the unlooked for success achieved in

the matter of illustrations. They certainly add much to the value of the book.

Now let all who belong to "the Warriner family of New England origin" take note that they need be strangers no more. With this volume in hand any one of them may trace his lineage to William Warriner, of Springfield, and determine in a very few minutes the nearness or remoteness of his kinship to any other member of the Warriner family.

The supreme good that such books may accomplish is the turning of our thoughts from the past to the future, and our learning the value of living for the welfare of those who are coming after us. In a short time our names will be written among the ancestors, and the harvests from our seed-sowing will be gathered by the generations yet unborn.

E. W.

STEPNEY, CONN., *June 15, 1898.*

Genealogy of the Warriner Family.

The original ancestor of the New England Warriners joined the settlers of Springfield, Mass., in 1638. His birthplace and ancestry are unknown. That England was the land of his nativity is probable beyond all doubt. He seems to have been one of the earliest of that name of whom history or tradition gives us any account. Tradition says that William Warriner, about the year 1600, eloped from Lincolnshire, England, with Lady Clifford (?), daughter of Lord Howe, or Howard, an English admiral, and made his escape — with other members of the family, who naturally would want to get out of the way of the offended and insulted nobleman — into Yorkshire. While crossing a river one or two of the Warriners were drowned. William and another were saved, also the lady. And the tradition further states that William settled in Yorkshire.

The English parish records of that period mention several Warriners, one of whom in particular bears the name William. The parish records, copied in the foot-note, establish a strong probability that the William Warriner mentioned many times in the Canterbury Cathedral register, who had children christened in that church from 1601 to 1614, who buried several children in the Canterbury churchyard, whose wife, Alice, was buried there in 1619, and of whom all records in the books of Canterbury Cathedral cease at that time, is the same William Warriner who eloped from Lincolnshire about 1600 with Lady (Alice) Clifford (?), and that he is the identical William Warriner who appeared among the pioneers of Springfield, Mass., in 1638. If this be the case, he was probably a widower, at least fifty-seven years of age when he married Joanna Scant in 1639, and about ninety- four when he died in 1676. And this is altogether credible, for some of his descendants have lived beyond that age.* There is here no discrepancy as to

---

* The following items are copied from ancient registers:
I. REGISTER OF CANTERBURY CATHEDRAL, 1564-1878.
(1) *Christenings.* — " 1601 June 5, Afra the daughter of William Warriner." " 1607 June 21, Elizabeth the daughter of William Warriner." " 1611 April 7 Roger, the sonne of William Warriner." " 1612 May 12, the sonne of William Warriner."

[One would naturally presume this to be the William Warriner who went to Springfield in 1638, since he would have been about twenty-six years of age at the time, but below are records of Canterbury which state that " William Warriner, son of William was buried in 1615," establishing clearly the fact that this child William died at three years of age.]

" 1614 July 19 Margaret the daughter of William Warriner." " 1615 July 30 Mary Warriner, daughter of Mr. Mathew Warriner, pety canon." " 1619 Oct. 21 John Warriner the sonne of Mr. Warriner." " 1617, July 27, Richard the sonne of Mr. Warriner." " 1643 July 9 Mathew the son'e of Richard Warriner and Sarah his wife."

(2) *Burials.* — " 1611 Apr. 10 Roger ye sonne of William Warrener." " 1615. Jan. 17 Margaritt, the daughter of William Warrener." " 1615 December 26 William Warriner the son of William Warriner." " 1610 Jan. 19 Alce Warriner ye wife of Mr. Warriner." " 1636 November 18, Marye Warrener, daughter of Mathew Warrener Petti cannon of this Church." [Next record]. " 1632 March 1. Recd of Do: Kingsley Archdeacon of Cant. Six shillings & Eight pence to be distributed to ye poore with in ye precincte of this Church wch he is to pay for a license to eate flesh granted to him and others by ye Archbishop of Cant. his Di ma til."

MAT. WARRINER, Sacrist.

dates. The principal objection that might be named to identifying the William Warriner of the Cathedral record with our William Warriner of New England, is the long distance of

"1643 January 10 Margaret ye wife of Mr. Mathew Warriner." "1643 February 14 Mr. Warriner." "1643 November 29 Mathew ye sonne of Richard Warriner."

II. REGISTER OF ST. DIONIS, BACK CHURCH, LONDON, — beginning 1538.

Burial. — "1698 abortive female of James Warrener's in South church yard."

III. REGISTER OF ST. GEORGE'S, HANOVER SQUARE, IN COUNTY OF MIDDLESEX.

Marriages. — "1751 Robert King and Susannah Warrenner." "1761 Feb. 4, Richard Wright B. and Catharine Warriner S." "1780 George Warriner and Elizabeth Grubb."

IV. REGISTER OF ST. JAMES', CLERKENWELL, 1551-1754.

(1) *Christenings.* — "1640 Oct. 11, William s. of Anthony Warrier & Elizab. his wife." "1642 July 3 Frances dau. of Anthonye Warrier & Eliz. vx." "1644 Apr. 14, Anthonye s. of Antho Warriner and Elizabeth vx." "1646, Oct. 18, Ann d. of Anthony Warrier & Elizabeth vx." "1649 April 8, Wm. s. of Antho Warriner and Eliz. vx." "1651 Jan. 11 Rachelle d. of Antho Warrier and Ellen." "1653 April 17 Judith d. of Antho Warriner." "1668 Dec. 6 Elizsabeth d. of Richard Waryner." "1690 Dec. 21, John son of Robert & Sarah Warrier." "1693 Sept. 3, James s. of Robert Warrier & Sarah his wife." "1696 Oct. 25 Robert s. of Robt Warrener & Sarah his wife born 11." "1679 Nov. 4, Sarah d. of Robt Warriner & Sarah his wife."

(2) *Marriage.* — "1665 May 21, John Wellum & Ann Warriner."

(3) *Burials.* — "1642, Aug. 18, Willm s. of Anthony Warriner." "1645 Jan. 9 ffreeman son of William Warr'ner." "1652 May 28, Rachell d. of Anto Warriner." "1690 Nov. 27, Elizabeth Warriner pentioner." "1700 Sep. 6 Sarah Warriner, wid."

V. PARISH REGISTER OF KENSINGTON. COUNTY MIDDLE-

Canterbury Cathedral in the county of Kent from Yorkshire, the traditional home of William Warriner. But this fact presents no difficulty if we locate his home in both places at different periods. The Cathedral records show that for about twenty years there were two Warriners, presumably brothers, William and Matthew, living in or near Canterbury; and William is conspicuous by his absence after 1619, while Matthew

---

SEX. *Christening.* — " 1620 Mar. 25, John the bastard son of John Bannister & of Anne Warrenner of Shure lane London."
VI. VISITATION OF LONDON, 1552-1610.
Marriage Licenses. — " 1572 Oct. 8, John Warryner and Alice Turner, spinster of Hackney: Gen. lic." " 1598 May 16, William Courti *alias* Smythe of St. Botolph, Aldergate, gent, about 27, a clerk in Sir William Spencer's office and Elizabeth Warriner of St. Botolph, Bishopgate, her parents dead 8 years: consent of her uncle and Guardian Thomas Crompton Esq. attested by his servant Clement Daubney, Gent. [In Vicar-General's Book she is called dau. of [blank] Warrener, late of Kendal, Co. Westmoreland, Gent. deed, to marry at St. Bodolph, Bishopsgate]." " 1607 Feb. 4, Moses Shoucke of St. Dunstan in the West London, Gent., and Margaret Warriner, of St. Andrew's, Holborne, widow of Thomas Warriner, late of same, coach maker, at St. Bennett, Paul Wharf, London." " 1625, April 11, Solomon Stroude, Baker and Catharine Warriner of St. Sepulchere's London, Spinster, dau. of Richard Warriner, Butcher, at St. Ethelburgh, London."
In addition to these the following items have been obtained:
Wm. Paver's MSS. in British Museum, Vol. III, p. 108. WATERHOUSE pedigree. Penelope dau. of Thos. Waterhouse mar. ——— Warriner.
Paver's Consolidated Visitation of Yorkshire, Vol. II, p. 17. GREENWOOD pedigree. Robert Greenwood of Wrenthorpe m. Anne dau. of ——— Warriner of Wakefield (between 1600-1610 I should say).
WATERHOUSE pedigree. Penelope dau. of Thomas Waterhouse of Halifax (living 1585) married Thomas Warriner. — Foster's Visitation of Yorkshire, p. 353.

remains until his death in 1643. The most natural supposition is that, after his wife's death, William Warriner left the county of Kent, and, after residing nearly a score of years in Yorkshire, emigrated to New England in 1638.

If there were any records or traditions concerning the religious tenets or church connections of William Warriner while he resided in Springfield, it would be easier to determine his identity and his antecedents. On the theory that he was the William Warriner of Canterbury Cathedral record, the baptism of his children may have been chiefly out of deference to his wife's attachment to the Church of England, or he may have been a strong churchman at that time and a dissenter afterwards. He had no prominence in church affairs in Springfield.

Several persons have alluded to traditions of the Welsh origin of the name and family, but in this connection no authority seems to have been found for anything definite as to localities or dates.*

The foregoing observations are not claimed to be conclusive. Until further facts are brought to light it will be impossible to positively know the antecedents of William Warriner. The name seems to have been spelled Warrener and Warriner interchangeably from the first. The word " Warrener " means the owner of a warren — a warren being a rabbit park, and sometimes a hunting reserve of large extent. It is said to have been applied by way of distinction, sometimes, to the owner of such lands. The first Warrener, therefore, may have been a person of privilege; that is, one who was entitled to convert his lands into a game preserve, and given the exclusive privilege of hunting on them.

There is little in the history of the British people to distinguish the family name. One man, at least (of the name of

---

* Rev. E. A. Warriner heard his father say that the name was originally spelled Warrinné, and was first applied to some person or persons in Wales. Some one with time and taste for the necessary research may yet reconcile what seems unreconcilable to us.

Warrener was celebrated as a warrior among the cavaliers. In a poetic volume written about 1600, called " Songs of the Cavaliers and Roundheads," is a poem entitled ' Wigan's Retreat," the first stanza of which is:

> " Hurrah! for the trumpeter blowing his best,
> Blood on his feather and blood on his crest;
> Here was old Warrener, trusty as steel,
> Fitting a crimson spur fast to his heel."

The career of Rev. William Warrener, of England, has made the name honorable in the annals of the church. He was received by John Wesley as a traveling preacher in 1779. After laboring in Great Britain for some years he went as missionary to the West Indies. Warrener, Hammet and Clark, in company with Dr. Coke, embarked September 24, 1786, for Nova Scotia to reinforce the Methodist missionaries there. They were a month in reaching the mid seas. There on the 24th of October, their ship sprang aleak. Three days later a most terrific storm arose, which continued until the middle of December, dismantled the ship and drove her with bare spars and in a sinking condition to a grateful though unexpected haven, in Antigua, on the Feast of the Nativity, a day of good omen to those islands of the west. There William Warrener remained and spent eleven years zealously and successfully ministering the Gospel to the negro slaves, be ng the first of the English preachers regularly appointed to that work. In 1779 he returned to England, and continued as a regular itinerant till 1818. After that, for a few years, he was a supernumerary supply. He died at his home in Leeds, November 27, 1825, in the 75th year of his age, " triumphing gloriously in death."*

---

* Condensed from Ethridge's Life of Coke and Minutes of Conferences, Vol. VI, p. 108. His travels are more definitely traced in the following record of appointments: 1779, Gainsboro circuit; 1780, Gainsboro cir., with George Shadford and others; 1781, Gainsboro cir. again; 1782, Aberdeen cir.; 1783, Dundee cir.; 1784, Berwick cir.; 1785, Brecon cir.; 1786,

William Warriner, the New England ancestor, was made a
freeman, or voter, in 1638. Under the first charter of the
Massachusetts Colony none were regarded as freemen, or
members of the body politic, except such as were admitted by
the General Court and took the oath of allegiance to the government here established. This custom continued in existence
until by the second charter the colony was transferred into a
province.*

We learn from the Springfield records that Wi liam Warriner was married to Joanna Scant in 1639.† The town clerk
made the following record of her death: "Johanna, wife of
Wm. Warriner, dyed ye 7th of ye 12th mon. 1660." On October 2, 1661, he married Elizabeth, widow of Luke Hitchcock,
of Wethersfield, Conn.‡ She was the mother of Hannah,
John and Luke Hitchcock. She survived Mr. Warriner and
became the third wife of Joseph Baldwin, of Hadley.§

This Warriner seems to have been, previous to his marriage
in 1639, the only person of the name residing in New England.

Angina, with J. Baxter; 1787, ditto, with J. Clark; 1788, ditto,
with J. Harper; 1789, not found; 1790, Antigua, with J.
Harper; 1791, St. Christopher's; 1792, ditto, with Richard Pat-
tison; 1793, ditto, with John Baxter; 1794, 1795, ditto, with
John Baxter and others; 1796-1798,   ; 1799,
1800, Buddington, York Dist.; 1801, 1802, Sunderland cir.,
Grimsby Dist.; 1803, Alnwick and Berwick cir.; 1804, Stock-
ton cir.; 1805, Darlington cir.; 1806, Malton cir., York Dist.

His wife is mentioned in the Minutes for several years after
1800, also his daughter, Ann, who was allowed eight pounds
eight shillings from the fund for the education of preachers'
daughters in Kingswood school.

* The freeman's oath may be seen in New England Histori-
can and Genealogical Register, Vol. II, p. 89.

† Boldwood reads the name Searl, and thinks she was the
daughter of John Searl. I have looked at the original record
carefully. The name is quite plainly written "Scant." — E. W.

‡ The town records show that they were married in Hadley.

§ Mr. Baldwin died Nov. 2, 1684, and she died Apr. 25, 1696.

One Ralph Warriner, who is once mentioned in the Old Colony Records, may have been brother to William. He seems to have been a transient person and not an inhabitant. At any rate no record in New England seems to contain any further mention of him.* There was a Ralph Warriner, whose name appeared in the records of Virginia about that time.†

In violation of a law made in 1640, William Warriner sold his canoe to some party outside the "plantation," and was fined therefor.‡ In 1642 a second division of the plantation was made, and "Will: Warriner," as one of the "maryed psons," had "10 rod bredth." Those having the "biggest familys" had "12 rod to begin upward at ye edge of ye hill" (Chestnut street). In casting lots for land he obtained several acres.

In 1664 Wm. Pynchon was taxed for purchase money to pay the Indians for land, 10 shillings. Another similar tax on 40½ acres, owned by "Will: Warrener," was 11 shillings 2 pence. "Wm. Warrinar" had one acre in lot 17, as part of the land "on ye Mile River, beginning lowermost on ye southeast branch, and so going up to ye little brooke, and then upward to ye —— 16 acres, and so on to ye north branch of ye upper end, and then come downward, and lastly to ye lake or pond."§

He owned a considerable part of what is now the heart of Springfield. His house stood near the spot where the old court-house now stands, on the north side of First Congregational church, in front of Court Square.

This venerable ancestor of all the New England Warriners died in Springfield, Mass., June 2, 1676, age not known. He was among the original white settlers of that part of Massa-

---

* This man "was fined 10s" by "a quarter court held at Boston 3d Day of the 7th month, 1639, for being at excessive drinking at Grayes at Marblehead." — Old Colony Records.

† For further account of him, see Appendix.

‡ Green's Hist. of Springfield. Here the name is spelled "Warrener."

§ Green's Hist. of Springfield, pp. 95, 110.

chusetts, and had been thirty-eight years a resident of the place. There is no record of his obsequies, and no memorial marks the place of his burial.

While he made no will, the following interesting record shows what disposition was made of his estate. The copy is *verbatim et literatim:*

" James Warriner, of Springfield Presented to this Corte Sepr 26, 1676 ye agreement of ye Persons Concerned as to ye Distribution of ye Estate of Wm. Warriner Deceased which Articles of agreement is upon ffile, & ye Corte haveing Considered it have Confirmed itt.

" Here ffolloweth a Coppy of ye Articles of agreement betwixt ye

" Legates of ye Estate of Wm. Warriner Deceased what each persons part of ye estate shall bee

Bee it known to all whome it may Concern that it is mutually agreed between Elizabeth Widdow on ye One part, & James Warriner, Joseph Warriner and Thomas Noble ye children of Wm. Warriner, her late husband on ye Other part what as to ye Devition of ye Estate of ye sayd Wm. Warriner the sayd widdow shall have & enjoy the third of her Husband's whole Estate during her naturall life, and moreover she is to enjoy ye whole house and house lott, ye half of ye homelott & ye whole meaddow yt lyeth against ye homelott & ye whole orchard except one Row of trees and alsoe so much of ye Barn as she needes to Bestow ye Product of her part of ye Land in, & ye Lott on ye other side of ye River Right against ye house Conteining three acres three Roods or thereabouts all these to be to he with ye Preveledges & Appurtenances thereto belonging During her naturall life or Widdowhood moreover ye sayd Widdow shall Receive out of ye state of her sayd Husband the sum of fifteene Poundes (which shall presently be set Out to her) to be hers and at her free Dispose for ever, also shall have ye whole Produce yt she can Rayse out of ye Premises by her Own Diligent & Prudent Labor & to be to her & at her free dispose for ever.

And ye Rest of ye Estate of ye sayd Wm. Warriner shall all

& every part of it be to ye children of ye sayd Wm. Warriner wholldly free & quit from all Claime or Challenge yt may be made by ye sayd widdow or any other by, from, or under her.

Hereto as our free and voulentary act & Deed we have for ye Preventing qarrl & Discord & for ye maintaineing of mutuall love & peace between us, given our free & full Consent except ye Corte see Cause to alter ye same or part thereof, and in Confirmation hereof we have subjoined our handes & seales ye Day & yeare above written

In Presence off   Elizabeth F her mark Thomas Noble
               Warriner
John Russell Jur   James Warriner   Joseph Warriner
Samll Marshfield

To ye abovesayd agreement were ffour seales affixed.

The abovesayd Instrumt being Presented to the Corte Septr 26, 1676 at Springfield & it being ye mutuall agreement of ye abovesayd Persons the Corte did Confirm it.

As Attests Samll Partrigg Recordr."

INVENTORY agreed upon by above-named legatees James Warriner, Joseph Warriner & Thomas Noble " Owned in Corte " same September 26, 1676.

	£	S.	D.
Impr To house & houselott at	060	00	00
to 5 acres of Land	006	00	00
to 4 acres of wet medow at	003	00	00
to 4 acres of Land at	001	00	00
to 2 Cows a heifer & Calf	009	00	00
to 2 Swine irons for wheels	002	10	00
to Beetle Rings wedges at	000	13	00
to tongs firepan exett at	000	08	00
to iron Pot & Kettell at	000	18	00
to Pewter at	002	05	00
to Chests & one bed at	007	00	00
to Sheets & Pillowbeers &c	004	00	00
to a hat table, Chairs	000	14	00
to Cart Rope & irones	000	08	06
to Debtes due ye Estate	000	1 ?	00

		£	S.	D.
Impr	to 12 acres of Ld on ye plaine	020	00	00
	to 4 acres of Ld over ye River	006	00	00
	to 4 acres of wet meadow at	001	00	00
	to an ox two Steers at	009	00	00
	to 3 yr olds 3 horses yearlings	008	00	00
	to plow irons harrow teeth	001	16	00
	to sett sules tramels pan at	000	14	00
	to Armes & Ashes at	001	15	00
	to Brass Kettels & Candle slides	005	00	00
	to Dishes & Coopery ware at	001	00	00
	to 1 Rug 3 Blanchets Coverlits	005	00	00
	to Cloathing & Bookes	056	12	00
	to Bedsteads hetchell hooke	001	06	00
	to an iron Pott at	000	06	00
	Total of ye above sayd Inventory is	165	15	06
	Debts due from ye Estate at	004	15	08
	Remains of ye Estate	160	19	10

Here begins an enumeration of all the descendants of William Warriner, of Springfield, Mass., in the male line, or under the family name.

1 WILLIAM WARRINER.

CHILDEN OF WILLIAM WARRINER (1):
(All three born in Springfield.)*

* If there were more than three children, there is no record of the fact. One person bearing the name has puzzled the genealogists. There is mention of the marriage of Elizabeth Warrinor to John Strong in 1664. She was his second wife. She died June 7, 1686, ten years after the death of William Warriner, and is not mentioned in the administration of his estate. She was baptized and admitted into Westfield Church in August, 1666. The children of John and Elizabeth (War-

2. James, born Nov. 21, 1640.*
3. Hannah, born June 17, 1643;† married, Nov. 1, 1660,
Thomas Noble, of Springfield, formerly of Boston. He removed to Westville in 1669, where he
was made a freeman in 1681. Before going thither
they had children born to them, namely, John,
Hannah and Thomas. Surviving Mr. Noble, who
died Jan. 20, 1704, she was married Jan. 24, 1705,
to Dea. Medad Pomeroy, and died prior to May
12, 1721.‡
4. Joseph, born Feb. 6, 1645.

2 DEA. JAMES WARRINER, son of William (1) and Joanna,
was born in Springfield, Mass., Nov. 21, 1640. He was among
the inhabitants of Springfield who took the oath of allegiance,
Dec. 3, 1678. He married in Springfield, March 31, 1664,
Elizabeth, daughter of Joseph Baldwin, the first settler of Milford, Mass.§ She died Apr. 24, 1687, and he married, on July
10, 1689, Sarah, daughter of Alexander Alvord. She died
May 16, 1704, age 44, and he married, on the 29th of December following, Mary, widow of Benjamin Stebbins, of Spring-

---

rinor) Strong were John, born 1665; Jacob, born 1673; Joseph,
born 1678.

This Elizabeth Warriner might have been a daughter of
William by a second marriage in England, but in that case
she would have appeared as one of his heirs after his death.
It has been presumed that she was his sister; but she was evidently too young at the time of her marriage to have a brother
84 years of age, as our reckoning makes him to have been at
that time. Savage suggests that the name should have been
written "Warner." Some cases have occurred of the con-
founding of these two names in the early records.

* See Town Records of Springfield for this date.
† Springfield Records.
‡ N. E. Hist. & Gen. Reg., Vol. XII, p. 123.
§ Hist. of Springfield says: "Elizabeth Baldwin of Hadley."

field, Mr. Warriner being her third husband. His name appears on the list of soldiers in King Philip's War.

He was a deacon in the First Congregational Church, as stated in the Historical Address by Judge Morris, page 2'. It is well known that Springfield was settled by a religious community. The earliest ministers were George Moxom, Wm. Hosford, Wm. Thompson, Samuel Hooker and Peletiah Glover. Mr. Moxom and Mr. Glover were settled pastors. Daniel Brewer followed Mr. Glover as settled pastor, and during his ministry Dea. James Warriner died. Our picture represents the third building erected by the First Congregational Church of Springfield. The following interest-

MEETING HOUSE IN SPRINGFIELD IN WHICH THE WARRINERS WORSHIPED FOR SEVENTY YEARS.

* Pynchon's Diary says: "Sept. 20, 1688, Samuel Phelps and William Randall crossing this evening from the Bay & informing me yt ye Inhabitants of Quabaug were in some danger, they being weak and few. * * * Sept. 21, I accordingly sent to their relief & to scout out & to make fortifications there these men, viz.: Henry Gilbert to command, John Hitchcock, James Warriner, Thos. Gilbert, Eben Parsons, Samuel Parsons. These returned the 27th, so they were in service seven days apiece."

From the Council Records, Aug. 1, 1693, it appears that Thomas Gilbert, of Brookfield, John Hitchcock, James Warriner and Samuel Parsons, of Springfield, were allowed from the State treasury "for services at Quabaug 10 shillings apiece." History of North Brookfield, Mass., p. 153.

ing statements are recorded in Hon. Henry Morris' Historical Address, delivered in 1875: "In the first meeting house, erected in 1645, about where the large elm stands, near the southeasterly corner of Court Square, the first pastor met his people as they assembled on the Sabbath at the sound of the drum, and proclaimed to them the words of eternal life. This meeting house was forty feet long and twenty-five feet wide, and faced south on the one-rod road leading to the training-field and burial ground, since made wider and called Elm street. It had two large windows on each side, and one smaller one at each end; one large door on the southerly side, and two smaller ones. It had a shingled roof — a rare thing in that day — and two turrets, one designed for a bell, the other for a watch tower. * * * Soon after the destruction of the town by the Indians in 1675, the original meeting-house, which had escaped the flames, was taken down and a larger and more commodious structure erected further west, mostly, if not wholly, within the limits of what is now Court Square, very near its southwestern angle. It was built in 1677. * * * Again the parish passed a vote in Apr., 1749, to built a new meeting house. It was erected the same year or the year following, so far as to be ready for use, although not entirely finished until 1752. It was 60 feet long by 46 wide, and 26 feet high between joints. This house, the third built, was the immediate predecessor of the present meeting house and stood directly east of the ground now occupied. The principal entrance was on the east side, but there was also an entrance through the tower. Some of the older inhabitants remember well this house with its high pulpit and square pews. * * * There are some things in our early parochial history which appear strange to our modern ideas. One of these is the practice that from the time of the erection of the first meeting house down to the present one seems to have prevailed, of a periodical assignment of seats to the congregation. Thus, in 1664, when the town and parish were identical, a vote of this kind is recorded: ' Dec. 30, 1664. It is ordered yt the Selectmen and Deacon or deacons shall from tyme to tyme seate persons in ye meeting house either higher or lower according as in their sound discretion they shall judge most meete.' A month later, in January, 1665, is found recorded an order of the selectmen, as follows: 'For as much as order is beautiful & especially in ye house of God & ye want thereof is displeasing to God & breeds disturbance among men — And whereas it doth appear yt divers young persons and sometimes others, not withstanding their being called upon Doe yet neglect to attend unto such order, as is prescribed them either for their sitting in ye meeting house, or for their reforming from disorders in & about ye meeting house in tyme of God's Publike worship — It is therefore hereby ordered that whosoever of this Towneship shall not, from tyme to tyme to their sittings in ye meeting house, submit themselves to the ordering of ye Selectmen & Deasons, or such as are empowered to seate & order persons in ye meeting house — All such persons as shall refuse or neglect to attend unto order as aforesaid shall forfeite as is herein after expressed, viz.: Hee or shee that shall not take his or her seate ordered ym fro tyme to tyme but shall in ye days or tymes of God's Publike worship Goe into & abide in any other seate, appointed for some other, Such disorderly person or persons for ye first offence shall forfeit three shillings four pence to ye towne's treasury.' By the same authority it was ordered that the seat formerly called the guard seat should be for smaller boys to set in ' that they might be more in sight of ye congregation.' In this seat none were permitted to sit ' above ye age of 14 or 15 yeares.' It appears that in the earlier period of our parochial history, care was taken that the men and women should be seated in separate seats." In the days of Dea. James Warriner and long after, some of these customs prevailed.

The records show that he was the first grantor of a deed in Hampden county by the name of Warriner.

"Here ffolloweth a Coppy of a Deed whereby James Warriner of Springfield hath sold & Passed over unto ye worshipfull major Pynchon Several Parcels of land lyeing & being within ye township of Springfield, with the acknowledgement of ye same before ye County Corte, &c.

"THESE PRESENTS testify ye James Warriner of

Springfield in ye Colloney of ye Massachusets for in good &
valueable Considerations him thereunto moving, Hath Given,
Granted, Bargained & Sold, & by these Presents Doth with
ye free Consente of Elizabeth his Wife fully Clearely, and absolutely, give Grant Bargain & sell unto Capt. John Pynchon
of Springfield aforesayed & his heirs & Assignes forever Certain Persells of Landes Lyeing & being in Springfield aforesayed
sayed viz: On ye West Side of ye greate River Impr A Persell of Land for a house lott Conteyning four acres more or
less, Being Bredth, Length, Extending from ye high way by
ye River to ye valley or greate Bottom westward & Bounded
by John Scotts Land Southerlie & By John Bakers Land
Northerlie; A Second Percell of Land hereby Sold is ten acres
more or less in ye Third Devition abutting on ye meaddow
wch Capt Pynchon Bought of Wm. Brantch, Southerlie; and
extending Northerlie One Hundred & Sixty Rodd from ye
old front of ye third Devition soe yt there is a little Persell
of Land Between ye sayd ffront of ye third Devition &
ye sayd meaddow wch makes this sayd Persell of Land hereby
sold ten acres more or Les, Alsoe this Persell of Land is in
Bredth thirteene Rodd by ye Meaddow & holdes that Breadth
as far as John Stewarts Land Extends Northerlie & then it
narrows so much in Breadth from thirteene Rodd as to take
out four acres on ye Westerlie Side of it which ye sayd James
Warriner sold to John Baker, ye sayd James Warriners Land
there haveing Been about fourteen acres. Another Persell of
Land hereby Sold is Six acres more or Less above ye Comon
ffence yt Extends from ye Greate River to agawome River this
Persell of Land is in Breadth twelve Rod & in Length four
Score Rod from ye high way by ye great River and Bounded
by James Taylor northerlie & by Abell Wrights Land Southerlie, All wch Persells of Land that is to say ye ffour & ten acres
& six acres above mentioned togeather wth the ffences &
ffencing Profitts, & ye appurtenances thereupon & thereunto
belonging ye Sayd Capt Pynchon is to have hold & enjoy for
himself his heirs & Assignes for Ever & in Respect of ffencing
for ye Land hereby Sold it is ye intent of these Presents yt ye
sayd Capt Pynchon is to maintaine only nine Rod & half

besides ye ffences at ye ffront of ye House Lott the sayd Rod & half, being Set out over agawome River by or nere Good man Miriks meadow, & ye sayd James Warriner is to Deffend Capt Pynchon from all Claimes of any person lawfully Claiming any Right or interest in ye Land hereby Sold by from or under him ye sayd James Warriner or any unto him belonging

In Witness whereof ye sayd James Warriner & Elizabeth his wife have hereunto Set their handes & seales March 25, $16\frac{9}{70}$.

Memorandum it is ye Intent of this Deed yt ye highway Lyeing by or through ye Land at ye third Devition hereby sold is not to be hereby prejudiced
Sealed Subscribed & Delivered
in ye Presence off

                                James Warriner
ELIZA HOLYOKE   The marke H of
THOMAS STEBBINS   Elizabeth   Warriner
The marke T Jonathan
    of   Taylor
To ye above Deed were too Seals affixed."

James Warriner died in Springfield, May 14, 1727. His widow died seven days thereafter.

CHILDREN OF DEA. JAMES WARRINER (2):

(Nine by the first wife; six by the second; all, or nearly all, were born in Springfield, Mass)

    5. Samuel, born Nov. 21, 1666; died in Springfield Feb. 12, 1667.
    6. James, born July 19, 1668.
    7. Elizabeth, born Aug. 1, 1670; married Henry Burt Jan. 16, 1689.
    8. William, born Jan. 6, 1672.
    9. Hannah, born Feb. 12, 1674, "about sun rising." A record of intention of marriage of Daniel Greaves, of Springfield, and Hannah Warriner was made in Springfield, Nov. 27, 1696.

10. Joseph, born Nov. 6, 1677.
11. Samuel 2d, born Jan. 26, 1679.
12. Ebenezer, born March 4, 1682.
13. Mary, born Apr. 1, 1685. Probably the Mary Warriner who married, Sept. 30, 1709, Increase Sikes, of Springfield.
14. Sarah, born Oct. 13, 1690; married Eb. nezer Thomas, of Lebanon, Apr. 23, 1712.
15. Jonathan, born Nov. 11, 1692.
16. John, born Nov. 29, 1694; died in Springfield, May 20, 1696.
17. John 2d, born in 1696; died young.
18. Benjamin, born Apr. 15, 1698.
19. David, born Oct. 8, 1701.

4 JOSEPH WARRINER, son of William (1) and Joanna, was born in Springfield, Mass., Feb. 6, 1645; married, Nov. 25, 1668, Mary, daughter of Richard Montague. He was at that time a resident of Hadley. The records say he was made a freeman in 1674. He participated in a great fight with the Indians at The Falls (Squakboag), May 19, 1676;* took the oath of allegiance Feb. 8, 1679, and was chosen tithing man that same year.

His name appears prominently in the history of Northfield.†

* " A list of ye soldiers yt were in ye Fall Fight under Capt. Wm. Turner approved off by ye Committee of ye Gen Cou t." This list, dated June, 1736, comprises 135 names, and among them is " Joseph Warriner, Hadley."

" A list of Soldiers and Descendants of such as are Deceased that were in the fight called the falls fight above Dearfie'd, who are intituled to the township granted by the Generall Court." The grant embraced the present town of Bernardston (at first called Fall-town), also Colraine, Leydon, etc. Among the 97 claimants was " Ebenezer Warriner, Endfield, son of Joseph Warriner." N. E. Hist. & Gen. Reg., Vol. XLI, pp. 212, 213.

† History of Northfield, by Temple & Sheldon, pp. 110, 123,

He removed in 1687 to Enfield, Conn.,* where his wife died July 22, 1689. He married, July 15, 1691, Sarah, widow of

---

has the following: "The land grant to Joseph Pomeroy, 1683, was forfeited and alienated to Joseph Warriner."

At a town meeting held Feb. 29, 1688, a vote was taken to build a meeting house and a bridge over Mill Brook. John Cleary, Jr., was chosen to present this vote to the committee for their approval. He went to Northampton with the following letter: " Ye town of Northfield considering ye necessity of a meeteing house for to meete in and alsoe to build a bridg over ye Mill brooke, being orderly met together did voat and were yunanimous in our voat to bild a Meeting hous and the sade brige, and also voated to make a Reat of fforty pounds, and to rate it upon grants of land for ye defraying of ye charges of sade meeting hous and brige as atteste

JOSEPH WARRINER
SAMUEL DAVIS

The following is from the record of home lots in the 3d settlement: " The Joseph Warriner lot 7½ acres, 20 rods wide, Nov. 1, 1711. Ebenezer Warriner, of Enfield, sells all his father's, Joseph's, rights in Northfield to Eleazer Mattoon, of Deerfield."

* Enfield records say that, April 7, 1687, Joseph Warriner, a settler of Enfield is assigned by the committee a lot. " Next Benjamin Jones lies the house lot of Joseph Warriner 10 rods in breadth and in length from the street on the west bank 160 rods easterly." He was possessed of other lots later; for example, one at Sehautuck river, also a parcel of meadow on Buckham brook. Enfield records contain the following, also, dated 1689: " Granted to Joseph Warriner as he is admitted an Inhabitant. An allotment 40 acres field Land 4 acres meadow and 10 acres house lot, that same House lot on the East side of the street, which James Harwood leaves, he the sd Warriner cuming to the place and continuing there 7 years, Defraying all charges and submitting to all the orders of the place — then all is granted to him, his heirs and Assigns forever."

A

Daniel Collins. She was daughter of Thomas Tibbals, of Milford, who mentioned her in his will.* An interesting document, well worthy to be here transcribed, was signed by him in 1694.

"Here ffolloweth a Coppy of a deed of Sale wr by Joseph Warriner did alienate a Certaine persell of Land in Hadley unto Peter Montague together with the acknowledgemt of the same.

THIS INDENTURE made on the fourth day of September in ye year of ye Lord one thousand six hundred and nintie four Betwn Joseph Warriner of Enfield with in his Majty Turitories and dominions America in New England with Sarah his wife On ye one pt & Petr Mountague of Hadley in ye dominion aforesd On ye other pt & Petr Witnesseth yt ye sd Joseph Warriner with Sarah his Wife for law ful reasons them moveing thereunto & in consideration of Seven pounds already received from Petr Mountague aforesd which hereby they are fully satisfied & doe hereby exonerate ye sd Petr Mountague or his Executors, administrators or Assigns any further payment hath clerely given, alienated Bargained sold and by these presents doth cleerely Grant Bargain & Sell unto Petr Mountague his heirs Executors, administrators or Assigns & to his & to their use forever these Persells of Land Being within the Bounds of the Township of Hadley One piece of which Land is Bounded northerly by a meadow called the School ffarme & Southerly by Land granted to Joseph Baldwin butting upon ye great River Westerly & the Bank Easterly containing Ten acres more or less, alsoe one piece of Land containing three roods & thirtie rod more or less On ye Southward Side of ye Mill Brook & Bounded by ye sd brook Northerly & by Land granted to Samll Gardner Southerly & the Great River Westerly & the Bank Easterly, alsoe one piece of Land more in ye tract of Land neere to ye fortracres conteining five acres more or less Bounded Northerly by Land of Phillip Smith & by the woods on hill Southerly & butts on the Comons Easterly & on ye high way and ten rodds in

---

* She was born Nov. 27, 1654.

breadth at the Rear, In all which prsells of Land & their appurtenances in manner & form prescribed wth all prveledges comodities appurtenances thereon or thereto belonging the sd Joseph Warriner with Sarah his Wife Doe for themselves their heirs exectrs administrators or Assigns absolutely utterly & forever Remit Remiss & Relinquish all and any former Right title powor claim interest appertaining or belonging to ye aforsd Joseph Warriner or Sarah his wife or their heirs executors etc. etc.

"Signed sealed &   Joseph Warriner
delivered in the presence   One seale
& Witness of   was Affixed"
John Smith
Ebenezr Smith

" October 26, 1694 Joseph Warriner personally appeared " etc

Aaron Coooke Justice of Peace
Entered Janry 24, 169⅗
Samll Partrigg Registr."

Joseph Warriner died in Enfield, Conn., Aug. 21, 1697, aged 52, and his widow married Obadiah Abbee, of Enfield.*

CHILDREN OF JOSEPH WARRINER (4):

(Eight by the first wife; three by the second.)

20. Mary, born Nov. 17, 1669; married, July 15, 1691, Zechariah Booth.
21. Joseph, born Jan. 16, 1671; died Nov. 1, 1672.
22. Joseph 2d, born Jan. 6, 1672; died young.
23. Hannah, born Sept. 10, 1674; married, 1691, Robert Pease, Jr. They had three sons born in Enfield, Conn., viz.: Nathaniel, 1702, Joseph, 1707, and Benjamin.†

* She was his second wife. Mr. Abbee had no children to be named in his will in 1752, the year of his decease.
† N. E. Hist. and Gen. Reg., Vol. III, p. 174.

24. Ebenezer, born Jan. 16, 1676.
25. Dorcas, born June 27, 1678.
26. Abigail, born Aug. 23, 1680; died July 21, 1689.
27. Joanna, born Nov. 8, 1682; married, Apr. 14, 1708, Thomas Colton, of Springfield, son of Capt. Thomas Colton. Their children were Thankful (1709-1735); Matthew (1711-1711); Dinah (1712-1759); Anna (1714); Elizabeth (1716); Thomas (1719-1808); Joseph (1721-1787).
28. Elizabeth, born Sept. 30, 1686; married, Nov. 13, 1713, Samuel Bliss, of Long Meadow, Mass. Their children were : Abigail, b. 1714; Josiah, b. 1716, d. 1716; Esther, b. 1717, d. 1718; Esther 2d, b. 1719, and Elizabeth.* Mr. Bliss died and she married 2d John Pease, of Enfield, on Nov. 12, 1729.
29. Abigail, born in Enfield, Conn., May 4, 1692.†
30. Mary, born May 4, 1692, twin sister of Abigail; probably the Mary Warriner who married Daniel Weld, Sept. 28, 1711.
31. Phebe, born in Enfield Sept. 5, 1694.

6 LIEUT. JAMES WARRINER, son of James (2) and Elizabeth, was born in Springfield, Mass., July 19, 1668; married, Jan. 20, 1692, Sarah, daughter of Thomas Rowland, granddaughter of Samuel Chapin. He was one of the active members of the East Side Parish Church,‡ held the offices of constable and selectman,§ and his name frequently appears in the records.**

* Ibid, Vol. XXXI, p. 420.
† One Abigail Warriner married, May 3, 1722, Samuel Ely. One of same name married Samuel Warner, Feb. 20, 172¾. See Nos. 66 and 69.
‡ History of Springfield by Green, page 205.
§ Ibid, pp. 194, 262.
** A record of Hampshire County Court, held at Northampton, March 25, 1684, has the following, and refers either to him or to his father: "James Warriner, of Springfield, being pre-

The town records of Springfield say: "James of Springfield Dyed the —— day of March Anno Dom. 173⅚. The date as elsewhere given is March 11, 1736.

CHILDREN OF JAMES WARRINER (6):

(All these births are recorded in Springfield town records.)

32. James, born March 7, 169⅔.

33. Sarah, born Apr. 1, 1694. She is probably the Sarah Warriner who married John Stebbins, Dec. 22, 1715.

34. John, born Aug. 20, 1696, in Springfield; baptized when three days old. Name spelled Warrinar in town records.*

---

sented for travelling on a publique day of thanksgiving, to give testimony against such abuses, this Corte has adjudged sd James and John Pees to pay to the Countie Treasurer 5d apiece."

Springfield voted, Dec. 22, 1726, that "the Removing of the Seats and Inlarging of the Seats for the judges to sit on in the Corte house be Don and effected at the Cost and Charge of the Town, & Lieut James Warriner & Thos. Merrick senr be a Committee to effect said Work."

Among the interesting documents is a record of sale of lands by Rowland Thomas to James Warriner Dec. 11, 1697. "In the County of West Hampshire within his majestie's Province of the Massachusetts Bay of New England For good Causes and valuable Consideration, Especially; for and in Consideration of the full, and Just sum of Sixty pounds, In Currant money of New England; to him in hand paid or assured to be paid before the Ensealing and delivering of these presents, By James Warriner Junr of the aforesd Springfield in the Province of the Massachusetts Bay, in New England.

* We hear nothing further from this John. He may have died young. A private record states that John Warriner (122) was killed in the French War. In that statement, more than likely, John is mistaken for Jonathan (15).

35. Elizabeth, born Dec. 23, 1697. In this birth record
    the town clerk spelled the name " Warryner."
36. Thankful, born Feb. 7, 1699-1700; married on Dec.
    31, 1722, to John Sikes.
37. Thomas, born Dec. 3, 1703. " Thomas Warriner,
    of Springfield, died —— day of June, 1740."
    Administrators on his estate were his brother and
    sister, " James Warriner and Elizabeth Warriner,
    both of Springfield."

8 WILLIAM WARRINER, son of James (2) and Elizabeth,
was born in Springfield, Mass., Jan. 6, 1672; married in
Springfield, Feb. 3, 1697, Elizabeth Weller,* daughter of John
and Mary (Alvord) Weller, and granddaughter of Richard
and Ann (Wilson) Weller. She died, it is presumed, before
1731, for in that year, Oct. 26, " Wm. Warriner, of Springfield," married Rebecca Lamb.

The following is an abstract of his will, which bears date
Nov. 13, 1738:

" IN THE NAME OF GOD AMEN. I William War-
riner of Springfield in the County of Hampshire and Province
of Massachusetts Bay in New England yeoman, being sick
and weak of body but of sound mind and understanding and
moved with the Consideration of the certainty of death and of
the uncertainty of the time when my Change will come do
make & ordain this to be my last will & Testament in the following manner and form viz First I remand my soul to God
who gave it," etc.

Impr, Whereas my wife Rebecca being by a Joynture made
with me before marriage Endowed fully for what she is to
receive out of my estate In case she survive me I therefore

* " Wm. Warryner came and entered his intention of marriage with Elizabeth Weller the 1st day of Feb., 1697, and
published the same day. Willyam Warryner and Elizabeth
Weller were joyned in maryage the 3d of February 1697." —
Springfield Records.

give her nothing in this my will save only that I give her &
order that she shall have three months Provision only for herself after my decease with fuel wood for that time and no
longer." He gives his sons William and Nathaniel, each ten
shillings, and adds: " The reason why I give my sd sons no
more in my will is because that I have heretofore advanced to
each of them by settlement respectively, what with what I
have in this my will given them I determine to be their Just
Proportion of my Estate." To " daughters Hannah Burt and
Experience Chapin 5 shillings each," having given them, etc.
To daughter Elizabeth Warriner 70 pounds not having given
her her portion; to daughter Martha 60 pounds; to son Moses
" homestead houselot," etc., on the " east side of the Great
River, where I now dwell." If the movable estate is not
sufficient to meet these demands, his son Moses is to pay the
balance. Executors: three sons, William, Nathaniel and
Moses. Witnesses: Jonathan Church, Edward Pynchon,
Wm. Pynchon, Jun.

He died not long after his will was executed, and his widow
died March 10, 1740.*

CHILDREN OF WILLIAM WARRINER (8).

(Birthplace, Springfield, Mass.)

38. William, born Jan. 12, 1698.
39. Elizabeth, born Feb. 4, 1700. "Aug. 13, 1780,
    Elizabeth Warriner, late of Wilbraham, decd.
    Power of administration committed to Noah War-
    riner." Supposed to be this Elizabeth Warriner.†
40. Luke, born Sept. 27, 1701; baptized Oct. 12 follow-
    ing; died Sept. 7, 1702.

---

* The record is as follows: " The widw Rebecca Warriner,
of Springfield Deceased Dyed the 10th day March Anno Dom
17 $3\frac{9}{40}$."

† One Elizabeth Warriner married Caleb Stebbins, Nov.
17 $3\frac{9}{40}$."

41. Nathaniel, born Feb. 22, 1703.
42. Luke 2d, born Aug. 5, 1705; died Dec. 30, same year.
43. Martha, born Oct. 21, 1706.
44. Moses, born July 24, 1708.
45. Hannah, born about 1710, probably; married, Jan. 11, 1733, Moses Burt. She is mentioned in her father's will.
46. Experience, born Sept. 27, 1702; married Isaac Chapin, of Springfield, June 27, 1734.
47. Samuel, born Oct. 16, 1714; died in Springfield, Aug. 3, 1721.
48. Mercy, born Aug. 12, 1716; died Jan. 20, 1736.

10 JOSEPH WARRINER, son of James (2) and Elizabeth, was born in Springfield, Mass., Nov. 6, 1677; married Hannah Bliss, intentions having been recorded Dec. 24, 1713. She was daughter of Samuel and Hannah (Stiles) Bliss, of Springfield, Mass. The will of "Joseph Warriner, of Springfield," is dated March 18, 1742, and provides as follows: To Hannah his "well beloved wife" the use and improvement movable estate, so long as she remains his widow; ditto one room in dwelling, etc.; to son, Joseph Warriner, real estate in Springfield, etc.; to daughter Hannah, and daughter Lydia, each fifty-five pounds, including what had been already given. Executors: his wife Hannah and his son Joseph. Witnesses: Benj. Chapin, Wm. Bliss, Wm. Pynchon.

Joseph Warriner died before 1757. His widow Hannah, on Sept. 21, 1758, leased the farm in Enfield to John Collins. The lease included "lands, buildings, tools and teams, and the cattle and sheep, and all things willed to me by my late husband." *

---

* Hannah Warriner and Samuel Warriner sold each to the other land located in Enfield, "on the 20th day of February in the twenty-sixth year of the Reign of our Sovereign Lord George of Great Britain, King, anno Dom. 1753." — *Enfield Records.*

CHILDREN OF JOSEPH WARRINER (10).

(All born in Springfield, Mass.)

60. Joseph, born Oct. 12, 1714; died in Springfield, Dec. 25, 1714.
61. Hannah, born Apr. 4, 1716; died in Springfield, Feb. 2, 1724.
62. Sarah, born March 23, 1720.
63. Joseph 2d, born Apr. 16, 1723.
64. Hannah 2d, born May 29, 1725.*
65. Lydia, born May 25, 1728; died in Springfield, Nov. 2, 1757.

11 SAMUEL WARRINER, son of James (2) and Elizabeth, was born Jan. 26, 1679, in Springfield, Mass.† He married

---

* Hezekiah Porter, of Hadley, filed intentions of marriage to Hannah Warriner, of Springfield, date not given.

† The name of Samuel Warriner appears, Apr. 7, 1707, on a list of 73 landholders in the part of Springfield lying west of the Connecticut river, signing a petition to the town authorities. This man may have been Samuel Warriner (11), but most likely another person of the same name.

Springfield has records concerning one Samuel Warriner, which evidently do not belong to the subject of the present sketch, nor to any other of the name known to have descended from William Warriner. In 1720 Samuel Warriner is named in a list of petitioners, like those mentioned above. This request was granted. The record is as follows: "June ye 6th 1720. Hear followeth an Account of the Divideing of the land given to the Inhabitants of the Precinct by the Town. And first the land on the hill. . . . And then there is twenty Rods for the highway. And the next lot to the highway is to Samll Warriner, which is in Number the eighth lot. Quantity ten acres. Length 80 Rods. Bredth 20 Rods, bounded on the highway South." (See N. E. Hist. & Gen. Reg., Vol. XXIX, p. 289.)

On May 20, 1720, Samuel Warriner drew lots for land in

Abigail Day in the same town, Feb. 18, 1703. His death occurred on March 30, 1713.* Letters of administration on his estate were granted to Abigail Warriner, his widow, on May 23, 1713. The inventory mentions house, land, cattle, gun, sword, ammunition, snow shoes, saddle, pillion, bridle, etc.

On Dec. 14, 1717, intentions of marriage of Thomas Mille: to Widow Abigail Warriner were recorded in Springfield.

CHILD OF SAMUEL WARRINER (11).

66. Abigail, born in Springfield, Dec. 8, 1703. One Abigail Warriner married, May 3, 1722, Samuel Ely, and one of the same name married Samuel Warriner, Feb. 10, 172¾. (See Nos. 29 and 69.)

12 EBENEZER WARRINER, son of James (2) and Elizabeth, was born in Springfield, March 4. 1682; married Joanna Dickinson, Jan. 8, 1701.† On Oct. 8, 1735, he, with eleven

---

Springfield. This same Samuel Warriner is in all probability mentioned in the following record: " Desire, daughter of Samuel and Sarah Warriner, was born Sept. 8, 1716." — *Springfield Town Records.*

We learn from the same source that Samuel Warriner died in Springfield, March 16, 1750.

It will be observed that the dates in the foregoing are all subsequent to the death of Samuel Warriner (11). From these records it may be inferred that there was in Springfield, in the first half of the eighteenth century, a Samuel Warriner, whose birth and marriage occurred elsewhere, and hence are not recorded in Springfield; whose wife was named Sarah; whose daughter was named Desire, and whose death took place in Springfield in the year 1750.

* " Samll, husband of Abigail Warriner was sick and died March ye 30th, 1713." — *Springfield Records.*

† " Ebenezer Warryner entered his intentions of marriage with Joanna Dickinson the 21st day of Dec. 1700, and weare published the same day." " Ebenezer Warryner and Joanna Dickinson were joyned in marriage Jan. 8, 1700-1701." — *Springfield Town Records.*

others, signed a protest or petition to the justices of Hampshire county against the settlement of an illegal ecclesiastical council.* He and twenty-two others recorded a protest against the support of Mr. Breck, the chosen pastor, on the ground that he was not an orthodox minister.†

His will is the oldest made by a Warriner, so far as the Hampshire county records show. It is dated " 21 Jan, 1736, in the 4th year of the reign of George II." The following are some of its provisions: " In the name of God Amen. I Ebenezer Warriner, of Springfield, in the County of Hampshire & Province of Massachusetts Bay in New England yeoman being now old with the consideration of the uncertainty of this mortal life, & the present indisposition of body I labor under, but of sound mind and understanding Do make & ordain this to be my last will & Testamt as follows First I recommend my Soul to Almighty God assured by trusting to the mercy of Christ Jesus for the Pardon of my Sins & Eternal life my body I remit to the earth by a decent Christian burial according to the discretion of my Executrix hereafter named, and as Touching my worldly Estate I give bequeath Devise and dispose of the same in the following manner & form, my debts and funeral Charges first being paid, That is to say

" Impr I give and Bequeath to Johanna Warriner my wife one third part of all my lands," etc.

He directs his son Ebenezer to pay to each of the daughters, Abigail Pease, Mary Cadwell and Elizabeth Stebbins, ten pounds, having given each sixty pounds before, making equal distribution. To David, Johanna, Martha and Rachel he gives seventy pounds each, they to receive the same when twenty-two years of age, or if they should marry sooner, at the time of marriage. The will gives to his son Ebenezer house, barns

* Green, History of Springfield, p. 248.

† Ibid, p. 251. The History of the First Church, Springfield, pp. 31, 32, says a committee was appointed to answer this complaint before the court, which " never actually adjudicated this delicate question of the orthodoxy of the Springfield minister. Subsequent events rendered it unnecessary."

and lands on east side of Connecticut river, etc. To his son Hezekiah are given lands, grants, etc., west of Connecticut river. He nominates his wife, Johanna, as sole executrix. Witnesses: Obadiah Cooley, Robert Harris, Wm. Pynchon, Jr.

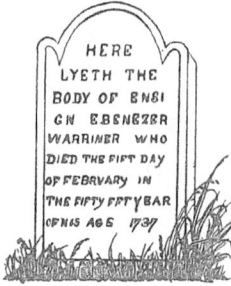

In a row of headstones bearing the name of Warriner in the Springfield cemetery, is one of slate, commemorating Ebenezer Warriner. It is represented in the cut.

His widow married Benjamin Chapin of Springfield. Intentions of the marriage were recorded Sept. 27, 1740.

CHILDREN OF EBENEZER WARRINER (12).

(All born in Springfield, Mass.)

67. Ebenezer, born July 4, 1701; died in Springfield June 8, 1713, in his 11th year.
68. Joanna, born June 24, 1703; died July 26, 1709.
69. Abigail, born Oct. 12, 1705.*
70. Joanna 2d, born Aug. 15, 1711; married Samuel Brooks, of Springfield, March 17, 1736; died March 27, 1756. Headstone in Springfield cemetery.
71. Elizabeth, born Jan. 16, 1713; married Caleb Stebbins, Nov. 23, 1732, both of Springfield.
72. Martha, born March 8, 1716; died, unmarried, Sept. 28, 1742.† Her grave is close beside that of Ensign James Warriner (32), and marked by a similar memorial.

---

* One Abigail Warriner married in 1722; one married in 1723. See Nos. 29 and 66.

† The record is as follows: " Martha Warriner of Springfield, daughter of Ebenezer Warriner late of Springfield, and Joanna Chapin late widw of Ebenezer, Dyed the 28th day of September Anno Dom. 1742."

73. Rachel, born Oct. 29, 1717; married Edward Bliss, of Warren, Mass., in 1743. (Record of intentions in Springfield Apr. 2, 1743.)
74. Ebenezer 2d, born Sept. 20, 1719.
75. Hezekiah, born Dec. 8, 1721. The following record shows he died in infancy.
76. Hezekiah 2d, born Oct. 13, 1724.

15 JONATHAN WARRINER, son of James (2) and Sarah, was born in Springfield, Mass., Nov. 11, 1692; married, Oct. 26, 1726, Mercy Burnham, of Hartford, Conn. The name of " Jona: Warriner " is found on the muster roll of Capt. Joseph Kellogg's company, raised in 1723 to fight the Indian Chief Gray Lock and his forces in Father Rolle's War.* " Jona: Warriner, Spg.," was also enrolled in Capt. Timothy Dwight's company at the Block House above Northfield.†

Jonathan Warriner (15) and Gideon Warriner (68) are on the list of members of the " First Parish " who lost their lives in the war with the French and Indians about 1745.

CHILDREN OF JONATHAN WARRINER (15).

77. Gideon, born June 5, 1727.
78. Cibbel, born Oct. 27, 1731, in Springfield.

---

* This statement is taken from the History of Northfield, p. 198. In the same book, page 207, concerning Capt. Kellogg's journal kept during that war, it is said: " The labor it recorded and the daring and endurance of these handfulls of men, thus striking off into the wild forests in the winter, fording bridgeless streams and climbing mountains slippery with ice and blocked up with snow, watching for the curling smoke from the red man's camp fire, and listening for the report of his gun, were a most exciting romance if they had not been a terrible reality. By such vigilance and fidelity and wear of soul and body was our village protected and our valley kept clear of blood."

† Ibid, p. 204.

18 BENJAMIN WARRINER, son of James (2) and Sarah, was born in Springfield, Mass., Apr. 15, 1698; married Mercy Bartlett, having recorded intentions in Springfield Oct. 20, 1726. His time-worn memorial is in the old cemetery in Wilbraham. It is represented in the cut. His widow, Mercy Warriner, was married to Joseph Wright, Feb. 4, 1768.

CHILDREN OF BENJAMIN WARRINER (18).

(All born in Springfield, Mass.)

79. Benjamin, born Sept. 3, 1727.
80. Mercy, born Jan. 31, 172$\frac{8}{9}$. She was probably the Mercy Warriner of Springfield who married Deliverance Atkinson, July 22, 1758.
81. Samuel, born March 23, 173$\frac{0}{1}$.
82. Reuben, born March 6, 173$\frac{2}{3}$.
83. Anne, born Jan. 10, 1735; probably the Anne Warriner, of Springfield, who married Ezra Barker, Aug. 22, 1756.
84. Aaron, born Nov. 13, 1736; died of small-pox, Jan. 25, 1761, in the 25th year of his age.
85. Eunice, born Apr. 3, 1739; married Aaron Parsons, Jr., Oct. 2, 1760.
86. Jacob, born May 19, 1724; died in Wilbraham, Oct. 10, 1766, aged 24.
87. Israel, twin brother of Jacob, born May 19, 1742.

19 DAVID WARRINER, son of James (2) and Sarah, was born Oct. 8, 1701; married Mary, daughter of Samuel Sikes. (Banns Feb. 9, 1738.) They settled on what is now the Wesleyan Academy farm in Wilbraham.

His wife died Sept. 22, 1774, five days after the death of her son Charles.

CHILDREN OF DAVID WARRINER (19).

89. Mary, born March 23, 1740; died Oct. 15, 1753, in Springfield. Her tombstone may be seen in the old cemetery in Wilbraham.
90. David, born May 13, 1742.
91. Charles, born Apr. 15, 1744; died Sept. 17, 1774.
92. Margaret, born in Springfield, Aug. 12, 1748; died July 8, 1824, aged 78. She was daughter of David, as the records say, and seems to have been unmarried.
93. Jonathan, born in Springfield Sept. 16, 1749. There is no record of his marriage. He died Apr. 15, 1819, in Wilbraham.

24 EBENEZER WARRINER, son of Joseph (4) and Mary, was born Jan. 16, 1676; went to Enfield (now included in Connecticut), where his father settled in 1687. He married Elizabeth ———. She died June 6, 1724, and he married Mary Field, Sept. 24, 1725. He was deacon in the Congregat.onal Church. We find him serving as selectman of the town in 1710 and 1723. He seems to have been one of the foremost men in Enfield.*

His father dying in 1752, Ebenezer inherited the home lot, "bounded west with the street, east with the Commons, north with Benj. Jones, south with Edward Kibbe containing 10 acres more or less." He became possessed of land by allotment in 1699, and at several times thereafter. Transfers of land with his name attached are found in the old Enfield records.† He was one of the grantees of the town of Bernardston on account of the military services of his father

---

* "At a Loyal meeting of ye eldest district or Precinct in Enfield, March ye 20th 1723-4, . . . Deacon Isaac Pease, Deacon Ebenezer Warriner, Azariah Booth, Thomas Jones and Joseph Sexton were chosen a committee for the Precinct or district for the year ensuing." — *Enfield Town Records*.

† A record of land sold May 6, 1748, " by Ebenezer Warriner, County Hampshire, Province of Massachusetts Bay for

CHILDREN OF EBENEZER WARRINER (24).

(All born in Enfield, Conn.)

94. Elizabeth, born Feb. 26, 1704-5; married David
     Hale. It is presumed that her son's name was
     David. Warriner Hale, of Enfield, who was
     born in 1776 and died young, was probably son of
     David and Ruth Hale, and grandson of this
     Elizabeth.
95. Joseph, born March 30, 1707. We have no further
     knowledge of him; he probably died in childhood.
96. Dorcas, born March 23, 1709; died in Enfield June
     19, 1719. The name is spelled in the record
     "Darkiss."

---

80 pounds to Ebenezer M'Gregory measured thus: Eastward
of Cold Meadow so called 39½ acres," etc. On June 13, 1751,
he sold another plot to Samuel Warriner, his son, for "200
pounds old tenor of Providence of the Mass. Bay." This
land was in Enfield, "so lying on the south side of Grape
brook, bounded east on the country road by estimation twelve
rods wide north on land of Benoni Gains, beginning for the
south east corner at a stone which stands on the north side of
a gutter west above the deep gutter so called, and by said
road running westward to a stone on the west side opposite
gutter on the side hill, thence northward to a stone by the
mouth of said deep gutter, then northward to land of said
Gains, be the same more or less than twenty acres with a
house standing thereon."

On Apr. 8, 1760, after Ebenezer Warriner's death, his heirs
signed a quit-claim deed with the following preamble: "That
whereas our honored father did in his life-time convey unto
Ebenezer M'Gregory a certain piece or tract of land in the
township of Enfield," etc. This instrument was signed:

"Samuel Warriner, David Hale, Elizabeth X Hale, Hannah X Hale, Jacob Adams."

97. Ebenezer, born Jan. 30, 1711; probably died young.
98. Mary, born Aug. 11, 1713; died June 6, 1724.
99. Hannah, born Apr. 17, 1716. She may have married ——— Hale. See Hannah Hale's name in note 45.*
100. Samuel, born Nov. 19, 1719.

32 JAMES WARRINER, commonly known as Ensign James Warriner, son of James (6) and Sarah, was born in Springfield, Mass., March 7, 1693; married Anny (sometimes written Almy) Sheldon, of Westfield, Sept. 8, 1720. She died March 30, 1759, and he married Deborah Wright, of Springfield, on July 10, 1760.

He was chosen selectman of Wilbraham precinct in 1751. His will is dated Springfield, April 29, 1765, 5th year of the reign of George III.† His death occurred a short time after-

* See note 34, which may possibly refer to this Hannah Warriner (99).

† Contents of the will are as follows: To Deborah his " well-beloved wife " is given the use of the northerly lower rooms and cellar of his dwelling near the meeting-house in Springfield, etc. To his son James several tracts and parcels of land; to his son Aaron his right in the saw mill in the lower part of Springfield, and improvement of considerable property which is to go to his (Aaron's) heirs after his death. If Aaron should die without issue, the aforesaid son, James, was to have a larger part, while his daughter Anny and his granddaughter Mercy (daughter of his son Stephen, deceased) were to have a smaller part of the property intended for Stephen's heirs. To his daughter, Anny Wells, he bequeathed the former possessions of his wife Amy, " saving that I allow to my present wife, Deborah, the use and improvement of a large brass kettle during the time she remains my widow." To daughter Anny and granddaughter Mercy Warriner he gave several tracts of land, Mercy being entitled to receive her portion when eighteen years of age. His son James was named as executor. The witnesses were Luke Bliss and William Pynchon.

ward, May 9, 1765. His widow, Deborah, married, Nov. 24, 1768, Luke Montague.*

IN MEMORY OF
ENSIGN
JAMES WARRINER
who after a Useful
& Exemplary Life
died May 9ᵗ 1765
In yᵉ 73ᵈ Year of
His age

Near the side entrance to the cemetery in Springfield a good-sized space is occupied by the remains and headstones transferred from the old cemetery, foot of Elm street, in 1848. At the end of this plot, nearest the gate in a conspicuous place, is a brown stone slab which appears as represented in the cut.

CHILDREN OF JAMES WARRINER (32).

(All born in Springfield, Mass.)

109. Anny, born Sept. 17, 1721; married Joseph Wells, of Springfield, Nov. 26, 1747. Records say "Anny Jr."
110. James, born Sept. 2, 1723.
111. Stephen, born March 17, 1726.
112. Aaron, born July 21, 1728.

37 THOMAS WARRINER, son of James (6) and Sarah, was born in Springfield, Mass., Dec. 3, 1703. In the record of deaths he is called "Thomas Warriner of Springfield." He was not married. Near Ensign James Warriner's headstone in Springfield cemetery is a memorial of this man, which appears as represented in the cut.

Here lyeth
The Body of
hᵉ Thomas
Warriner Son of
LieutᵗJames Warriner
and his wife who dye
d June 7ᵗ 13ᵗʰ in the
39 year of his age
anno 1740

38 WILLIAM WARRINER, son of William (8) and Elizabeth, was born in Springfield, Mass., Jan. 12, 1698; married Sarah Bostwick; died in Brimfield,

* Springfield Records.

Mass., Nov. 16, 1765. On the 20th of Sept. preceding he made his will. The will grants to his wife Sarah the use of a third part of the real and personal property during her lifetime; to his son William the house lot north of J. Sherman, Esq., etc., etc.; to his daughter Mercy land in Brimfield; to daughters Sarah Worthington, Eunice Bostwick, Elizabeth Thompson, Abigail King, Lois Browning, Mercy Warriner and Eleanor Cooley, all the rest of his estate both real and personal, to be divided equally for quantity and quality between them. Executors: wife Sarah and son William. Witnesses: James Bugham, Bezaleel Sherman, Nathan Abbott.

CHILDREN OF WILLIAM WARRINER (38).

(All born in Brimfield, Mass.)

114. William, born Sept. 25, 1727; died May 18, 1833.
115. Eunice, born June 3, 1729; married ――― Bostwick.
116. Elizabeth, born March 8, 1731; married Jonathan Thompson, of Brimfield, son of James Thompson, ensign to the celebrated Count Rumford. She died Aug. 28, 1808, aged 73.*
117. Abigail, often called "Nabby," born Jan. 1, 1733; married ――― King, of Vermont. Their son James was a missionary to Greece.†
118. Lois, born Dec. 21, 1735; married ――― Browning, of Brimfield, Mass. Nine children.
119. Will, or William 2d, born Aug. 14, 1736; died in infancy.
120. Mercy, born Aug. 13, 1737; married Col. Bannister. Three children.
121. Eleanor, born Aug. 7, 1739; married ――― Cooley.
122. John, born Oct. 3, 1741; said to have been killed in

* N. E. Hist. and Gen. Reg., Vol. XIII, p. 376.
† Memorandum by Miss Emmeline Warriner, of Jamaica Plain, Mass.

the French War, but the truth of this report is questioned.*

123. William 3d, born Jan. 2, 1744.

41 NATHANIEL WARRINER, son of Willard (8) and Elizabeth, was born in Springfield, Feb. 22, 1703; married Margaret Mirrick, of Springfield, March 1, 1723; died Jan. 10, 1780, aged almost 77. His wife died Dec. 25, 1764. They left no children. He was one of the first settlers in Wilbraham, moving there in 1734.† It was then called "Outward Commons," or "Springfield Mountains," and was at that time about twenty-five miles square. When that section was established as a separate precinct in 1741 the warrant was issued to Nathaniel Warriner to call the first meeting. He was on the committee of the precinct for the year ensuing, and was chosen collector. At his home the first minister, Rev. Noah Mirrick, was ordained, and some members of the committee were entertained there over night.‡

In 1749, 1753 and 1761 he was on a committee to apply to the town and general court to have Wilbraham set off as a separate town. The appeal was finally successful. He was moderator of many of the precinct meetings, and almost exclu-

* Miss Emmeline Warriner's record. But see sketch of Jonathan Warriner (15), and see John (34).

† He located where Mrs. Gale and Mrs. Mears resided in 1863. — *Stebbins' Centennial of Wilbraham.*

‡ The church voted to pay him six pounds, one shilling and six pence for "keeping the ministers, delegates and scholars at the time of the ordination," and eleven pounds ten shillings "for keeping Mr. Mirrick and his Mair." When the committee met to decide where to build a church, Deacon Nathaniel Warriner was paid one pound twelve shillings and sixpence for procuring the committee, and two pounds twelve shillings and sixpence "old tenor" for keeping said committee and their horses. "Old tenor," or paper money, was then worth one-tenth its face value in coin or lawful money. (See Stebbins' Centennial of Wilbraham, pp. 32, 33.)

sively moderator of the town meetings for the first seven years to 1770.

He led the singing in the public religious services.* He was deacon of the church from the first, and one of its chief supporters — a staunch defender of the Standing Order. In his will he divided his estate between his church and the public schools. Those two funds are a permanent benefaction.† The parsonage occupied by the Congregational pastors of Wilbraham is "the Nathaniel Warriner parsonage."

He is buried in the old cemetery in Wilbraham. His tombstone is conspicuous — a large slab supported by five pillars, and on which a long inscription is carved. The letters are moss covered and difficult to read.

44 MOSES WARRINER, son of William (8) and Elizabeth,

---

* When the meeting house was first occupied, the "worthy Rev. Noah Mirrick, with wig and powdered hair, and cue, bands and small clothes, and silk stockings, and shoe buckles of silver, entered the house, the congregation all rising as a token of respect. He read a hymn, then handed the book over the top of the rough pulpit — for there was but one hymn book in the precinct, and that was the minister's — to Deacon Nathaniel Warriner, who named the tune, gave the pitch, read one line of the hymn and commenced singing it; Warner, and Brewer, and Langdon, and Stebbins, Moses, and David, and Hosea, and Huldah, and Jemima, and Ruth followed after, as ability and strength permitted; the deacon, conscientiously and as became the service of God's house, waiting before he gave out another line till the most dilatory had finished." (Stebbins' Centennial of Wilbraham, p. 57.)

† The amount was four hundred pounds, "lawful money," and it was "to be one-half given to the support of the Gospel Ministry, the other half to the use and support of Schools. Provided that all other Churches which are or may be in this town of a Different constitution from the Standing Order of churches in the Land Shall Forever be excluded from Receiving any Benefit from the same." (Stebbins, p. 99.)

was born in Springfield, Mass., July 24, 1708. Moses Warriner (probably this one) and Miriam Ferry, of Springfield,
had banns recorded in that town, Feb. 24, 1738. There is no
record of marriage. If they married she probably died soon,
for he married Anne Cooley, of Springfield, having recorded
" intentions " Nov. 7, 1741. The History of Connecticut Valley states that he and Benjamin Warriner (79) were among the
twenty-two soldiers from Wilbraham precinct in the French
War, 1755-1760. He belonged to Capt. John Bancroft's company, Col. Timothy Ruggles' regiment.

The will of " Moses Warriner, of Springfield," is dated
March 11, 1762. It declares its author to be in a " languish-
ing state of health, but of sound mind and understanding."
It gives to Anne his " well-beloved wife," south half of dwelling house, free use of barn and barn yard; also sufficient of
firewood to be provided for her by their son Moses so long
as she remains his widow; also third part of land and one-half
of movable estate during her natural life. To eldest son,
Moses, dwelling house, subject to wife's privileges; also one
or two farms. To Noah, third son, a certain amount of land.
To sons Samuel, Nathaniel, Abner and Daniel, to be divided
as they or their guardians shall agree, land on Brimfield line.
To Anne, eldest daughter, 13 pounds 6 shillings 8 pence, when
18 years of age, and the same to Miriam. His wife was named
as executrix, and the witnesses were Moses Burt, James War-

riner, Jr., and Moses
Burt, Jr. Moses
Warriner, his eldest
son, was to be guar-
dian of minor sons,
Abner and David.

Moses Warriner
died in Wilbraham
and is buried there.
The dates of his and
his wife's death are
inscribed on their
tombstones as in
the cuts.

CHILDREN OF MOSES WARRINER (44).

(Births of all except the first recorded in Springfield.)

124. Moses, born 1742.
125. Samuel, born Aug. 30, 1744.
126. Anne, born Aug. 10, 1746; died in Springfield, Sept. 9, 1748.
127. Noah, born Oct. 27, 1748.
128. Nathaniel, born Oct. 18, 1750.
129. Anne 2d, born Dec. 12, 1752; probably the Anne Warriner who married Judah Ely in Wilbraham, May 24, 1781.
130. Abner, born Dec. 12, 1752; twin brother to Anne.
131. Daniel, born Jan. 16, 1756.
132. Miriam, born Apr. 1, 1758; probably the Miriam Warriner who died in Wilbraham, Feb. 10, 1831.*

63 JOSEPH WARRINER, son of Joseph (10) and Hannah, was born in Springfield, Mass., Apr. 16, 1723. Joseph Warriner was with Gideon Warriner (68) in Col. Joseph Dwight's regiment, 6th company, Capt. Isaac Colton, of Louisburg. He married Sarah Howard, of Mansfield, " intentions " having been filed in Springfield, Nov. 28, 1747.

CHILDREN OF JOSEPH WARRINER (63).

(All born in Springfield, Mass.)

133. Joseph, born Dec. 8, 1748.
134. Theodora, born May 9, 1753; died May 6, 1754, in Springfield.
135. William, born Oct. 28, 1756.
136. Nathan, born Dec. 18, 1758.
137. Lydia, born March 18, 1761; married Arriel Cooley, of Springfield, Sept. 27, 1781.

74 EBENEZER WARRINER, son of Ebenezer (12) and Joanna,

* It may, however, have been Miriam (229) who died in 1831.

was born in Springfield, Mass., Sept. 20, 1719; married, Oct. 23, 1746, Sarah Chapin, of Springfield. She died in that town, Apr. 6, 1773; he died there Jan. 19, 1813, in his 94th year.

CHILDREN OF EBENEZER WARRINER (74).

(All born in Springfield, Mass.)

140. Sarah, born Sept. 17, 1747; married Jesse Warner, Jr., May 11, 1769, "both of Springfield." This was "Sarah Warriner 3d." They moved to Long Meadow, Mass., thence to Conway, Mass., and moved again, about 1796, to Phelps, Ontario Co., N. Y. Their children: Elijah, 1770; Lewis, 1772; Rufus, about 1775; Jesse, 1777; John, about 1781; Oliver, about 1783; Jesse 2d, about 1786; Lucinda, about 1796, who married ——— Peck.
141. Martha, born Nov. 25, 1749.
142. Azeuba (spelled "Zeuba" by the town clerk), born June 23, 1752; married, in Springfield, to John Root, Dec. 10, 1775.
143. Ebenezer, born July 18, 1754.
144. Lucy, born July 7, 1757; died in Springfield, Jan. 20, 1759.
145. Martin, born Oct. 16, 1759.
146. Daniel, born Nov. 9, 1763.

76 HEZEKIAH WARRINER, son of Ebenezer (12) and Joanna, was born in Springfield, Oct. 13, 1724. On the death of his father, his mother was constituted his guardian, Aug. 29, 1739. He married Mary, daughter of Capt. Ebenezer and Mary (Morgan) Hitchcock, of Springfield, June 11, 1747.*

---

* The Hitchcock Genealogy says she was sister to Abner and Joseph Hitchcock, who were among the early inhabitants of Ludlow, Mass.

She was somehow nearly related to Gad Hitchcock, D. D. (1718-1803), a distinguished Unitarian minister.

Hezekiah Warriner died intestate, July 5, 1785, aged 61, and power of administration was granted to Gad Warriner. His widow died May 24, 1802, aged 78. She is buried in Agawam.

CHILDREN OF HEZEKIAH WARRINER (76).

(All born in Springfield, Mass.)

160. Hezekiah, born July 14, 1748; died Aug. 23, 1748.
161. Mary, born Dec. 7, 1749; probably the Mary Warriner, of Springfield, who married Gideon Leonard, Aug. 1, 1771.
162. Tabitha, born Jan. 1, 1753.
163. Lois, born June 16, 1754; married in West Springfield, May 29, 1800, to Samuel Partridge, of Springfield, Mass. (?)
164. Hezekiah 2d, born Apr. 29, 1756.
165. Abiah, twin sister to Hezekiah, born Apr. 29, 1756; married Oliver Leonard, Oct. 24, 1785 — both of Springfield.
166. Gad, born March 1, 1758.
167. Lewis, born Dec. 13, 1759.
168. Dinah, born Oct. 27, 1761. She was a Methodist; lived some years with Gad Warriner; died, unmarried, in Long Meadow, Mass., June 26, 1833, aged 72.
169. Eunice, born Sept. 8, 1765; married Calvin Cooley, in West Springfield, June 17, 1790. He died Feb. 19, 1846. She died Oct. 30, 1842, aged 77. They had Lewis, Norman and a daughter. The sons went west.

77 GIDEON WARRINER, son of Jonathan (18) and Mercy, was born in Springfield, Mass., June 5, 1727. He, with Joseph Warriner,* was in Col. Joseph Dwight's regiment, 5th Co., Capt. Caleb Johnson, commissioned to serve in the memorable expedition against Louisburg in 1745. The regiment did

---

* N. E. Hist. & Gen. Reg., Vol. XXV, p. 265.

not go, however, but built Fort Massachusetts. The name of Gideon Warriner is on the roll of the same regiment.* He and his father lost their lives in that war.†

79 Benjamin Warriner, son of Benjamin (18) and Mercy, was born in Springfield, Mass., Sept. 3, 1727; married Persis Willard, June 28, 1749. He and Moses Warriner (41) were among the twenty-two soldiers from Wilbraham in the French War.‡

Children of Benjamin Warriner (79).

(Births of the first seven recorded in Springfield; those of the rest in Wilbraham after it became a town.)

180. Persis, born Jan. 5, 1750.
181. Benjamin, born March 3, 1751.
182. Willard, born Feb. 17, 1753.
183. Esther, born Feb. 19, 1755. Asahel Cooley recorded intentions of marriage with Esther Warriner (probably this person) Aug. 11, 1778.
184. Lydia, born Nov. 5, 1757.
185. Bathsheba, born Feb. 10, 1760.
186. Gad, born Jan. 29, 1762.
187. Elijah, born Jan. 25, 1764.
188. Mercy, born March 16, 1766. Lewis Wright recorded intentions of marriage to Mercy Warriner July 8, 1786. Both were of Springfield. Probably this Mercy Warriner is meant.
189. Zadok, born Feb. 29, 1768.
190. Phebe, born Apr. 13, 1770. This is probably the Phebe Warriner who married Israel Dwight, of Great Barrington, Mass., March, 1795, and who died in Hartwick, N. Y., March, 1802 — "a woman of large-hearted generosity, and of a win-

---

* N. E. Hist. & Gen. Reg., Vol. XXV, p. 265.
† See sketch of Jonathan Warriner (15).
‡ Hist. Conn. Valley.

ning and affectionate disposition."* She left four
children: Eliza, Lyman, Harriet and Jedediah
Bushnell. Ann S., wife of S. Lyman Smith, of.
Ithaca, N. Y., is daughter of Harriet.

191. Zeruiah (dau.), born Aug. 22, 1772.

81 SAMUEL WARRINER, son of Benjamin (18) and Mercy,
was born in Springfield, Mass., March 23, 1730; married, Nov.
6, 1753, Ruth, daughter of Ebenezer and Sarah (Colton) Bliss
— both of Springfield.† She was born in Long Meadow,
Mass., Jan. 16, 1732.

CHILDREN OF SAMUEL WARRINER (81).

(The births are recorded in Springfield records except the
last; John was born in Wilbraham after it became a town.)

192. Ruth, born May 4, 1754.
193. Samuel, born May 24, 1760.
194. Aaron, born Dec. 30, 1761.
195. John, born Dec. 10, 1764.

82 REUBEN WARRINER, son of Benjamin (18) and Mercy,
was born in Springfield, Mass., March 6, 1733; married, Feb.
3, 1756, Sarah Willard, of Springfield. He died Dec. 29, 1758.
Power of administration was granted to Sarah, his widow,
March 12, 1759, and she was appointed guardian of their son,
Reuben, on July 10, 1759. She married Asa Colton, Apr. 20,
1761, and they had nine children.‡

* Dwight History, p. 700.
† The town clerk of Long Meadow says there is a record to
this effect, that Samuel Warriner married Ruth, daughter of
Ebenezer Bliss in Long Meadow, on Sept. 6, 1733. This was
an error in copying — else there must have been another Sam-
uel Warriner, and another Ruth Bliss, daughter of Ebenezer
Bliss.
‡ N. E. Hist. and Gen. Reg., Vol. XXXIV, p. 187.

54

CHILDREN OF REUBEN WARRINER (82).

(Both born in Springfield.)

196. Reuben, born Nov. 7, 1756.
197. Sarah, born Dec. 12, 1757; died Jan. 17, 1758, in
Springfield.

87 ISRAEL WARRINER, son of Benjamin (18) and Mercy,
twin brother of Jacob, was born May 19, 1742.* He married,
July 10, 1766, Mara, or Molly, Hitchcock, or Mary Heaton.†
Israel Warriner was selectman in Ludlow, Mass., seven years.

* The town record of Springfield says 1742; the record kept
in the family has 1743.

† The Springfield books plainly say " Mary Heaton," both
in record of intentions and record of marriage, the latter bearing date July 10, 1766. The family record says: " Israel Warriner, married, July 10, 1766, to Mary Hitchcock." She was
probably daughter of Abner Hitchcock, of Ludlow. He was
son of Ebenezer Hitchcock, of Springfield. Abner appears in
Ludlow a few years later than his brother Joseph, who was
one of the first settlers of that town. At a meeting in Ludlow,
in March, 1774, the two brothers, Abner and Joseph Hitchcock, also the two brothers, Isaac and Israel Warriner, were
present. The three last-named were elected to office.
The descendants of Israel Warriner claim that his wife's
name was Mary Hitchcock, and that in her later days she often
talked of Ludlow. While it seems best to accept this version,
the records in Springfield are a puzzle hard to solve. There
are no Heaton marriages in Springfield records except Mary's.
No death of Heaton is recorded. Savage, Gen. Dic., has
Nathaniel Heaton, of Dedham, freeman, 1761. By his wife
Mary he had Sarah, James (25 March, 1690) and Abigail —
perhaps others earlier. Nathaniel, New Haven (perhaps son
or brother of James), proprietor 1685.
Isabel Hitchcock, daughter of Caleb Hitchcock, married
Jonathan Heaton, Apr. 26, 1777. Was he brother of Mary
Heaton?

55

He moved thence to Oneida county, N. Y., thence to Adams Center, in the same State, where he died March 26, 1810. He is buried there. Molly Hitchcock Warriner was born June 5, 1748; died in Adams Center, N. Y., Jan. 15, 1834.

CHILDREN OF ISRAEL WARRINER (87).

(All born in Mass. — some in Springfield, some in Ludlow.)

201. Mary, born in Springfield, Dec. 7, 1766; married ——— Caulkins.*
202. Israel, born in Springfield, Oct. 29, 1768.
203. Luther, date of birth unknown.
204. Lucy, born May 18, 1780; married Asher Kinney, March 3, 1802. Mr. K. was born in 1767. Their children: Hewit, 1803; Asher, 1805; Emily M., 1807, married Phineas C. Miller; Giles, 1809; James F., 1811; Sylvester, 1813; Lucy Ann, 1816; married Alfred B. Mason; Sabra L., 1823, married Myron Keith.
205. Reuben, born Apr. 7, 1781.
206. Calvin, born Apr. 4, 1784, in Ludlow, Mass.
207. Eunice, date of birth not known; married Ebenezer Bartlett. Their children: Betsey, Pamelia, Mary Emiline, Festus, Julius King, Chauncey L. A son of Chauncey L., namely, Homer A. Bartlett, resides in Watertown, N. Y. (1898). Eunice Bartlett died in North Adams, N. Y.
208. Lucina, born July 2, 1788; married, Feb. 19, 1812, Heman, son of Capt. John Colton. She died Apr. 9, 1857. Children: Emily J., born 1813, died 1813; Heman, born 1816, died 1816; Chauncey, born 1817, died 1892; Mary, born 1819, married Ralph Mack, died 1890; Julia Ann, born 1822, died 1843; Marie Antoinette, born 1826, died 1842; Emily, born 1828, died 1842.

* Letter of Parley E. Warriner.

88 ISAAC WARRINER, son of Benjamin (18) and Mercy, was born in Springfield, Mass., Aug. 28, 1745; married Lydia Fury, of Wilbraham, in 1767. Banns were recorded Apr. 11 of that year. He lived in Ludlow for some time after 1771.* He made his will March 11, 1803, and bequeathed to his wife, Lydia, his entire estate, real and personal. Nevertheless small sums were given to his two sons, Jacob and Justin, and to his daughters, namely Sally, wife of Joseph Hatfield, Rachel Warriner, and Chloe, wife of John Collins. His wife refused to execute the trust as executrix, and the court appointed Edward Pynchon administrator. Amount to be divided among creditors was $145.93.

Isaac Warriner died three days after making his will, on March 14, 1803, and his widow, Lydia, died on July 25, 1815, in her 72d year.

CHILDREN OF ISAAC WARRINER (88).

209. Jacob, born in Wilbraham, Apr. 18, 1768.
210. Sarah, born in Wilbraham, Aug. 13, 1769; died in the same town, Jan. 20, 1770.
211. Sarah 2d, or "Sally," born in Wilbraham, July 10, 1771; married in Springfield in 1791 to Joseph Hatfield.
212. Rachel, born in Ludlow, probably in 1774; died, unmarried, Sept. 4, 1844, in her 70th year.
213. Chloe, born in Ludlow, probably; married, 1799, John Collins, "both of Springfield."
214. Justin, born in Springfield, Apr. 27, 1783.
215. Isaac, born in Springfield, Oct. 14, 1788; died in Springfield, Jan. 7, 1803, in his 15th year.

90 DAVID WARRINER, son of David (19) and Mary, was born in Springfield, Mass. (now Wilbraham), May 13, 1742. He married Joanna Moody, of Hadley. In company with Wm. Rice he kept a public house in Wilbraham. The original boarding house of the academy was the old Warriner

* See † note on page 54.

WARRINER HOMESTEAD—WESLEYAN ACADEMY, 1825.
(The house with swinging sign in front was the Warriner Hotel.)

tavern and farm house. One-half the homestead, sixty acres, became the property of the academy. The tavern was enlarged and fitted up, and the school was opened for the reception of students Nov. 8, 1825.

David Warriner made his will in Wilbraham, Jan. 4, 1783. He gave to David, his eldest son, a farm at Stony Creek, etc.; to his son Jonathan, lands at Cowper's Meadow Bridge, etc.; to his " only daughter, Peggy, . . . land in the mountain . . . value of a good cow, a free lease of lower north room of dwelling, so long as she shall remain in an unmarried state." Witnessed by Ezra Barker, Abel King and Ezra Barker, Jr. His widow died in Springfield, May 6, 1820, aged 77.

CHILDREN OF DAVID WARRINER (90).

(All born in Wilbraham.)

216. Mary, born Jan. 17, 1792; died in Wilbraham, Sept. 2, 1774.
217. Joanna, born March 14, 1774; died Apr. 9, 1776.
218. Jerusha, born Nov. 17, 1775; died Jan. 17, 1777, in Wilbraham.
219. David, born Jan. 3, 1778.
220. Joanna 2d, born Dec. 5, 1779; married John Rice, Dec. 23, 1802.
221. Charles, born Oct. 7, 1782.
222. Jerusha 2d, born March 15, 1785; married, Sept. 17, 1809, Wm. Rice; died July 20, 1869. Children: Cornelia, who died unmarried; Jerusha, who married Norton Norton; William; * Joseph Benson — died in infancy.

---

* This was the Rev. Wm. Rice, D. D., founder of the City Library of Springfield, Mass. He was a member of the committee to revise the Methodist Hymnal in 1876, and is widely known as an author. Among his published works are " The Pastor's Manual," and " Religous Quotations from the Poets." He was married in 1843 to Caroline Laura, daughter of Wm. North, of Lowell, Mass. Children: Wm. North Rice, Ph. D.;

Some of her descendants have a letter written by Amos Binney to Charles and David Warriner, asking how much they would take for the farm. The purchase was made, Mrs. Rice (Jerusha Warriner) giving her part of the sixty acres as a donation.

100 SAMUEL WARRINER, son of Ebenezer (24) and Elizabeth, was born in Enfield, Conn., Nov. 19, 1719; married Martha Hale in 1748, record of intentions having been made on May 12. He was constable in 1765, also tithing man, school committeeman, and selectman at different times till 1774. He is frequently mentioned in the old records of Enfield.* He died in Enfield, Conn., Dec. 31, 1787, in his 68th year.

His widow, Martha Warriner, executed a lease to Horace Burt, of Long Meadow, the property leased being all the real estate formerly owned by her husband — two pieces of land in Enfield. The lease extended through her lifetime, and Mr. Burt was to provide for her a good and comfortable support, viz.: " good house room, fire wood, clothing and lodging, meat, drink, washing physick, and attendance both in sickness and in health, and in every way provide for her, the said Martha, every convenience of life during her life, and also to pay annually to Martha Bliss five dollars worth of provisions during the natural life of the said Martha Warriner."

110 CAPT. JAMES WARRINER, son of James (32) and Anne, was born in Springfield, Mass., Sept. 2, 1723; married Miriam Parsons, Oct. 27, 1744. We find his name, James Warriner, Jr., among the selectmen of Wilbraham precinct in 1759. He

Professor in Weslyan University; Edward H. Rice, Ph. D., classical teacher in Worcester High School; Rev. Charles F. Rice, A. M., New England Conference; Caroline L. Rice, graduate of Wesleyan University.

* July the 22d Samuel Warriner entered the mark of his creatures, a half cross the upper side of each ear, and a slit the under side " of the near ear."

was town clerk of Wilbraham, 1773-1778 and 1781-1785. He was the Capt, James Warriner who commanded the first soldiers from Wilbraham in the Revolutionary War. Roused by the news of the firing at Lexington, he led a company of militiamen to the defense of American liberty. In Stebbins' Centennial of Wilbraham may be found a roll of his company copied from the State rolls. To this roll the following statement is affixed: "Dec. 5, 1775. The persons above named living in the town of Wilbraham, who marched with their arms and ammunition, occasioned by Lexington fight, some before and some after me, who pray that they may have pay, agreeable to a late resolve of the Genll Court of this colony, agreeable to the services that are affixed to their names, which is the time of service affixed to each name in this Roll according to ye best of my knowledge.

Attest. JAMES WARRINER, Capt."

He, with a majority of his company, served ten days, for which he received two pounds seventeen shillings nine pence. The Revolutionary rolls in the office of the Secretary of State in Boston, Mass., contain a record of his service as captain, serving on the alarm of Apr. 19, 1775.

He made his will Dec. 2, 1791.*   His death occurred June

---

* He bequeathed to his wife, Miriam, household furniture, wearing apparel, use and improvement of one-third of the farm, etc. To the two elder sons, James and Thomas, " in equal shares all my house lot or farm on which I dwell," etc., except partly to the other sons; to his " son Solomon the farm or lot on which he now dwells," etc.; to his son Stephen " land in Monson; " to his son Ethan, " part of house lot, 16 rods on north side," etc.; to his daughter Miriam, " Lot of land in sd Wilbraham on the east side of the mountain," etc.; to his daughter Amy Charlotte, land in Monson, etc.; to his two daughters, in equal shares, the use of one-third part of dwelling house while they remain single. His son Solomon was named as executor, also as guardian to the " two eldest sons, James and Thomas, they being incapable of taking care of themselves." Witnessed by John Buckland, Reuben Hitchcock, Samuel F. Merrick.

20, 1793. His name and those of his wife and youngest daughter may be seen on tombstones in the old cemetery in Wilbraham. Two of the stones are here pictured by our artist.

CHILDREN OF CAPT. JAMES WARRINER (110).

226. James, born Sept. 18, 1745, in what was then Springfield township. There is no record of his marriage. He died in Wilbraham, Apr. 17, 1824, aged 79. Some incapacity of mind or body is mentioned in his father's will. His tombstone is in the old cemetery in Wilbraham.

227. Thomas, born Jan. 2, 1747, in Springfield. He probably never married. He died May 9, 1821, aged 74. He is mentioned in his father's will in the same way as his brother James, and is put under the guardianship of his brother Solomon. His tombstone in Wilbraham cemetery is well preserved.

228. Solomon, born Aug. 16, 1753.

229. Miriam, born in Springfield, Jan. 22, 1756. It was either she or Miriam Warriner (132) who died in Wilbraham Feb. 10, 1831.

230. Stephen, born June 8, 1760.

231. Ethan, born July 8, 1763.

232. Anny Charlotte, born Feb. 26, 1768; died in Wilbraham, May 25, 1792, aged 24.

111 STEPHEN WARRINER, son of James (32) and Anne, or Almy, was born in Springfield, Mass., March 17, 1726; mar-

ried Mercy Burt, May 23, 1750 — " both of Springfield." She died in Springfield, Aug. 15, 1751, and he married Hepzibah, daughter of Samuel and Hepzibah Chandler, of Enfield, Conn. He died Feb. 3, 1760, and his widow married Stephen Chandler.*

CHILDREN OF STEPHEN WARRINER (111).

(Both born in Springfield.)

223. Stephen, born July 5, 1751; died Aug. 15, 1751.
224. Mercy, born Sept. 7, 1755; named in the will of her grandfather, James (32). In 1769 her guardians were James Chandler and Hepzibah Chandler.

112 AARON WARRINER, son of James (32) and Anne, or Almy, was born in Springfield, July 21, 1728, and died Jan. 17, 1798, in the 70th year of his age. Probate records state that he was adjudged insane, and Moses Bliss became his guardian in 1790, and an order was issued by the court to sell his real estate, farm, sawmill, etc. The property was appraised at 901 pounds 6 shillings; debts 605 pounds 11 shillings 11 pence.

123 WILLIAM WARRINER, son of William (38) and Lois, was born in Brimfield, Mass., Jan. 2 (or 14), 1744; married Lois Morgan, Oct. 10, 1776. She was born Apr. 26, 1750.

CHILDREN OF WILLIAM WARRINER (123).

235. Nabby, born Dec. 15, 1778; married David Hyde, Apr. 9, 1801.
236. Lois, born 1780; died, unmarried, in 1850, in New York City.
237. Ruth, born Sept. 22, 1782; married David Bacon, M. D., of Buxton, Me., Dec. 12, 1802.
238. William Bostwick, born Feb. 3, 1785.
239. Abner Morgan, born Apr. 15, 1787; married in Feb., 1813, Mary N. Green, of Providence, R. I.

* N. E. Hist. and Gen. Reg., Vol. XXIII, p. 69.

124 MOSES WARRINER, son of Moses (44) and Anne, was born in 1742; married Mary Warner, "intentions" having been recorded Aug. 30, 1763. He died in Wilbraham, Mass., Oct. 4, 1809.*

CHILDREN OF MOSES WARRINER (124).

(Born in Wilbraham.)

240. Mary, born Sept. 24, 1764.
241. Susannah, born Sept. 18, 1766; married Isaac Lewis, March 28, 1787.
242. Lydia, born March 22, 1769; died in Wilbraham, Sept. 16, 1771. A headstone marks her grave in the old cemetery.
243. Moses, born May 24, 1771.
244. Lydia 2d, born June 15, 1773; married Noah Dean, Jan. 30, 1800 — both of Wilbraham.
245. Elizabeth, born July 4, 1775; married Jonathan Kilbourne in Wilbraham. Her name is written "Betsey" in the marriage record.
246. Flavia, born Feb. 14, 1782; married on Feb. 10, 1803, Thomas Glover — "both of Wilbraham." He died in 1849; she died Nov. 4, 1864. Her tombstone is in the old cemetery, Wilbraham.

125 SAMUEL WARRINER, son of Moses (44) and Anne, was born in what was then part of Springfield (now Wilbraham), Mass., Apr. 30, 1744; married Chloe, daughter of Martin Nash,† Feb. 26, 1766. They moved to Brattleboro, Vt., in

---

* One "Widow Mary Warriner," probably widow of this man, died in Wilbraham, Jan., 1830.

† She was born Feb. 26, 1746. Rev. Sylvester Nash, A. M., in his Nash Genealogy, says Chloe Nash married Capt. Daniel Warriner. Daniel (118), brother to Samuel, died young. Samuel's son, Daniel (249), was captain. The author of Nash Genealogy has evidently put "Capt. Daniel Warriner" in place of Samuel (112).

1774, and settled in the woods. A correspondent of the Vermont Phœnix, on Aug. 13, 1897, says: " Samuel Warriner of this town (Brattleboro) enlisted Sept. 24, 1777, into Capt. Josiah Boyden's company of Col. Williams' regiment and served 23 days.

Samuel Warriner built a new house in 1800, which remains

HOME OF SAMUEL WARRINER, BUILT IN 1800.

almost unchanged in outward appearance. It was built of hard wood, and it took 70 men to raise it. The large chimney has been removed and blinds have been added. Henry Warriner (717), a grandson of Samuel Warriner, resides there at the present time (1898). In the History of Eastern Vermont, by Benjamin H. Hale, the name of Samuel Warriner appears signed to important papers relating to the formation of the State in 1777. He took strong ground in the controversy. In his own town he was a prominent man, holding the office of justice of the peace. At a town meeting in Brattleboro in

1778, he was chosen moderator, and he was coroner 1778-1780.* He was by occupation a farmer, and he was a deacon in the Congregational church. He died in Brattleboro, Vt., Sept. 25, 1808, aged 64, and his widow died July 4, 1830, aged 84. Their graves with headstones are in West Brattleboro.

CHILDREN OF SAMUEL WARRINER (125).

(First two or three were born in Wilbraham, Mass.; the others in Brattleboro, Vt.)

247. Samuel, born June 17, 1769; died in Brattleboro, Vt., Aug. 22, 1803.
248. Chloe, born Oct. 8, 1770; married Cushing King; died March 22, 1836.
249. Martha, born Nov. 8, 1772; died Feb. 22, 1835, unmarried.
250. Laurania, born Oct. 8, 1774; married ——— May; died in Brattleboro, Vt., July 27, 1800.
251. Elizabeth, born Feb. 25, 1777; married, 1st, David White; 2d, S. Keep; 3d, S. King. It is believed that she died in Salt Lake City.
252. Nancy, born Dec. 16, 1779; married Daniel Melendy; died probably in Bainbridge, Vt.
253. William, born June 23, 1782.
254. Daniel, born Nov. 5, 1785.
255. Cynthia, born Feb. 10, 1789; married John Hadley. From her son, Judge Daniel B. Hadley, of Kansas City, Kan., we learn that she was a marked character among the early Methodists of Western New York. In 1815 she accompanied her husband as an early settler of a town named Elba, in Genesee county. An incident illustrates her conscientiousness and decision. Before she married John Hadley she made him promise not to play the violin for dancing parties. At a gathering where they

* See History of Eastern Vermont, pp. 292, 319, 480, 467.

were on one occasion, dancing was proposed and
he was drawn into playing his fiddle, which had
been sent for. She indignantly stepped up to the
fiddle, flipped out the bridge, and the music
stopped.

They moved from Elba, in 1822, to Batavia,
thence, in 1828, to Bennington, twenty miles
south, where they escaped fever and ague, which
had tormented them from the time they first went
to the new country.

She was a singer, and a remarkable exhorter,
and greatly gifted in prayer. She gloried in the
old-time Methodist camp meetings, and took an
active part in them.

Their children all left home to seek their for-
tunes, save John Jones, who died Aug. 20, 1837,
and Herman, who bought a part of the farm in
1840, and lived there till his death in 1852. Jones,
as he was called, went to the seminary at Lima to
fit himself for the Methodist ministry, but died as
stated above. John Hadley and his wife sold out
after Herman's death, and moved to Attica, N. Y.,
in 1855. They remained there till 1858, and then
went to live with their son William in Williamsburgh, L. I. There they died. The date of her
death is Feb. 11, 1865. They are buried in
Cypress Hills Cemetery. Their daughter Chloe
married the Rev. Mr. McKinstry in 1858, and died
about 1891.

256. Pliny, twin brother of Cynthia, born Feb. 10, 1789.
Probably he died unmarried.*

* Judge D. B. Hadley, of Kansas City, Kan., writes: " My
parents often said Pliny visited them at Elba, Genesee county,
N. Y., about 1818, and left there to go to Hamburgh to visit
Dr. William Warriner, but never reached Hamburgh, and was
never heard of by any of the family thereafter."

127 DEACON NOAH WARRINER, often called Lieutenant
Noah Warriner, son of Moses (44)
and Anne, was born in Wilbraham,
then part of Springfield township,
Mass., Oct. 27, 1748; married Grace
Gregory. She died of small-pox
in Wilbraham, July 14, 1778, in her
31st year. His second wife was
Mary Ainsworth, of Providence,
R. I. He signed the non-con-
sumption pledge in 1774. In the
Revolution he was sergeant in
Capt. Paul Langdon's company,
Col. Davidson's regiment. He
served among the eight months'
men encamped at Roxbury, and,
with Abner Warriner, his uncle, in
the army that besieged Boston after
the Lexington alarm. He was
town clerk of Wilbraham in 1779
and 1780. His will bears date
Aug. 11, 1796.* He and his wife
died in Wilbraham, and are buried

MEETING HOUSE IN WILBRA-
HAM IN WHICH MANY WAR-
RINERS WORSHIPED. (Re-
built and steeple added in
1797.)

in the old cemetery in that town. In copying the inscriptions
for the cuts we omit the poetry, which is moss-grown and hard
to decipher. (See cuts on following page.)

---

* This will gives to his wife, Mary, use and improvement of
dwelling-house, barn, etc., "stand on lot lately belonging to
my honored uncle, Noah Warriner, deceased, during the time
she remains a widow;" ditto, other real estate, etc. To
daughter, Anna Gregory, "wearing apparel of her late mother,
deceased, mother's movable goods, and $80 at 20 years of age,
or at her marriage, with interest, should she marry before
reaching that age." Other property is divided among the
daughters, Anna G., Grace, Polly, Linda, Margaret, Sophronia and Dolly, and a nephew, Noah Warriner Sheldon.
Executors: Mary Warriner and Joshua Frost. Witnesses:
William Pynchon, Joseph Sexton, Francis Sexton. Codicil
names Mary Warriner as guardian of all the daughters.

CHILDREN OF DEA. (LIEUT.) NOAH WARRINER (127).

(All born in Wilbraham.)

257. Anna Gregory, born May 4, 1778; married Rev. Samuel Colton, of Long Meadow, March 6, 1799. Children: Leroy, 1799; Samuel, 1801; Mary Ann, 1802; Emeline, 1804-1863; Flavia, 1805.* Mr. Colton died in 1811. His widow, Anna Gregory Warriner, married Rev. Gilbert Burt in 1816.

258. Grace, born Nov. 7, 1781.

259. Polly, born July 27, 1783; drowned in Nine Mile Pond, Apr. 29, 1799.†

260. Linda, born July 23, 1785; married Chester Sexton, May 28, 1806. She died at West Point, N. Y., June 22, 1860. He died at the same place soon after. Children: Lucinda, Bezaleel, John Gregory, Hannah, Mary.

---

* One daughter married E. W. Storrs, of Springfield; another married ——— Lawton; a third married ——— Wright; a fourth married Hon. John H. Brockway, M. C., from Hartford district. (N. E. Hist. and Gen. Reg., Vol. V, p. 168.)

† In the year 1871 Walter Warriner (275), when 90 years of age, wrote the following to his niece, Victoria S. Warriner: "A sailor by the name of Shepherd came to Wilbraham and built a house on the banks of a pond called Nine Mile Pond, being nine miles from Springfield. He likewise built a sail-boat with two masts and sails accordingly, for pleasure trips.

261. Margaret, born Aug. 1, 1787. Her husband's name was Smith.*

262. Sophronia, born July 11, 1790; married Pynchon Bliss; died June 4, 1813, aged 23. Her husband married again, and died in 1868, aged 82. See headstone in Wilbraham. His second wife was Betsey Warriner (632).

263. Dolly, born July 6, 1793; married Col. Warren Lincoln.† Children: William, born 1814, died

---

One pleasant day a company of young persons were on a visit to the house of Levi Bliss near the pond. I will give the names of the company: Mary Warriner (same person named Polly on tombstone), Abigail Merrick, Ascenath Bliss — all in their 16th year — also Guy Johnson, Leonard Bliss and Gordon Bliss. These six persons all went inti eternity together. A little circumstance — while taking tea at Mr. Bliss', Abigail Merrick, as was customary, turned up her cup to find her fortune. 'Oh!' says she, 'I'm going to be drowned.' The others made light of it. Soon all repaired to the pond and got aboard the boat and set sail. The pond was in the shape of a pair of spectacles. They steered for the nose, coming within six rods of it. A gust of wind came round the nose, took the sails, turned over and sank the boat, and there the six young persons perished together. Gordon Bliss, Leonard Bliss, Ascenath Bliss, brothers and sister, three from one family, in perfect health, were drowned at the same time. Comment on the parents' feelings is useless. 1798 was near the time of the disaster; it was in the month of April."

The inscription on her gravestone in the old cemetery in Wilbraham is as follows: "In memory of Miss Mary, Daughter Dr Noah and Mrs. Mary Warriner was drowned in the pond in Wilbraham, together with five others on the 29th day of April, 1799, in the 16th year of her age. Bost not thyself of tomorrow, for thou knowest not what a day may bring forth."

* Letter of Mrs. S. C. Warriner, granddaughter of 263. One Margaret Warriner married George Cooley, Jr., June 30, 1812.

† His family was one of the most influential in the nation. It is stated that President Abraham Lincoln, Gen. Benjamin

1883; Albert W., born 1819; Charlotte Maria, born 1821; Eliza, born 1823.

128 NATHANIEL WARRINER, son of Moses (44) and Anne, was born in what was then Springfield, Oct. 18, 1750; married Diadema, daughter of Thomas and Jemima (Wright) Hancock.* She was born in Springfield, March 2, 1753. They

---

Lincoln, who received the sword of Lord Cornwallis on his surrender, and was secretary of war; Enoch Lincoln, governor of Maine, 1827-1829; Levi Lincoln, attorney-general of the U. S., 1801-1805; lieut.-governor of Mass., 1807, 1808, and acting governor, 1809; Levi Lincoln, LL. D., lieut.-governor of Mass., 1825-1834, and first mayor of Worcester, 1845, were all of the same family.

Col. Warren and Dolly Lincoln's eldest son William was a man of wealth and influence in western Mass., well known in the insurance business. He married an intelligent lady, Elizabeth Bucknam Ellis, daughter of Capt. Shepard Ellis. She was a descendant of Rev. Thomas Shepard, of England, and of Cambridge, Mass. (1623), and of Rev. Nathan Bucknam, of England, and of East Medway, Mass. (1724). She was related to John Quincy Adams and Judge Josiah Quincy on her father's side, and to Gen. Benedict Arnold and John Alden on her mother's side. The Ellis family, it is claimed, descended from the early French kings. The name was spelled de Lys, and the family were entitled to wear the royal fleur de lis in their coat-of-arms.

Ida, daughter of William and Elizabeth B. Lincoln, wife of Col. S. C. Warriner (1260), of Springfield, Mass., has a copy of this coat of arms in water colors.

Albert W., another son of Col. Warren and Dolly Lincoln, was a wealthy broker. He married Mary Ann Blair. Charlotte Maria Lincoln married Prof. David M. Kimball, of Yale. Elizabeth Lincoln married Danforth Keys, a descendant of the first settlers of Warren, Mass., and of Col. Danforth of Revolutionary fame.

* Thomas Hancock, of Long Meadow, son of John and

moved to Adams, N. Y., in 1805, and found there an almost unbroken wilderness — two or three log cabins and a small sawmill. He is said to have lived some time in Norwich, N. Y., probably before going to Adams. He died about 1833, at the home of his daughter, Nancy Spencer, in Clayton, N. Y., aged 83. His wife died in the same village, aged 96.

CHILDREN OF NATHANIEL WARRINER (128).

(All born in Wilbraham, Mass.)

265. Nathaniel, born July 7, 1776.
266. Diadema, born July 17, 1777; married Leonard Reynolds. He died at John Spencer's, in Clayton, N. Y.; she died in Pamelia, N. Y., at the home of her son Lorenzo. Children: Betsey, Maria, Harriet, Franklin, Lucy Ann, Lorenzo, Irene — all born in Lorraine, N. Y. The family moved to Pamelia.
267. Daniel, born Apr. 6, 1779.
268. Nancy, born Apr. 11, 1781; married John Spencer. Their life was mostly spent in Clayton, N. Y. Children: Sidney, Jason, Hannah, Ambrose, Otis, Alonzo, Tryphena, Tryphosa, Irving. Otis lived in Clayton.
269. Ethni, born March 21, 1784.
270. Luther, twin brother of Ethni, born March 21, 1784.
271. Sarah, born Feb. 16, 1788. She moved to Adams, N. Y., with her parents when seven years of age. On reaching maturity she married Titus Bassett. Mr. Bassett was a soldier in the War of 1812, and one of the sturdy men who assisted in carrying from the mouth of Sandy Creek to Sacketts Har-

Anna Hancock, was born in Springfield, Mass., May 10, 1727, and married Jemima Wright, daughter of Benjamin and Mary Wright, of Chicopee, Nov. 16, 1749. John Hancock married Anna Web, Nov. 19, 1713.

bor, the ponderous cable which was to be used in fitting out the war ship at the latter place, and which stood there as a monument to their patriotism for many years. Sarah Warriner Bassett was the mother of three children, Laura, Harvey and Marvin. Marvin was living recently in Oswego, N. Y.

272. Cynthia, born July 9, 1791; married Joseph Rowe. Children: Roswell and a daughter. Mr. Rowe died in Oriskany, N. Y., and Cynthia went to live with her children in Wisconsin.

273. Loren, born about 1800.

130 ABNER WARRINER, son of Moses (44) and Anne, was born Dec. 1, 1752. He and his brother Daniel being minors when their father died, James Warriner was appointed guardian over them. He married Elizabeth Wright, Nov. 27, 1817. Abner Warriner, fifer, was among the eight months' troops encamped at Roxbury, Mass., and in the army that besieged Boston after the Lexington alarm. His brother, Noah Warriner, was there also.

Abner Warriner died in Wilbraham, Mass., and a picture of his gravestone in the old cemetery is here shown. His wife died at her daughter's in Enfield, Conn., Sept. 6, 1849, aged 90.

CHILDREN OF ABNER WARRINER (130).

(All born in Wilbraham, Mass.)

274. Abner, born Aug. 30, 1779.
275. Walter, born Apr. 30, 1781.
276. Ira, born Apr. 4, 1783; died young.
277. Warren, born Jan. 10, 1785.
278. Pamelia, date of birth not given; married Asher

Hitchcock, intentions having been recorded in Springfield, Dec. 5, 1807. Their children: John, Lyman, Franklin, Sophronia. A granddaughter, Mrs. E. P. White, resides in West Springfield, Mass.

279. Julia, born Dec. 17, 1788; died suddenly, not married.
280. Alford, born May 30, 1791.
281. Theodore, born March 20, 1793.
282. Samuel, born Apr. 22, 1795.
283. Elizabeth, born May 20, 1797; married in Wilbraham, Nov. 27, 1817, to Obadiah Hurlburt. Their home was in Enfield, Conn. She died Feb., 1886. Children: Julia, Elizabeth, Clarissa E., Eleanor, Olive, Edwin, Ossian, Corydon, Franklin. Ossian Hurlburt, of Glastonbury, Conn., is the only son living in 1898, and all the daughters are dead except Elizabeth (Mrs. Hugentobler, of Hartford, Conn.), and Clarissa (Mrs. Lester, of East Hartford Meadow, Conn).
284. Noah, born May 14, 1799; died young.

131 DANIEL WARRINER, son of Moses (44) and Anne, was born in Springfield township, Jan. 16, 1756. He enlisted in the Continental service, and died Aug. 27, 1777, in Albany, N. Y., in the 22d year of his age. The Revolutionary rolls in the custody of the secretary of the commonwealth of Massachusetts mention his enlistment and his death. He was of South Hadley, and served in 1775 and 1777.

136 NATHAN WARRINER, son of Joseph (63) and Sarah, was born in Springfield, Mass., Dec. 18, 1758; married Hannah Butler, Sept. 23, 1779. She died Nov. 3, 1817, and on Sept. 8, 1819, he married Rhoda Truesdell, in Wilbraham. She survived him. They resided in Monson, and children were born to them as recorded below.

CHILDREN OF NATHAN WARRINER (136.)

(All born in Monson, Mass.)

300. Sarah, born Sept. 9, 1780; died Sept. 23, 1816, aged 36, unmarried. Buried in Wilbraham.
301. Joseph, born Sept. 5, 1782.
302. Barbara, born Feb. 22, 1785; married Elijah Osborne; died Jan. 29, 1835, in Monson, Mass.
303. William, born May 10, 1787.
304. Theodora, born Feb. 23, 1790; married John Butler, 1815 — both of Monson. He died 1859, aged 75. Children: Marcus, John, Theodosia, Jane, Abel, Linus.
305. Nathan, born May 29, 1792.
306. Benjamin Howard, born Apr. 6, 1794.
307. Hannah, born Jan. 2, 1796; married Rev. John Borden, and had children. They went to Pennsylvania.
308. Lydia, born Sept. 23, 1798; married Joseph Palmer; lived and died in Delmar, Tioga county, Pa. They left no children.
309. Abel, born Jan. 31, 1801.
310. James, born Sept. 15, 1803.

143 EBENEZER WARRINER, son of Ebenezer (74) and Sarah, was born in Springfield, Mass., July 18, 1754; married, Feb. 21, 1781, Tryphena Farre, of Springfield; died Nov. 18, 1836, aged 80.

CHILDREN OF EBENEZER WARRINER (143).

(Born in Springfield, Mass.)

311. Sarah, born Feb. 5, 1782.
312. Moses, born March 30, 1785; died in Springfield, Nov. 22, 1805, in his 21st year.
313. Walter, born Sept. 9, 1789.
314. Jonathan, born July 1, 1793; died of consumption in Springfield, Dec. 22, 1813, in his 21st year.

145 MARTIN WARRINER, son of Ebenezer (74) and Sarah, was born in Springfield, Mass., Oct. 16, 1759; married, Oct. 5, 1780, Sabra Hancock — "both of Springfield." She was born July 23, 1755, and died Jan. 23, 1809. Martin Warriner died in Springfield, July 23, 1818.

CHILD OF MARTIN WARRINER (145).

315. Ebenezer, date of birth not given; drowned in Mill River, March 21, 1802, aged 5 years.

146 DANIEL WARRINER, son of Ebenezer (74) and Sarah, was born in Springfield, Mass., Nov. 9, 1763; married Lucy, daughter of Archelaus and Jane C. Russell, Jan. 2, 1792 — "both of Springfield." He died in Springfield, March 16, 1804. His widow died Sept. 10, 1863, aged 89.

CHILDREN OF DANIEL WARRINER (146).

(Born in Springfield, Mass.)

316. Fanny, born Sept. 6, 1794. Fanny Warriner married Edward Gorman, Apr. 29, 1814 — "both of Springfield." This one or 408.
317. Lucy, born Sept. 29, 1796.
318. Daniel, born Feb. 24, 1800.
319. Mahala, born Oct. 18, 1802; married Charles Ball, Oct. 24, 1822, in Springfield.

164 HEZEKIAH WARRINER, twin brother of Abia, and son of Hezekiah (76) and Mary, was born in Springfield, Mass., Apr. 29, 1756. He married, Dec. 4, 1783, Katharine Leonard — "both of Springfield," and, after her death, he married (1811) Elizabeth Cooley, widow of Justin Bliss, of Springfield. He was first selectman in 1795 and for some years thereafter, in the town of Hawley, Franklin county, Mass. He died in Hawley about 1866, at the age of 83.

CHILDREN OF HEZEKIAH WARRINER (164).

(All born in Agawam, Mass.)

319. Cynthia, born about 1787; married Benjamin
Andrews about 1816; died in Conway, Mass.,
Nov., 1864. Her children: Lewis Warriner, 1817;
Benjamin Allen, 1819; James, 1820; Hezekiah,
1822; Cynthia Olivia, 1824. The eldest, Lewis
W., never married. Benjamin A. resides (1898)
in Conway, Mass., and has two daughters, Bertha
and Bessie, one of whom is a graduate of the State
Normal School, Westfield, Mass. James resides
in Chicago, Ill. His two sons are E. H. Andrews,
of San Bernardino, Cal., and J. P. Andrews, of Chicago. His daughter is Katharine Andrews, graduate of Smith College, Northampton, Mass., and
teacher of a private school in Evanston, Ill. The
children of Hezekiah are R. B. Andrews, of Leo-
minster, Mass.; H. O. Andrews, of Fitchburg,
Mass, and Rose Andrews Hitchcock, of Springfield, Mass. Cynthia Olivia is unmarried.

320. Hezekiah, born Nov. 8, 1788.

321. Catharine, born about 1790; married Henry Childs;
died in Deerfield, Mass.; no children of her own;
she was stepmother to four. One of the stepsons,
Henry Childs, Jr., graduate of Yale, married a
niece of Pres. Hitchcock, of Amherst; died a
prominent citizen of Buffalo, N. Y.

322. Lois, born about 1792; married Ezra Howes. She
died in Buckland, Mass. Her only daughter died
in infancy. Her husband was a widower when he
married her. His former wife was Lydia Spaulding, daughter of Rev. Josiah Spaulding, pastor for
28 years of the Congregational Church in Buckland. Mrs. Lois Warriner Howes endeared herself greatly to all who knew her. Her step-
daughter, Mrs. Mary W. Goddard, of Tacoma,
Wash., writes: " Hers was a domestic life, full of

sunshine even in sorrow. Her first great sorrow was the death of her little girl, the child of her old age; next, the death of her husband, with whom she had lived 17 years, and whose memory she cherished to the day of her death. Had her early life been attended with the educational advantages of the present, she would have been a marvelous woman; as it was, the light of her life was chiefly confined to the home circle where it was ever beautiful and never dimmed."

166 MAJOR GAD WARRINER, son of Hezekiah (76) and Mary, was born in what is now Agawam, then part of Springfield, Mass., March 1, 1758; married Eunice Worthington. She was born in 1764, and died May 23, 1820, aged 56. Gad Warriner married, 2d, Miss Phelps. No children by second wife. He died May 19, 1842, aged 84, and was buried in Agawam, where his tombstone may be seen. He was prominent in town affairs, serving as selectman for a number of years. He was a member of the Mass. Legislature from Springfield in 1805 and 1809, and from West Springfield, 1814, 1815. He lived in a house next to the horse ferry in West Springfield, as shown on a map printed in 1831. Reuel Warriner was his nearest neighbor. The Gad Warriner homestead is in good repair, and is owned and occupied (1898) by Elijah D. Abbee.

CHILDREN OF MAJOR GAD WARRINER (166).

(All born in Agawam, then West Springfield.)

326. Tabitha, born Feb. 10, 1785; married Seth Adams, son of Seth and Elizabeth (Lane) Adams. He died June 12, 1833; she died Dec. 9, 1841. They had one son, Ralph Adams, who died in Cleveland, O., in 1897. His only daughter, Eliza, is wife of Rev. George O. King, of Cleveland, Ohio.

327. Reuel, born

328. Harriet, born March 15, 1789; married Marvin, son of Jabez and Eunice (Burnham) Kirkland. She

died in Worcester, Mass., Nov. 14, 1783; buried in Agawam. He died Apr. 15, 1860. They had eight children, namely: Bela Burnham, dec'd; Albinus Theodorus, dec'd; Eunice Ann (Mrs. Corbin O. Wood, of Worcester, Mass.); Sarah Caroline, dec'd; John Augustus, dec'd; Edward; Edwin, of New Haven, Conn.; Rachel Warriner, dec'd.

328. Philura, born Feb. 9, 1791; married, Sept. 20, 1821, in Agawam, to Anson Bingham, of Springfield, son of Ithamar and Hannah Bingham. She died Feb. 28, 1863, and was buried in Agawam. Her son, Anson Bingham, was a very dear friend of the author of this book. He was born March 12, 1828; married, Nov. 30, 1848, Margaret Graves. He died in Forestville, Conn., Dec. 16, 1887. His widow, and son and daughter are residents of Forestville (1898).

330. Rachel, born Sept. 20, 1793; married, 1st, Joel Worthington, son of Stephen and Lydia (Rogers) Worthington; married, 2d, Joshua Howes. Children by first husband: William Worthington, dec'd, and Rev. Henry Worthington, who died in Michigan in 1881.

331. Orpha, born Dec. 26, 1798; married, Apr. 6, 1824, David Worthington, son of David and Mary (Rogers) Worthington, of Agawam. She died at their home in Agawam, Jan. 5, 1871; he died Aug. 20, 1883, in Suffield, Conn. Their first child was Orpha Warriner Worthington, who married Joseph Creighton Hastings, son of William and Lydia (Remington) Hastings, of Suffield, Conn. She died in Suffield, Nov. 12, 1866. J. C. Hastings married, 2d, Lucy Jane Ball, daughter of Norman and Betsey (Warriner) Ball. Residence (1898) Suffield, Conn. Children: John Worthington Hastings, physician in Agawam, town clerk and treasurer, 1888-1898; and Charles William

Hastings, grocer, residing in Agawam. The second child of Orpha (Warriner) Worthington was Harriet, born 1829; died 1837.

332. Gad, born May 13, 1801; died in infancy.
333. Gad Hitchcock, born Sept. 3, 1803.

167 CAPT. LEWIS WARRINER, son of Hezekiah (76) and Mary, was born in Springfield, Mass., Dec. 13, 1759. He married " Betty " (Elizabeth) Remington, in West Springfield, March 8, 1787. He died Nov. 11, 1805, aged 45. That year administrators made an inventory of his estate. Gad Warriner was made guardian of his two minor sons. An original commission as lieutenant, issued by Gov. Samuel Adams to Lewis Warriner in 1793, has been preserved.

CHILDREN OF LEWIS WARRINER (167).

340. Betsey, born Apr. 19, 1790; married, 1st, Alfred Leonard; married, 2d, Norman Ball, son of Eli Ball, of Agawam. Norman Ball died Nov. 30, 1862; Betsey Warriner Ball died Sept. 14, 1859. Six children, all living (1898): (1) Alfred Leonard Ball, shoemaker in Springfield, unmarried; (2) Cynthia Ball (widow of Wm. Chapman Clark, of Worcester, Mass.);* (3) Elizabeth (widow of Dexter Winter, of Belchertown, Mass.), residence (1898), Springfield, Mass.; (4) Norman Ball, captain and major in the Civil War, residence, Haddam, Conn.; (5) Mesheck Warriner Ball, of Springfield, Mass.; (6) Lucy Jane Ball, second wife of Joseph C. Hastings, of Suffield, Conn.
341. Lewis, born June, 1792.
342. Norman, born 1794.
343. Mesheck, date of birth not given; probably the Mesheck Warriner who died in Springfield, July 6, 1808.

* Their children are William, who died, and Ida, who resides in Worcester, Mass.

181 BENJAMIN WARRINER, son of Benjamin (79) and Persis, was born in Springfield, Mass., March 3, 1751.* He married Rachel, daughter of Amos Tolles, and they resided some time in Bennington, N. Y., where he died May 8, 1823, and she died Nov. 1, 1825. They are buried in Bennington.

CHILDREN OF BENJAMIN WARRINER (181).

358. Sally, born May 5, 1793; married Jeremiah Jones; died in North East, Pa.
359. Zerniah (a daughter), born Aug. 25, 1795; married Alvin Jones; died in Johnsonburgh, N. Y., where her grandson, J. W. Jones, resides (1898).
360. Chloe, born March 14, 1796; married Smith Rogers; died in Crawford Co., Pa.
361. Philena, born June 4, 1798; married Joel Crandall; died in Independence, N. Y.
362. Clarissa, born Apr. 19, 1800; married Sidney Riley; died in Ohio.
363. Hiram, born Dec. 18, 1802.
364. Rachel, born Nov. 18, 1804; married Thomas Church; died in Chicago, Ill., in March, 1839. Has one child living (1898), namely: Mrs. Mary Ingalls, Oak Park, Ill. Another daughter was named Melissa. Thomas Church died in 1871.
365. Eliza, born July 23, 1807; married Barney Crandall; died in Andover, N. Y., March 10, 1891; left 4 daughters, namely: Mrs. Catharine Clark, of Andover, N. Y.; Mrs. Esther Bassett, of Alfred, N. Y., dec'd; Mrs. Philena Remington, of Andover, N. Y., and Mrs. Marcella Bassett, of Andover.

---

* The date in the town record book of Springfield is March 3, 1750; but it follows another entry bearing date Oct. 18, 1750, and should probably be March 3, 1751.

In the year 1750 England adopted New Style, so March 14, 1751, the date Mrs. Alger gives, may be reconciled with our record.

366. Amanda, born in Bennington, N. Y., May 23, 1809;
married Kirtland Doty; died in Alexander, N. Y.,
Apr. 11, 1855. Children: Phebe S., dec'd; Benj.
F., dec'd; James, G.; Alvin N., dec'd; Sylvia N.;
Henry L.; Helen F., dec'd; Mary R.; Frank K.,
dec'd; Emma E. Those who are living reside
(1898) in Attica, N. Y.
367. Sophia, born in Bennington, N. Y., Nov. 22, 1811;
died in Buffalo, N. Y., in 1828.
368. Laurinda, born in Bennington, N. Y., Apr. 14, 1814;
married Joel Bailey; died in Battle Creek, Mich.,
Sept. 17, 1879. O. W. Bailey, of Battle Creek, is
her only living child (1898).

182 WILLARD WARRINER, son of Benjamin (79) and Persis, was born in Springfield township, Mass., Feb. 17, 1753.
He enlisted under Capt. Enos Chapin, in Col. Porter's regiment, in March, 1775, and served as fifer one year. He was
married, Nov. 27, 1779, to Lois, widow of Elijah Hancock
(maiden name Lois Stebbins, born Sept. 11, 1759).*
He moved from Wilbraham, Mass., to Canaan, Columbia
county, N. Y., in 1794. His occupation was farming. He
died in Martinsburgh, N. Y., March 9, and is buried in the
Hough burial ground. His widow died July 26, 1839.

CHILDREN OF WILLARD WARRINER (182).

369. Bathsheba, born in Wilbraham, Mass., Apr. 22, 1780;
married Rufus Chase; lived in Tolland Co., Conn.
Her daughter, Lucina, married and lived (1814)
in Palmer, Mass.
370. Lucinda, born in Wilbraham, July 30, 1782; married,
Oct. 6, 1806, Ephraim H. Merrill, of Oneida

---

* Letter of Mrs. Polly H. Farr, of Frederica, Ia., who states
that Hancock was a comrade of Willard Warriner in the Revolution, and that Lois Hancock had a son named Elijah
Hancock.

county, N. Y.; died at the home of Mrs. Jason
Farr, near East Martinsburgh, N. Y. Their chil-
dren were, Lucy, William G., Lucinda, Ephraim
H. and George W.

371. Jeremiah, born Oct. 26, 1784.
372. Lois, born Nov. 21, 1786; married, Sept. 7, 1808,
Jared Stiles, of Tolland, Conn. They moved to
Turin, Lewis county, N. Y., thence to East Martinsburgh, and settled on a farm, now (1898)
owned by their son Dwight Stiles. Jared Stiles
died Sept. 18, 1857; Lois died Apr. 11, 1884, aged
98. Children: Belinda, Jared, Alford, Alfred,
Anson, Mary and Dwight.
373. Eunice, born Nov. 26, 1789; married Pierce Squires,
of Canaan, N. Y., Dec. 17, 1807. Mr. Squires
died in Dempster, N. Y., Jan. 11, 1861. His wife
Eunice died in the same place, June 25, 1873.
Children: Nehemiah (Smyrna, N. Y.), who has a
son James and a grandson Arnon L.; * Emily,
dec'd; Lavinia, dec'd; Harriet (Glendale, N. Y.);
Edward A., dec'd; Francis W., dec'd, 1897; Willard W., New Haven, Oswego Co., N. Y.
374. Rhoda, born June 26, 1793; married Orrin Squires,
Feb. 14, 1814. Children: William H., killed by
lightning, 1829; Charlotte, dec'd; William H., 2d,
Hamilton, N. Y. Rhoda Warriner Stiles died
Oct. 19, 1872; her husband died in 1860.
375. Willard, born Oct. 7, 1795.
376. Sterling, born June 26, 1800; by trade a painter;
died, unmarried, previous to 1874, in East Martinsburgh, N. Y.; buried there.

186 GAD WARRINER, son of Benjamin (79) and Persis, was
born in the township of Springfield, Mass., Jan. 29, 1762; married Lucy Reed, of Springfield. He was a soldier in the Revo-

* Arnon Lyon Squires, of Keating & Squires, Counsellors-
at-law, 34 Nassau street, New York City.

lution.* He and his cousin, Daniel Warriner (193), emigrated to the Green Mountain State soon after the Revolutionary War. He moved from Pawlet, Vt., to Western New York in 1812, and died in Gainsville (now Silver Springs), June 12, 1837, aged 75, and his widow died June 13, 1849, aged 85.

CHILDREN OF GAD WARRINER (186).

377. Chester, born Jan. 1, 1784.
378. Willis, Born July 16, 1785.
379. Lucy, date of birth not given; married Aaron Wing. They had Harriet, Willis W., Asahel, Angeline and Alford, twins, Horace, Philip and Henrietta.
380. Ezra Bushnell, born in 1792.
381. Lydia, date of birth not given; married Ezekiel Gardner. They had Drusilla, Lucy, Perry Ira, Harriet, Daniel, Jacob, Henry, Willard, Rosannah.

187 ELIJAH WARRINER, son of Benjamin (79) and Persis, was born Jan. 25, 1764 or 1765; married Elizabeth Waite, or Wait, who was born May 12, 1770, and died Aug. 12, 1800. His second wife's name was Poles. He lived in Durham, Greene Co., N. Y., and gave a lot for a cemetery in that place. He died July 20, 1815.

CHILDREN OF ELIJAH WARRINER (187).

(Six by the first wife. These were born in West Durham, N. Y.; probably the others also.)

382. Henry(born Nov. 24, 1788.
383. Benjamin, born May 3, 1891.
384. Betsey, born March 31, 1792; married, March 25, 1813, Elihu Moss. She died Aug. 13, 1878. Children: Mrs. Olive W. Kelsey, Bristol

* His grandaughter, Mrs. Laura A. Abbott, of Portageville, N. Y., writes: " I have heard my father's father tell with pride that George Washington took his gun from his hand, and asked him if he had a good gun."

Springs, N. Y.; Mrs. Esther C. Fellows, Bristol
Springs, N. Y.; Orville, Durham, N. Y.; Emma,
dec'd; Reuben, Cornwallville, N. Y.; Mrs. Emma
B. Hughson, Bristol Springs, N. Y.
385. Elijah, born Apr. 21, 1794; died young.
386. Phebe, born Aug. 26, 1796; married James Hubbard. They had six children.
387. Belinda, born Aug. 9, 1798; married Eli Hubbard, Feb. 27, 1817. He died May 6, 1833; she died Sept. 24, 1871. Children: Louisa, Andrew, Kate, Mary, Miriam, Lucy, Ruah, Sylvester, Phares, Teressa.
388. Persis, born Jan. 30, 1802; married Zachariah Brainard. They had seven children.
389. Lucy, born March 24, 1803; married James Smith; no children.
390. Anna, born May 1, 1805; married Richard Kirtland; no children.
391. Elijah 2d, born March 28, 1809.

189 ZADOK WARRINER, son of Benjamin (79) and Persis, was born Feb. 29, 1768; married Mary, daughter of James and Chloe Maxwell in 1788. He died Apr. 20, 1838, in Springfield, Mass., and was buried there. His wife, who was born Aug. 9, 1768, died Dec. 10, 1864, in Unadilla, N. Y.

CHILDREN OF ZADOK WARRINER (189).

(First two born in Wilbraham, Mass.; others in Vermont.)
392. Wheeler Reed, born Dec. 18, 1789.
393. Polly, born June 28, 1792; died 1793.
394. Polly 2d, born Feb. 12, 1795; married, 1825, Simmons Lewis; died in Unadilla, N. Y. One child, Lorilla, who married Wm. T. Cook.
395. Phebe Higgins, born June 16, 1797; married Jacob Boalt, March 1, 1823; died in Unadilla, N. Y., Oct. 14, 1878. Children: Charles Augustus, Sarah Elizabeth, John Henry, Eben Wheeler,

Sarah Eliza (Mrs. Chase, of Washington, D. C.).
396. Persis W., born Apr. 15, 1804; married, Sept., 1830,
to Samuel Davis; died in Franklin, N. Y., Oct.
24, 1891. Children: Margaret L., Albert W. and
Mrs. Mary E. Fisher, of Sidney Center, N. Y.
397. Eliza E., born in Vermont, Feb. 1, 1807; died,
unmarried, in Sidney Center, N. Y., Apr. 12, 1840.

193 SAMUEL WARRINER, son of Samuel (81) and Ruth, was
born in Springfield, Mass., May 24, 1760; married Keziah,
daughter of Job Pease, of Norwich, Conn. He died in Gainsville (Silver Springs), N. Y., in 1812. His grandchildren, Mrs.
Laura A. Abbott and Mrs. S. P. Warriner, say he was a Revolutionary soldier and a pensioner. Not long after his marriage he and his cousin, Gad Warriner (186), emigrated to
Vermont, and moved from there in 1812 (it must have been
just before his death) to " the Genesee country " in New York
State. He was a farmer and a member of the Baptist church.

CHILDREN OF SAMUEL WARRINER (193).

(The first was born in Conn.; the others in Tinmath, Vt.)

398. Polly, born in 1796; married James Lowing; died in
Gainsville (Silver Springs), N. Y., in 1850.
399. Keziah, born in 1778; married Joseph Thayer; died
in Spring Valley, Minn., in 1876.
400. Betsey, born in 1790; married Zephron Broughton;
died in Conneaut, Pa., in 1860.
401. Pliny, born in 1792; died in Vt. in 1807.
402. Samuel, born in 1794; died in 1794.
403. Ruth, born in 1796; married Ezra B. Warriner (380);
died in Gainsville (Silver Springs), N. Y., in 1833.
404. Eunice, born in 1798; married Richard Brownson;
died in Buffalo, N. Y., in 1878.
405. Lucy, born Aug. 6, 1800; married Gerdon Kennedy;
died in Kingsville, O., Dec. 19, 1870. Children:
Eunice, who married ——— Scoville and has four
children (Post-office, Seneca, Kan.); Keziah, who

married S. P. Warriner (1001); Rachel, dec'd; Elizabeth, resident of Conneautville, Pa.; Ellen, dec'd; Amy, who married —— Reed (Post-office, Avoca, Ia.); William, of Elgin, Ill.

194 AARON WARRINER, son of Samuel (81) and Ruth, was born in Springfield, Mass., Dec. 30, 1761. His wife's name was Phebe. Some of his descendants have the impression that he moved to Ohio.

CHILDREN OF AARON WARRINER (194).

(Born in Wilbraham, Mass.)

407. Phebe, born Dec. 27, 1789.
408. Fanny, born Apr. 11, 1792. Fanny Warriner married Edward Gorman, Apr. 29, 1814 — "both of Springfield." This one or 316.

196 REUBEN WARRINER, son of Reuben (82) and Sarah, was born in Springfield, Mass., Nov. 7, 1756; married Sarah, daughter of Gideon Colton, Feb. 15, 1783. He entered the volunteer service at the Bennington alarm. The Revolutionary rolls in the custody of the secretary of the commonwealth of Massachusetts, contain a record of this man serving as private in Capt. James Shaw's company, Col. Pynchon's regiment in 1777, and as corporal in Capt. Abel King's (Springfield company) in 1781. After the war was over he settled in Vershire, Vt.

CHILDREN OF REUBEN WARRINER (196).

419. Sarah, born May 11, 1783; married Samuel Porter; moved to Utah.
420. Justin, born about 1785.
421. Lucinda, date of birth not given; married Stephen Russ; lived in Thetford, Vt.; had two children; moved further north.

422. Reuben, born in 1800.
423. Ascenath, date of birth not given; married Ezra
Hutchins; lived in Bethel, Vt. Children: Ezra,
Orson, Warren, Charles, Milton, Ascenath.

202 ISRAEL WARRINER, son of Israel (87) and Mary, was
born in Springfield, Mass., Oct. 29, 1768; resided for a time in
New York State, and, on reaching his majority, emigrated to
Meigs county, Ohio. He married Anna Calkins in Conn.,
Apr. 19, 1792. His death occurred in Meigs Co., Ohio, Aug.
3, 1824. He was a farmer and a member of the Baptist
denomination. His widow died at the home of her daughter,
Lucy, in Greensburgh, Ind., Jan. 31, 1843, aged 72. She was
a most estimable woman.

CHILDREN OF ISRAEL WARRINER (202).

450. Chauncey, born Apr. 3, 1793; died Apr. 6, 1796.
451. Ella (a son), born Jan. 15, 1795, in Saratoga county,
N. Y.
452. Chauncey 2d, born Apr. 27, 1798; died Apr. 18, 1803.
453. Zebina, born Nov. 30, 1799.
454. Reuben, born Aug. 31, 1801; died March 12,
1802.
455. Lucy, born March 2, 1803; married James Gageby;
lived in Greensburgh, Ind.; died Apr., 1893. Two
of her children resided in Greensburgh, Ind., in
1898, namely: Mrs. Milton Siling and Mrs. Charles
Porter.
456. Calvin, born Aug. 15, 1805; died Aug., 1806.
457. Franklin, born Dec. 27, 1807.
458. Linus, born Aug. 12, 1809.
459. Lester, born June 11, 1813.

203 LUTHER WARRINER, son of Israel (87) and Mary, was
born in Ludlow, Mass., probably. He married Eunice
Barker. After her death he went to Paris, N. Y., and married

88

a widow named Hill. He died in Hounsfield, N. Y., at the home of his son, Orrin, about 1837. He is buried in Adams Center, N. Y.

CHILDREN OF LUTHER WARRINER (203).

460. Orrin, born in 1803, in Fairview, Pa.
461. Eliza, date of birth not given.
462. Polly, date of birth not given.
463. Samuel, date of birth not given; died when a young man.
464. Lydia, date of birth not given; married ——— Freeman; died.
465. Emily, date of birth not given; married Charles Ward; died.
466. Henry, date of birth not given.
467. David, date of birth not given; went to Mt. Morris, N. Y., to live with his brother Orrin, and died young, unmarried.

205 REUBEN WARRINER, son of Israel (86) and Mary, was born in Ludlow, Mass., Apr. 17, 1781; married Betsey, daughter of Jared and Elizabeth Chittenden. He was a farmer and a Presbyterian. He died in Adams, N. Y., and is buried in Adams Center. His widow married Gen. Calvin. She died in Adams, Apr. 20, 1854. The only surviving child of Calvin and Betsey Britain in 1898 is Mrs. Martha C. Burgess, of Baton Rouge, La.

CHILDREN OF REUBEN WARRINER (205).

468. Walter, born Apr. 7, 1807.
469. Betsey, born Nov. 20, 1809; married John Fish, Apr. 3, 1832; died in Belleville, N. Y., Nov. 11, 1863. Children: Thomas Angel, dec'd; Caroline, dec'd; Augustus Chittenden, dec'd; William Edward, dec'd; Mary Ermina, dec'd; Frances Amelia, married Alanson Kilby (residence [1896] Syracuse,

N. Y.) Augustus Chittenden Fish has two sons, Nathan and Arthur (residence [1896] Watertown, N. Y.) William Edward Fish had a son, Edward W.

470. Harriet Jane, born Feb. 5, 1812; married Roswell Barber; died Nov. 7, 1864.
471. Clarissa H., born Dec. 20, 1813; died in Belleville, N. Y., Sept. 22, 1818.
472. William E., born Jan. 19, 1816; married Delia Clark; died 1887, in Detroit, Mich.; left two daughters, Fannie and Delia; no son. The widow died and daughter resides (1898) at 75 East High st., Detroit, Mich.
473. Virgil Chittenden, born Nov. 29, 1819.
474. Clarissa Angeline, born June 16, 1822; married Wm. Tamblin; died 1885, in Lincoln, Neb.

206 CALVIN WARRINER, son of Israel (87) and Mary, was born in Ludlow, Mass., Apr. 4, 1784. At sixteen years of age he moved with his father to Oneida county, N. Y. He married Mrs. Abia Rice in North Adams, N. Y., in 1823; died in North Adams, Apr. 8, 1858. A tombstone designates the place of his burial in Adams Center. His wife, daughter of Roger and Lydia Reed, was born in Bennington, Vt., and died in North Adams, N. Y., June 7, 1856.

CHILDREN OF CALVIN WARRINER (206).

475. Parley Ephraim, born in North Adams, N. Y., Apr. 27, 1827.
476. Mary Elizabeth, born in North Adams, N. Y., May 21, 1830; married Eber L. Mansfield; died at Cedar Rapids, Ia.

209 JACOB WARRINER, son of Isaac (88) and Lydia, was born Apr. 18, 1768; married three times. His first wife was Sabra Bush, and she was the mother of all his children. They were married Apr. 10, 1795, in Springfield, Mass.* His descendants say he was a Congregationalist and a farmer. He died in Claridon, O., Sept. 4, 1857, in the 90th year of his age. His likeness was taken a short time before his death.

CHILDREN OF JACOB WARRINER (209).

477. Oliver, born Dec. 30, 1795.
478. Reuben, born July 5, 1797.
479. Dorcas, born in Springfield, Mass., Jan. 12, 1799. She married and had four daughters and one son.
480. Eli, born Oct. 23, 1800.
481. Isaac, born Feb. 7, 1802.
482. Lydia, born Nov. 5, 1804; married Garret Martin. She died in Mt. Pleasant, Ia., March 3, 1875. Children: Altana, died young; Jason Homer (residence, Olds, Ia., 1898, and his father, Garret, lives with him); Fanny, died young.
483. Jacob, born August 11, 1806; died young.
484. Willard, born May 11, 1808.
485. Orrin, born in Rodman, N. Y., Apr. 15, 1810.
486. Orson, twin brother of Orrin, born in Rodman, N. Y., Apr. 15, 1810.
487. Henry, born June 15, 1812.
488. Jacob 2d, born March 21, 1814.
489. Polly, born May 19, 1816; married Benajah Brewer. Children: Ruth Abigail, dec'd; Mrs. Melissa Eleanor Martin, of Franklin, Neb.; Justin Warriner, of Columbus, O.; Clinton.
490. Lucy, born Aug. 22, 1818; married Garret Martin after her sister's death; died in Henry county, Ia., Jan. 27, 1893.

214 JUSTIN WARRINER, son of Isaac (88) and Lydia, was born in Springfield, Mass., Apr. 27, 1783; married Anna

---

* The town record says " Jared Warriner," but that seems to be an error.

Chapin, May 19, 1806 — "both of Springfield." He was employed in the Springfield armory. He died in his native city June 8, 1846, aged 63. His widow died in Chicopee, Nov. 21, 1850, aged 69. She was a Congregationalist.

FIVE SONS OF JUSTIN WARRINER.

RALPH.   FRANCIS.   ISRAEL C.

ISAAC F.   WILLIAM C.

CHILDREN OF JUSTIN WARRINER (214).

491. William Church, born Feb. 2, 1807.
492. Isaac Ferre, born Nov. 13, 1808.
493. Israel Chapin, born July 24, 1810.
494. Mary, born May 10, 1812; resided in Springfield, Mass.; died in New York City, Jan. 9, 1861, unmarried.
495. Justin, born March 8, 1815.
496. Francis, born Feb. 9, 1817.

497. Charles, born March 6, 1819; died in Buffalo, N. Y.,
 Feb. 8, 1847, aged 28, unmarried.
498. Ralph, born Feb. 15, 1822.

219 DAVID WARRINER, son of David (90) and Joanna, was born in Wilbraham, Mass., Jan. 3, 1778; married Fanny McCray. He was a farmer and a member of the Congregational church. He died in Wilbraham, as did also his wife. Their tombstones are in the old Wilbraham cemetery, and the engravings show how they appear.

Mr
David Warriner
died
March 26 1827
Æ 49

Mrs.
Fanny
Wife of
David Warriner
died
Nov. 9 1827
Æ. 40

CHILDREN OF DAVID WARRINER (218).

(Born in Wilbraham, Mass.)*

551. Charlotte Wells, born Aug. 23, 1816; married Alvah
 S. Davis, of Amherst, Mass., Dec. 14, 1847; no
 children.
552. Emeline, born July 26, 1818; married Lyman Wood,
 Sept. 10, 1836; died May 31, 1860; had a daughter,
 Mary Jane, and a son; both died.
553. John McCray, born Oct. 28, 1820.
554. Mary Jane, born Nov. 9, 1823; married Samuel Dale,
 Nov. 14, 1845; died Jan. 20, 1857. No children.
555. David McCray, born Oct. 28, 1820; died Aug., 1851,
 in New York City.

_____

* Caroline M., half sister to David Warriner's children, was born in 1805; married Joel M. Lyman, July 1, 1824. He died and she was living, a widow, in Wilbraham in 1892.

221 CHARLES WARRINER, son of David (90) and Joanna, was born in Wilbraham, Mass., Oct. 7, 1782; married Priscilla Paddock, June 27, 1834. He died of consumption, June 3, 1852, aged 69. His tombstone in the old cemetery of that town commemorates his virtues. Our artist has reproduced the inscription.

CHILDREN OF CHARLES WARRINER (221).

556. Charles Moody, born Oct. 23, 1834.
557. George Paddock, born Aug. 10, 1836.

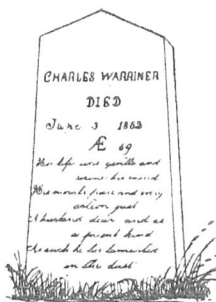

228 SOLOMON WARRINER, son of Capt. James (110) and Miriam, was born in what was then part of the township of Springfield, now Wilbraham, Aug. 16, 1753; married Mary Moore. She died March 9, 1794, aged 40. He married for his second wife, Betsey Jones, in Wilbraham, March 1, 1795. A sketch of Wilbraham in the History of Connecticut Valley, states that he joined the Continental army at the Bennington alarm. The Revolutionary rolls in the custody of the secretary of the commonwealth of Massachusetts give his name as a private serving in Capt. James Shaw's company, Col. Pynchon's regiment, in 1777.

In February, 1808, he gave $5 toward $100, amount raised in Springfield to buy a runaway slave from her master. The original bill of sale and subscription paper are in the Springfield city library.

A white marble slab, as shown in the cut, marks the grave of Solomon Warriner, and contains also a record of his first wife and two of his children.

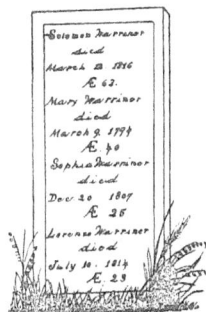

CHILDREN OF SOLOMON WARRINER (228).

(All born in Wilbraham, Mass.)

625. Solomon, born March 24, 1778.
626. Polly, born Jan. 29, 1780; married Samuel Holman, of East Windsor, Conn., Nov. 27, 1800; lived in Wilbraham. Her daughter, Mary, married Henry Sargent; her daughter Abby married Otis Childs; her sons were Ralph and Edwin. Edwin married Mrs. Heminway.
627. Sophia, born May 11, 1782; died in Wilbraham, Dec. 20, 1807, aged 25. See tombstone.
628. Jeremy, born June 10, 1785.
629. Ralph, born July 1, 1787; died 1816, unmarried.
630. Nabby, born Oct. 19, 1790; married Otis Colton, Oct. 26, 1814; had two daughters.
631. Lorenzo, born Aug. 30, 1792; died in Wilbraham, July 10, 1814, aged 22. See tombstone in old cemetery.
632. Betsey, born June 19, 1795; married Pynchon Bliss, May 15, 1816 — "both of Wilbraham." This Pynchon Bliss had been the husband of Sophronia Warriner (262).
633. James, born Aug. 5, 1797.
634. Eunice, born Dec. 10, 1800; seamstress; died, unmarried, in Wilbraham, July 26, 1875, aged 74. Tombstone in the old cemetery.
635. Lyman, born June 20, 1802.
636. Wells, born June 11, 1807; lived in Wilbraham and Springfield; never married.

230 STEPHEN WARRINER, son of James (110) and Miriam, was born in what was then part of Springfield township, now Wilbraham, June 8, 1760; married Elizabeth Ely, and settled in Monson, Mass. He died there July 10, 1842, aged 82. His wife, Elizabeth, died Feb. 1, 1818. She was born June 8, 1760, same day as her husband. Stephen Warriner was selectman of Monson in 1811 or later; he also represented the town in the Legislature in 1811, and several terms thereafter.

CHILDREN OF STEPHEN WARRINER (230).

640. Laura, born in Wilbraham, Dec. 14, 1789; married
Calvin Patten, of Stafford, Conn., intentions having been recorded in Monson, Apr. 4, 1818. The
marriage took place Apr. 22. They had four
children: Laura Elizabeth (Mrs. R. H. Mellen),
Calvin Warriner, Alfred Ely, Emerson Wood-
ward.

641. Daphne, born in Wilbraham, March 19, 1791; married and had four children: Mary Elizabeth, Parsons, Foster, Melissa Mack. The eldest son left
home and was never heard from. It was under-
stood that he went to the Sandwich islands.

642. Stephen Orlando, born in Monson, Nov. 15, 1793.

643. Amy, born in Monson, Feb. 27, 1796; married Au-
gustus Webster about 1832; her husband died in
Pelham, Mass., and she died in Vineland, N. J.
No children.

231 ETHAN WARRINER, son of Capt. James (110) and
Miriam, was born July 8, 1763 — the first child born in the
Fourth Precinct after it was set off as the town of Wilbraham.
He married Sally Colton, of Wilbraham, Sept. 29, 1799. He
died March 28, 1815, in Wilbraham, aged 52. His widow
died Feb. 1, 1846, in Wilbraham, aged 84.

CHILDREN OF ETHAN WARRINER (231.)

(Born in Wilbraham, Mass.)

644. Miriam, born July 29, 1800; married Elisha Pratt,
May 28, 1822 — " both of Wilbraham."

645. Ethan, born Oct. 22, 1802.

646. Harriet, born Aug. 5, 1805; married Shelden Cady,
of Ellington, Conn., June 6, 1833.

238 WILLIAM BOSTWICK WARRINER, son of William (123)
and Lois, was born in Malden, Mass., Feb. 3, 1785; married

Rebecca Rich, of Athol, Mass., June 30, 1808. He died in Boston, 1819. He was by creed a Unitarian; by occupation a wholesale grocer.

CHILDREN OF WILLIAM BOSTWICK WARRINER (238).

675. Emmeline, born Nov. 24, 1809; died, unmarried, Jan. 4, 1893, in Jamaica Plain, Mass. Her niece, Miss Florence Plune Warriner, writes: " She was greatly interested in the genealogy of the family. She lived to be eighty-four years of age, a handsome, intelligent old lady to the last."
676. William Bostwick, born in Apr., 1811.
677. Sarah R., date of birth not given; died young in Apr., 1816.
678. Julia Alice, born Jan. 28, 1815; died in Boston, unmarried, May 14, 1861.
679. Daniel Charles, born May 25, 1818, in Charlestown, Mass.

243 MOSES WARRINER, son of Moses (124) and Mary, was born in Wilbraham, Mass., May 24, 1771; married Anna Maxwell, Feb. 2, 1795 — " both of Wilbraham." He was by religion a Baptist, by occupation a shoemaker. In his later days he was a resident of West Pawlet, Vt. He died in New York, Feb. 2, 1834. His widow died in the same city, May 8, 1851.

CHILDREN OF MOSES WARRINER (243).

701. Millie, born in Wilbraham, Mass., March 20, 1796; married ——— Baldwin; died May 13, 1821.
702. Phanuel, born in Wilbraham, March 17, 1798.
703. Hiram, born in Wilbraham, Sept. 12, 1800; died Sept. 12, 1810.
704. Alexander, born in Wilbraham, Aug. 21, 1802; died Jan. 20, 1805.
705. Alexander 2d, born Apr. 10, 1805.
706. Lutetia, born May 24, 1807; married Erastus Pitcher; died in Sylvania, O., May 6, 1846.

707. Harvey Lewis, born Sept. 23, 1809.
708. Chloe M., born June 17, 1812; died June 28, 1833.
709. Hiram 2d, born July 17, 1815.
710. Dimnis Maxwell, born in East Gainsville, N. Y.,
May 9, 1819; married Giles Loring; died in Grand
Rapids, Mich., June 26, 1893 — the last of her
father's family. Her eldest daughter is Mrs. H.
S. Hayes, 337 Lyon st., Grand Rapids, Mich.
Her son, C. A. Loring, resided (1894) in Misha-
wako, Ind.

253 Dr. WILLIAM WARRINER, son of Samuel (125) and
Chloe, was born in Brattleboro, Vt., June 23, 1782; married
Lydia, daughter of Jotham and Ascenath Bemis; practiced
medicine in Hamburgh, Erie Co., N. Y.; died there May 20,
1820. His widow died in the same place, July 1, 1821. Their
orphan children were taken care of by their grandmother
Bemis until they were old enough to care for themselves.

CHILDREN OF DR. WILLIAM WARRINER (253).

(All born in Hamburgh, Erie Co., N. Y.)

711. Lucius Hector, born Aug. 17, 1814.
712. Helen Mars, born Nov. 18, 1816; married Alexander
Jamison, about 1838. Her husband died; she
then moved to Jackson, Ia. She also is dead.
Children: Henry, Lydia, Alonzo, Ida, Alexander.
713. Marcus Brutus, born June 14, 1819.

254 DANIEL WARRINER, son of Samuel (125) and Chloe,
was born in Brattleboro, Vt., Nov. 5, 1785, and on Jan. 10,
1824, in Chesterfield, N. H., he married Mary, daughter of
Isaiah and Esther Richardson. He was a farmer; taught
school for some time; was captain of a military company and
deacon in a Congregational church. He died in Brattleboro,
Apr. 21, 1846, and is buried in West Brattleboro. His wife, a
native of Vermont, died in West Brattleboro, July 10, 1880.

CHILDREN OF DANIEL WARRINER (254).

(All born in Brattleboro, Vt.)

714. Harriet Maria, born Oct. 20, 1824; resided (1894) in West Brattleboro, Vt., unmarried.
715. Samuel, born Feb. 12, 1827.
716. William, born Aug. 8, 1829.
717. Henry, born Dec. 28, 1831.
718. Chester, born Oct. 13, 1831.
719. Mary Esther, born March 12, 1836. Residence (1894) West Brattleboro, Vt.; not married.
720. Fanny Matilda, born March 4, 1838; married, Oct. 18, 1877, Edward Wells Colton. She resided (1894) in East Northfield, Mass., where her husband died Dec. 2, 1887. Her son, an infant, William Clayton, died in 1880.
721. Daniel Clifford, born June 6, 1841; died in Brattleboro, Nov. 26, 1861, unmarried.

DANIEL WARRINER.

265 NATHANIEL WARRINER, son of Nathaniel (128) and Diadema, was born in Wilbraham, Mass., Apr. 6, 1779; married Lucy Stewart, July 14, 1805, in Granville, N. Y.; moved from the vicinity of Watertown, N. Y., to Watertown, Wis., in 1844; died there Oct. 31, 1854, aged 75. His widow died Feb. 17, 1862. Both are buried in Watertown, Wis.

CHILDREN OF NATHANIEL WARRINER (265).

(All born in New York State.)

722. Daniel Stewart, born Nov. 15, 1805.
723. Ira, born Nov. 12, 1807; died Aug. 11, 1808, in the State of New York.

724. Lydia Almira, born July 23, 1809; died Aug. 6, 1867, in New York State.
725. Lucy, born Jan. 8, 1811; died in New York State, Jan. 8, 1817.
726. Sophia Maria, born Feb. 13, 1814; married Quarter G. Carley.
727. Alvah, born Sept. 6, 1816; died Jan. 28, 1822, in New York State.
728. Celinda, born about 1812; died May 3, 1843.
729. Harvey, born Dec. 1, 1821.
730. Charlotte, born July 30, 1824; married John Gill.
731. Mary Jane, born Sept. 6, 1827; married Sylvester Cleaveland; died in Eureka, Wis., Oct., 1873.
732. Wesley, born May 22, 1831; died in California, Apr. 4, 1853.
733. Orlando, born June 15, 1835; drowned in Lake Michigan, Aug. 6, 1860. He was a sailor.

269 ETHNI WARRINER, twin brother of Luther, son of Nathaniel (128) and Diadema, was born in Wilbraham, Mass., March 21, 1784, and moved with his father to New York State when thirteen years of age. He married Rebecca, daughter of Jonas and Rebecca Wheeler, in Galway, N. Y., about the year 1806. After 1810, he moved to Lorraine, Jefferson Co., N. Y. Some 30 or 40 years afterward he moved to the then new State of Michigan. He died in Mosherville in that State, May 19, 1880, aged 96. At the time of his death he was father of 10; grandfather of 50; great-grandfather of several. The records of the War Department in Washington show that he was in Elisha Allen's company, 55th (Sprague's) regiment of New York militia, War of 1812. He drew a pension in his last years. He was a total abstainer from the use of

ETHNI WARRINER.

intoxicating drink, and desisted from the use of tobacco at the age of 94, after indulging in the habit over 80 years. He was by faith a Baptist, by occupation a farmer. He is buried in Mosherville. His wife died in Scipio, Mich., July 16, 1856.

CHILDREN OF ETHNI WARRINER (269).

735. William, born July 23, 1808, probably in Galway, N. Y.

736. Laura Almira, born July 23, 1810; married Harvey Austin, in Lorraine, N. Y. He died in Freedom, Ill. To them were born two children, Alvaro and Herbert Eugene. For second husband she married Jeremy Rogers and they had two children, George and Frank. Alvaro lived in the southern part of Illinois. Herbert married and lived in Iroquois, Ill. George and Frank, when reported, lived at home. Laura A. Warriner Rogers died in the year 1880, her husband having died about two years prior to that date.

737. Julia Elvira, born in Lorraine, N. Y., May 6, 1812; married, in that town, Isaac Chafa, and there were born to them Alonzo, Rosalia, Melissa, Levi, George, Addis, Deloss and Delano. The first died in infancy; Rosalia married James Crum, and died in Chicago; Melissa married Peter Morgan and lived in Henderson, N. Y. The parents moved with most of the children to Wisconsin. The mother, Julia E., died in 1879. Levi Chafa, of Fontenelle, Adair Co., Ia., has seven children, all living, and some of them have families of their own. Addis, not married, has a home with Levi.

738. Levi, born in Lorraine, N. Y., probably March 24, 1814.

739. Solomon Johnson, born in Lorraine, N. Y., Oct. 31, 1816.

740. Mary Melissa, born in Lorraine, N. Y., July 25, 1818; married Benjamin French. He died in 1881. Their six sons are Charles, James, George,

John, Clarke and William. They are all farmers and have families of their own. Charles married his cousin, Emma Warriner (1408) and resides in White Rock, O. T. James and John live near their mother, and their P. O. is Mosherville, Mich. George resides in Litchfield, Mich., and Clarke in Foston, Polk Co., Minn. William occupies the old home in Mosherville, Mich.

Mary Warriner French wrote from her home in Mosherville in 1893: "I feel as though my pilgrimage is

MRS MARY M. FRENCH.

nearly ended. In a little while I shall pass over the river to join father and mother, brothers and sisters that have gone before. Although I feel unworthy, yet God's grace is sufficient for me, and in him is my trust."

741. Ormina Mahitabel, born May 4, 1821; married John F. Blois, a lawyer, author of a Gazetteer of Michigan. She died in Jonesville, Mich., in 1875. He died June 9, 1886. Their children, Ida and Edward, reside (1898) in Wayne, Ill.

742. Orel Calvin, born Sept. 7, 1822, in Lorraine, N. Y.

743. Alfred, born Dec. 3, 1827, in Lorraine, N. Y.

744. Melinda Melvina, born Oct. 3, 1829, in Lorraine, N. Y.; married Horace Button when 16 years of age; died, 1847, in Mosherville, Mich., leaving a daughter, Jessie, only six months old, who now lives (1898) in Chillicothe, Mo.

270 LUTHER WARRINER, twin brother of Ethni, son of Nathaniel (128) and Diadema, was born in Wilbraham, Mass.,

March 21, 1784; married Freelove Steele (adopted name Johnson). He died in Oriskany Falls, N. Y., in 1873. She died in
Pitcher, Chenango Co., N. Y., in 1867. Both are buried in
Oriskany Falls. He was a farmer. His home, in his old age,
was with his son David.

CHILDREN OF LUTHER WARRINER (270).

745. Ira, date of birth not given; died young.
746. Orrin, born March, 1808.
747. Johnson, born in 1809, in Lorraine, N. Y.
748. Laura, born in Lorraine, Jefferson, Co., N. Y., in
1811; married, 1841, to Harvey Carrington. Children: James E., Alice, who married ———— Blackman; Helen, who married ———— Dix.
749. Lyman, born in Lorraine, N. Y., in 1811.
750. David, born in 1816.
751. Sarah Maria, born in 1819; married, 1st, Henry Bur-
lingame, by whom she had two children. She
married, 2d, Daniel Page. Her death occurred in
Oriskany Falls, about 1897. She was a member
of the Methodist Episcopal church.
752. Abigail, born 1821; married Erastus Young; died
1895. Children: Charles, Bryant and Adeline.
753. Charles, born in Oriskany Falls, N. Y., in 1832; died
1834.

273 LOREN WARRINER, son of Nathaniel (128) and Diadema, was born in Wilbraham, Mass., probably about 1795;
married Hester G. Van Ness, who belonged to a large family
that came from Holland.

Loren Warriner died in Manlius Square, N. Y., March 5,
1842; his wife died in Jan., 1844. Both are buried in Manlius
Square. He was a cooper by trade and a member of the
Methodist Episcopal church. His daughter, Mrs. Baldwin,
writes: " Father was handsome in appearance and refined in
manner; he was honest and too free-hearted for his own good.
He lost his house in Verona. . . . He sang beautifully,
and played the flute and fife to perfection."

CHILDREN OF LOREN WARRINER (273).

(The first six were born in Sherburne, Chenango Co., N. Y.)

754. Samuel Miller, born in 1821 or 1822.
755. Thomas Orlando, born Dec. 9, 1825.
756. Philip Philander, born in 1827.
757. George Washington, born about 1828. In 1853 he visited his sister Amanda M. (759) at her home in Utica, N. Y. He was then running a coal boat on the Erie canal and making his last trip. He told his sister that his plan was to move with his family, consisting of a wife and two children, to Indiana, where it is supposed he intended to take up a government claim and locate for life. He told her that after finding his home in the west he would write to her, directing his letter to Utica. This he probably did; but that same year the sister married and moved away, so that the letter was lost and the brother was lost as well.
758. William Gates, born about 1836. He accompanied his sister, Mrs. Baldwin, on an overland tour to California. All crossed the river at St. Joseph, Mo., May 4, 1854, with a large drove of cattle and horses. He returned and died, unmarried, July 30, 1861, at the home of his brother, P. P. Warriner, in Holland Patent, N. Y.
759. Amanda Melvina, born Jan. 14, 1831, in Sherburne, N. Y.; married James William Baldwin, of Utica, N. Y., Oct. 17, 1853. Mrs. Baldwin's early married life was romantic and adventurous in a very marked degree. The Baldwins, particularly James and Edward, though reared in the midst of refinement and wealth, preferred the rougher life of the frontiersman, and spent many years in prospecting and conducting trains and droves of cattle across the plains to California. Edward Baldwin is distinguished as the first white dis-

coverer of Yellowstone Park. He made his discoveries while on his way to meet his brother James W. Baldwin, who had taken a large train across the plains to Virginia City, Montana, for the Gold and Silver Mining Company of New York City. A printed memorial of J. W. Baldwin says that after his marriage to Miss Warriner, " the young couple came to St. Louis, Mo., and remained through the winter. During that time Mr. Baldwin bought a large lot of stock in Illinois, and early in the spring of 1854 started it across the plains. Mr. and Mrs. Baldwin took the steamer Mayflower, and met their train at St. Joseph, and then proceeded on the long journey over the plains. They wintered in Weber Valley, at the mouth of Weber Canon, and in the spring reached California. Here Mr. Baldwin disposed of his entire outfit, and in July of that year started back for the States. It was a wild, lonesome trip, but husband and wife had grown used to the rough life on the plains, and they reached the Missouri river safely in September, 1856. Mr. Baldwin died in 1884. Their children were named John, Frederick, Mary Ella, Harriet Ann and William James. The last is married and lives in the same house with his mother (1898). The others are dead.

MRS. AMANDA M. WARRINER BALDWIN.

MRS. CAROLINE E. CARROLL.

760. Sarah Jane, born in Sherburne, N. Y.; died there, aged 16.

761. Caroline Elizabeth, born in Sangerfield (Oriskany

Falls), N. Y., Nov. 24, 1835; married, May 13, 1852, Henry D. Carroll, who died March 21, 1880, in the 46th year of his age. He enlisted in the Union army in the first year of the war, and was made lieutenant soon thereafter. Mrs. Carroll has been a member of the Methodist Episcopal church from childhood. She has lived in Utica, N. Y., and in Lincoln and Omaha, Neb. She has had four children: Ardella A., dec'd; William Henry, dec'd; James Henry, dec'd; Pamelia Almira (Mrs. Gasten), of Portland, Oregon.

762. Clarissa Angelica, born in Verona, N. Y. 1836; died of scarlet fever at 6 years of age.

763. Elmina Jane, born in Verona, N. Y., about 1839; married a man named Stephens in 1861, in South Richland, Oswego Co., N. Y.; died there.

764. Cordelia Sophia, born in Verona, N. Y.; died in childhood.

765. Cornelia Adaline, born in Manlius, N. Y., in 1839, and died in 1841 of scarlet fever.

274 ABNER WARRINER, son of Abner (130) and Elizabeth, was born in Wilbraham, Mass., Aug. 30, 1779. Some one states that he·had a wife named Mary, but Ossian Hurlburt, of Glastonbury, Conn., says he never married. He removed to New York State. Lucius A. Warriner (774) says he was blind.

275 WALTER WARRINER, son of Abner (130) and Elizabeth, was born in Wilbraham, Mass., Apr. 30, 1781; married Betsey Horton, in Wilbraham, Sept. 18, 1805. She was born in Westfield, Mass., Feb. 22, 1781, and died in Frankfort (or New Graefenberg), N. Y., May 19, 1851, and he married, in August, 1851, Catharine Barnes. His death occurred in Frankfort, July 9, 1874, at the age of 93, and his grave in that town is marked by a monument erected by his son, Lucius Albert. He belonged to the Presbyterian church, and was a school teacher 45 years.

CHILDREN OF WALTER WARRINER (275).

(All born in Frankfort, N. Y.)

770. Sarah Maria, born May 3, 1809; married Charles R. Mix; died in Auburn, N. Y., 1836. She had several children.
771. Jere Horton, born March 14, 1811.
772. Albert Werter, born Jan. 2, 1813; died in infancy, in Frankfort, N. Y.
773. Frances Fidelia, born Nov. 30, 1813; married Dr. D. G. Maltby; died in St. Louis, Mo., in Oct., 1888.
774. Lucius Albert, born Apr. 11, 1816.
775. Dwight, born June 20, 1817; died young, in Frankfort, N. Y.

277 WARREN WARRINER, son of Abner (130) and Elizabeth, was born in Wilbraham, Mass., Jan. 10, 1785; married Catharine Fullington, of Claverack, N. Y. He served for another man, as cook, in the War of 1812. His wife died in Springfield, Mass., May 7, 1851. He died in the same city.

CHILDREN OF WARREN WARRINER (277).

(Place of birth, Wilbraham, Mass.)

779. Lorenzo, born Nov. 6, 1807.
780. Roxanna, born Feb. 23, 1809; married Simeon Chapin. She died in Springfield, Mass. Her husband died in Long Meadow. Children: Marshall, Charlotte, William, Julia. Charlotte and Julia living (1895).
781. Alford, born June 10, 1811.
782. William Fullington, born Sept. 19, 1813; killed by diving in the water, in Wilbraham, when 19 years of age.
783. Louisa, born Nov. 21, 1815; married John Church. Her children were named Emeline, Amelia and

William. William served his country as a Union soldier, was captured and died in Libby prison.

784. Eliza Ann, born Sept. 16, 1821; married Austin Keep. She died in Dana, Mass. Children: Maria, who married George Ellis, of Unionville, Mass., and two other daughters who died years ago.

785. Julia, born Nov. 12, 1824; married Francis Keep. She died in Holyoke, and left one son, Stuart, who resided in Maine (1895).

786. Emeline, date of birth not given; burned to death when 8 years of age.

787. Janette, born Feb. 7, 1831; married William Wallace Pomeroy, June 9, 1853 — "both of Springfield." He died from accident in East Hampton, Mass., aged 36. The widow resides in Northampton, Mass., 1898. Her children were named Ada Louella and William Warren. The latter died in East Hampton, Mass., aged 4 years.

788. Horace, date of birth not given. His mother died when he was a child, and he was adopted and his name changed to Allen. He is dead.

280 ALFORD WARRINER, son of Abner (130) and Elizabeth, was born in Wilbraham, Mass., May 30, 1791, and was married, Sept. 22, 1819, to Eliza, daughter of Charles and Elizabeth (Newton) Angier. He followed farming and shoemaking. He also learned the tanner and currier's trade in Springfield when young. He was a consistent and devout member of the Congregational denomination, having joined in Massachusetts at the age of 12. He spent most of his married life in Frankfort, N. Y.

ALFORD WARRINER.

He was foremost in temperance reform; anti-slavery in politics, voting the abolition ticket for years when only four abolition votes were cast in the town, and attending conventions where such men as Alvan Stewart, Gerrit Smith and Wm. Lloyd Garrison were mobbed. He died in peace, in Washington Mills, N. Y., Dec. 22, 1877, and is buried in New Graefenberg (Frankfort), N. Y. His wife was born in Southbury, Mass., Jan. 4, 1798, and died in Washington Mills, N. Y., Sept. 5, 1882; "a woman of great faith and much prayer." She and her husband lived together 58 years. The wagon shed in the picture was their home for many years, and there their older children were born.

HOME OF ALFORD WARRINER, FRANKFORT HILL (NOW NEW GRAEFENBERG, N. Y.)

CHILDREN OF ALFORD WARRINER (280).

(All born in New Graefenberg, N. Y.)

789. Solomon Newton, born March 22, 1820.
790. Betsey Ann, born Nov. 2, 1822; died, unmarried, in New Graefenberg, N. Y., March 14, 1851.

791. Martha Cornelia, born Jan. 1, 1827; died in New Graefenberg, N. Y., July 29, 1851, unmarried.
792. Cordelia Eliza, twin sister of 793, born Apr. 20, 1830. She died Apr. 2, 1898, in Utica, N. Y., unmarried. She was first a Congregationalist and then a Baptist.
793. Frances Beattie, twin sister of 792, born Apr. 20, 1830; married Edward D. Williams. P. O. (1894) Brinkerhoff ave., Utica, N. Y.
794. Victoria Sabrina, born Sept. 18, 1839; married John O. Clark. Residence (1898) 188 Oneida st., Utica, N. Y.

281 THEODORE WARRINER, son of Abner (130) and Elizabeth, was born in Wilbraham, Mass., March 20, 1793; married Betsey Greene. As to church membership he was a Congregationalist; as to occupation a tanner and currier, and shoemaker. He died in Davenport, Ia., in 1874. His wife died in the same city in 1878.

CHILDREN OF THEODORE WARRINER (281).

795. Abner Eaton, born in Wilbraham, Mass., date not given.
796. William Chandler, born in Wilbraham, Mass., Sept. 10, 1833.
797. Samuel Horton, born in Frankfort, N. Y., date not given. He died young.

282 SAMUEL WARRINER, son of Abner (130) and Elizabeth, was born Apr. 22, 1795; married Harriet Turner, July 14, 1844. She died without children, and he married Laurette Goodrich. He died in the month of Jan., 1865, in East Windsor, Conn., and was originally buried in Obadiah Hulburt's private ground in Enfield, Conn., and afterward removed to the cemetery in Enfield Street.

SON OF SAMUEL WARRINER (282).

800. Nathaniel, born Aug. 1, 1855, in Farmington, Conn.
In 1895 he was employed in the transportation
department of the G. N. R. R. Post-office, 216
Sixth ave., St. Cloud, Minn.

301 JOSEPH WARRINER, son of Nathan (136) and Hannah,
was born in Monson, Mass., Sept. 5, 1782; married Naomi
Cleaveland, of Wilbraham, Jan. 26, 1806. His wife was born
in Palmer, Mass., Feb. 10, 1788. He died in Monson, Apr.
12, 1849, aged 67; she died in the same town, June 4, 1855.

CHILDREN OF JOSEPH WARRINER (301).

820. Amos, born May 16, 1808.
821. Miriam C., born May 5, 1810; married Giles Hatch,
in Monson, Mass.; died in the same town, Dec.
28, 1883. Children: Almira, Jane and Linus.
822. Linus, born Sept. 23, 1812; died Sept. 23, 1813, in
Monson.
823. Naomi M., born March 3, 1815; married Reuben
Burt, of Chicopee, Mass.; died Oct. 19, 1845; no
children.
824. Elias Turner, born May 31, 1818.
825. Hannah, born March 17, 1824; married Watson I.
Durkee, in Monson. He is a farmer, a son of
Amos Durkee, of Pittsfield, Mass. Children:
Elna Augusta, Florence M. A., Sarah, John.
826. Nathan, born Oct. 8, 1829; died March 22, 1831.

303 WILLIAM WARRINER, son of Nathan (136) and Hannah, was born in Monson, Mass., May 10, 1787; married Lucy,
daughter of Selden and Anne Borden; died Nov. 24, 1867, in
Stony Fork, Pa.; buried there.

CHILDREN OF WILLIAM WARRINER (303).

827. William Lombard, born in Monson, Mass., Apr. 8,
1812.

III

828. Hiram, date of birth not given.
829. Samuel Borden, born in Delmar, Pa., date not given.
830. Louisa, date of birth not given; married Elder Jacob Decker; died in Addison, N. Y.
831. Sarah Ann, date of birth not given; married Simeon Decker.
832. Laura, date of birth not given; married Vernam Northrop; died in Addison, N. Y.
833. Cornelia, date of birth not given; married William A. Warriner (842).
834. Sabrina, born Dec. 28, 1834; married Bela Borden; died in Stony Fork, Pa.

305 NATHAN WARRINER, son of Nathan (136) and Hannah, was born in Monson, Mass., May 29, 1792; married in Monson, Apr. 23, 1815, Abigail S. Cleaveland, who was born in Wilbraham, Mass., May 23, 1796. The wife died Feb. 26, 1829; the husband died suddenly, Oct. 8, 1829.

CHILDREN OF NATHAN WARRINER (305).

(All born in Monson, Mass.)

835. Eliza, born Apr. 2, 1816; died in infancy.
836. Levi Clark, born May 19, 1819.
837. Abigail Marilla, born Feb. 12, 1821; married Horace Walker, in Belchertown, Mass.; died in Greenwich, Mass., June 4, 1854, aged 33. One of her three children, Mrs. Newcomb, resided (1894) in Enfield, Mass.
838. Perlin Nathan, born July 24, 1822.
839. James Monroe, born July 11, 1825.

306 BENJAMIN HOWARD WARRINER, son of Nathan (136) and Hannah, was born in Monson, Mass., Apr. 6, 1797. They resided some time in Vt.; afterward moved to Stony Fork, Pa. He died and was buried in Delmar, Pa., and his widow died in Hornellsville, N. Y., Dec. 11, 1855. Both were members of the Free Will Baptist denomination.

CHILDREN OF BENJAMIN HOWARD WARRINER (306).

840. Washington Lathrop, born in Braintree, Vt., Nov.
19, 1815; married Clarissa C. Kingsbury, Nov. 23,
1841; died in Berlin, Vt., March 18, 1891; buried
in Northfield, Vt. He was a carpenter by trade,
but lived on a farm. He was in poor health for
many years. No children.
841. Almira Matilda, born Nov. 1, 1817, in Brookfield,
Vt.; married Stillman Davis, Aug. 4, 1837. She
died Apr. 4, 1896, in New Lisbon, Wis. Her husband was a native of Vt. He died in New Lisbon
in the year 1850. She was a Baptist; he a Spirit-
ualist. Children: Francis S., Marcia M., Melinda
S. The first two died; the last married M. B.
Heath, of New Lisbon, Wis.
842. William Allen, born July 5, 1820, in Brookfield, Vt.
843. Chauncey Howard, born March 25, 1822, in Brookfield, Vt.
844. Sarah Monora, born in Roxbury, Vt., July 17, 1829;
married Francis Ferry, March 31, 1856. They
reside (1898) in the town of Monson, and their
post-office address is Palmer, Mass. They are in
comfortable circumstances. Children: Nellie
Jane (Mrs. L. B. Colburn), deceased; Inez Viola;
Francis Elliott, deceased.
845. Jahiel Mann, born June 30, 1830; died Jan. 5, 1831.
846. Ira Mann, born in Roxbury, Vt., March 10, 1837.

309 ABEL WARRINER, tenth child of Nathan (136) and
Hannah, was born Jan. 31, 1801; married Sophia Ferry, Dec.
29, 1822. They moved to Delmar, Pa., and he died there Feb.
17, 1877. He was a farmer and a member of the Free Will
Baptist church.

CHILDREN OF ABEL WARRINER (309).

850. Mary Ann, born in Monson, Mass., March 15, 1824;
marrier her cousin, Samuel B. Warriner (829).

851. Elvira, born in Delmar township, Pa., Feb. 4, 1826; died, unmarried, Nov. 15, 1828.
852. Philena Janette, born in Delmar township, Pa., Feb. 18, 1828; married, 1st, Valentine Webb; married, 2d, Samuel Reynolds.
853. Abel Silas, born June 18, 1830.
854. Aurelia Jane, born in Monson, Mass., May 14, 1832; died Dec. 13, 1832.
855. Sophronia Cordelia, born in Monson, Mass., Oct. 12, 1833; died Oct. 10, 1835.
856. James Nelson, born in Monson, Mass., Feb. 26, 1835.
857. Harriet Ellen, born Oct. 27, 1838; married Edward Osborne.
858. Charles Royce, born in Delmar township, Pa., Jan. 26, 1841.
859. John Ferry, born in Delmar township, Pa., March 10, 1844; died.
860. Juliette, born in Delmar township, Pa., June 8, 1847.
861. Lanis Lafitte, born in Delmar township, Pa., Nov. 29, 1849; married Jennie Brill. He is a farmer and has four sons, but their names have not been given.

310 JAMES WARRINER, son of Nathan (136) and Hannah, was born Sept. 15, 1803, in Mass.; married Cretey Butler. They located on a farm in Pa. He died Aug. 25, 1862, in West Union, N. Y., aged 58; his wife died Oct. 23, 1871, aged 62.

CHILDREN OF JAMES WARRINER (310).

(All born in Pennsylvania, probably.)
862. James Wilson, born March 11, 1828.
863. Cretey Paulena, born Feb. 18, 1829; married Henry Lawton; died 1897.
864. Amelia, born Aug. 26, 1830; married Alanson Jearles; died 1886. She died in Wellsboro, Pa.
865. Betsey Harkness, born July 16, 1832; married Spencer Newbury. P. O., Delmar, Pa.

866. Amy Maria, born March 13, 1835; married Ethan
      Kennedy; died 1895.
867. Volarus B., born Jan. 15, 1839.
868. Nathan Allen, born Nov. 17, 1842.
869. Susanna A., born Nov. 18, 1847.

313 " CAPT." WALTER WARRINER, son of Ebenezer (143)
and Tryphena, was born in Springfield, Mass., Sept.
9, 1789; married Sophia Collins, Nov. 9, 1816. She died in Springfield, Apr. 29, 1824, aged 31, and he married Tirzah Hancock,
June 4, 1825. The town record says they were " both of
Springfield." She died and he married, as his third wife, Miss
Mary Henry, of Chester, " intentions " having been recorded
June 1, 1830. She died March 3, 1841, aged 52. He was a
farmer. He died of apoplexy in Springfield, Mass., Oct. 4,
1871, aged 82.

CHILDREN OF CAPT. WALTER WARRINER (313).

(All born in Springfield, Mass.)

875. Moses, born Aug. 1, 1817.
876. Sarah, born June 29, 1821; died, unmarried, Aug.
      21, 1849, aged 28.
877. Caroline, born March 21, 1823; married Col. Sam-
      uel Henry. They had two daughters, Amelia and
      Eliza.

318 DANIEL WARRINER, son of Daniel (146) and Lucy, was
born in Springfield, Mass., Feb. 24, 1800; married, Apr. 24,
1824, Rebecca, daughter of Zeanus and Dorothy Darling, of
Woodstock, Conn., a native of Spencer, Mass. She died of
consumption, Dec. 9, 1856, and is buried in Springfield.*

CHILD OF DANIEL WARRINER (318).

890. William D., born in Springfield, Mass., May 6,
      1826.†

---

* Springfield records.
† Stiles' Ancient Windsor.

320 HEZEKIAH WARRINER, son of Hezekiah (164) and Katharine, was born in Agawam, Mass., Nov. 8, 1788; married Hannah, daughter of Rev. John and Mehitabel Porter, May 29, 1817. He spent most of his life in Hawley, Mass.; there he died Jan. 13, 1843, and there he was buried. He was by trade a cooper. It is said that he was a soldier in the War of 1812. He was a well-read man and spent his evenings with his boys, discussing various literary and scientific subjects, the benefits of which the boys proved in after life.

CHILDREN OF HEZEKIAH WARRINER (325).

(All born in Hawley, Mass.)

910. Justin Bliss, born March 15, 1818.
911. Edwin, born May 10, 1819.
912. Benjamin Leonard, born Sept. 15, 1820.
913. Hezekiah Ryland, born July 23, 1822.
914. Henry Augustus, born Sept. 21, 1824.

327 REUEL WARRINER, son of Gad (166) and Eunice, was born in West Springfield (now Agawam), Mass., Jan. 12, 1787; married in 1814, Anna, daughter of William and Mary (Whipple) Chaffee.

Reuel Warriner is honored by his descendants as a true Christian

REUEL WARRINER.

MRS. REUEL WARRINER.

gentleman. He died June 19, 1854, aged 67. A stone marks his grave in Agawam. His wife's grave is there also. She died Jan. 29, 1882, aged 88. The old homestead is in excellent repair, standing on land originally granted to William Warriner as proprietary settler of Springfield.

THE REUEL WARRINER HOMESTEAD, AGAWAM, MASS.

CHILDREN OF REUEL WARRINER (327).

(All born in Agawam, Mass.)

925. Adaline Antoinette, born June 18, 1815; married Barnabas Norton Cooley, in Agawam, Nov. 27, 1839. She died Feb. 3, 1885. One child: Anna Adaline, deceased.
926. Samuel Dexter, born Feb. 11, 1816.
927. Reuel, born March 2, 1819; died in infancy.
928. Anson, born Feb. 11, 1821; died in infancy.

929. Anna Augusta, born Apr. 8, 1822; married Monroe
Bates, of Springfield; died Feb. 11, 1873. Children: Laura A. (Mrs. Cros-
sett, of Springfield); Martha
A. (Mrs. Wilson, of Aga-
wam); Martha A.(Mrs. Wil-
kinson, of Brooklyn, N. Y.)
930. Laura, born June 8, 1824;
died at three years of age.
931. Philura Amelia, born July 28,
1826; died, unmarried, Apr.
22, 1893.
932. Edward Augustus, born Feb.
18, 1829.
933. Martha Miranda, born March
2, 1832; married, in 1857,
Rev. Jacob Conklin

PHILURA A. WARRINER.

Dutcher, D. D. He was a son of William and
Anna (Van Wart) Dutcher. His mother was a
daughter of Isaac Van Wart, one of the captors of
Andre. Dr.
Dutcher was
born on the old
Dutcher place
at Irvington-on-
the-Hudson,
Oct. 8, 1820;
graduated at
Rutgers College,
1840; studied for
the ministry;
was pastor of the
following
churches: Owas-
co, N. Y.; Ber-

REV. JACOB C. DUTCHER, D.D.

MRS. MARTHA M. WAR-
RINER DUTCHER.

gen Point, N. J.; old Market Street Church, New
York City; Bound Brook, N. J.; when failing

health compelled cessation of his labors. In 1882 he was appointed consul at Port Hope, Canada, by President Arthur, and he remained there until 1887, when he removed to Springfield, Mass., where he died Nov. 27, 1888. In the war times of 1861-5, Dr. Dutcher was a strong supporter of the Union, and his services on the rostrum were in much demand. He published a number of works and was a writer of fine literary taste as well as an eloquent speaker. The children of Dr. Jacob C. and Martha M. Warriner Dutcher were: Jacob C., born Dec. 18, 1859, died Feb. 6, 1887, and Anna M., born May 17, 1862, died July 19, 1863.

JACOB C. DUTCHER, JR.   **333** GAD HITCHCOCK WARRINER, son of Gad (166) and Eunice, was born in West Springfield (Now Agawam), Mass., Sept. 3, 1803. He married, first, Abigail, daughter of Israel and Abigail (Runnell) Carpenter. She died July 25, 1840, and he married, second, Fanny C. Morley. Mrs. Fanny Warriner died March 8, 1855; Gad H. Warriner died Sept. 11, 1879, in New Haven, Conn., at the home of his daughter, Lucy M., where he had resided eleven years. He was a ship carpenter by trade.

CHILDREN OF GAD H. WARRINER (333).

934. Sarah Eunice, born Dec. 25, 1828; married Roswell Clark Ramsdell. Children: Mary M.; Edward (P. O. Middletown, Conn.); Clara (P. O. Washington, D. C.); Kate, Charles, William, Nellie. Mrs. Ramsdell's post-office is Hartford, Conn.
935. Orpha Electa, born Jan. 1, 1831; residence (1898) Springfield, Mass.
936. Lucy Maria, born Aug. 16, 1832; married John R. Turner; resides (1898) in New Haven, Conn., 40 Exchange street. Children: Mary (Mrs. Merwin), Ella, Addie, Ona, Emma, Alice, Nettie.

937. Jane Abigail, born Oct. 18, 1834; married George F. Cornwell; died March 3, 1893; one son, George I., survives.

341 LEWIS WARRINER, son of Lewis (167) and Betty, was born in West Springfield town (Agawam), Mass., in June, 1792; married, 1st, Fanny Wilson; married, 2d, Sabra Grout, Apr. 8, 1824. He was selectman in Agawam for years, also a member Mass. Legislature two or more terms. He was likewise in the State Senate in Indiana — "well and favorably known." He emigrated to Lake county in the State of Indiana in 1837. He died in Prairie Grove, Ark., May 24, 1869.

CHILDREN OF LEWIS WARRINER (341).

(All born in West Springfield — now Agawam — Mass.; first two were children of the first wife.)

940. Lewis Franklin, born probably about 1818; died, unmarried, in Cedar Lake, Ind., "one of the noblest young men the community of the county." He was not married.

941. Sylvester Wilson, born about 1820; died, unmarried, in Louisville, Ky. By trade a silversmith.

942. Edwin Baldwin, born Jan. 25, 1826.

943. Fanny C., born about 1828 probably; died at Cedar Lake, Ind., unmarried.

944. Sabra, born about 1830, probably.

342 REV. NORMAN WARRINER, son of Capt. Lewis (167) and Betty, was born in West Springfield in 1794; married in the same town, Mirilla, daughter of Roger Fowler. He moved to Lake county, Ind., in 1837. In 1843 he became pastor of the Baptist church in Paw Paw, Ill., and continued in that relation until a few months before his death. He was nearly fifty years old when he began to preach. His daughter, Mrs. Sollis, writes: "His character as a man and a Christian was all that is noble and pure, and of good report. His record as a minister of the Gospel was one of uncompromising loyalty

to truth and right, and of untiring and unselfish labor for the
cause of Christ, and for the benefit of all whom he could reach.
His work in the west at that date was necessarily of a pioneer
character, involving much of hardship and sacrifice, but he
fought a good fight, and kept the faith, and doubtless received
the crown." He is described as " pleasant, gentlemanly, grave
and earnest in the pulpit." He died in Paw Paw, Ill., in Jan.
1876. His wife was a woman of intelligence and strength of
character, though frail in body, and stood nobly by her husband in his work.

CHILDREN OF NORMAN WARRINER (342).

(All born in West Springfield, Mass.)

945. Hannah Caroline, born in 1823; married, 1841, Wm.
A. Taylor; died in 1850, leaving one daughter,
Mrs. James Radley, of Earlville, Ill.
946. Oliver Fowler, born Nov. 11, 1825.
947. Mirilla Fowler, born Dec. 18, 1828; married, 1868,
Thomas Sollis, M. D. He died in 1885. Her
P. O. address (1898) is Ann Arbor, Mich.
948. Remington, born July 17, 1833.

363 HIRAM WARRINER, son of Benjamin (181) and Rachel,
was born Dec. 18, 1802; married Lucinda Storm, Apr. 27,
1823. He was by occupation a farmer. He died Dec. 9,
1874, in Alden, N. Y., and was buried in Bennington Center.
His widow died in the month of Nov., 1888.

CHILDREN OF HIRAM WARRINER (363).

(All born in Bennington, N. Y.)

960. Louisa, born Nov. 1, 1824; married Lafayette Jones;
died in Bennington, N. Y., Jan. 6, 1866.
961. James, born May 29, 1827.
962. Clarissa, born Feb. 5, 1829; married Alonzo Mooers.
P. O. (1895) Alden, N. Y.
963. Chester, born June 29, 1831.

964. Gurdin, born Apr. 22, 1833; died Oct. 29, 1838.
965. Storm, born Dec. 1, 1835; died Feb. 4, 1862.
966. Rachel, born Jan. 3, 1836; married M. G. Alger.
P. O. (1895) Alden, N. Y.

371 JEREMIAH WARRINER, son of Willard (182) and Lois, was born in Conn., Oct. 26, 1784. At the age of 10 he moved with his parents to Sherburne, Chenango Co., N. Y.; married, on July 3, 1813, Eunice Hall, a native of Claremont, N. H. She died in 1844, June 17. He died in Hamilton, N. Y., on Jan. 14, 1868, and both were buried in North Norwich, N. Y. He was a member of the Baptist denomination, and by trade a carpenter. He was a man of sterling character, and was universally loved and respected. Of him

JEREMIAH WARRINER.

and his wife it may be said: "Their children rise up and call them blessed."

MRS. POLLY H. FARR.

CHILDREN OF JEREMIAH WARRINER (371).

(All born in Sherburne, N. Y.)

970. Reuben Lyon, born Feb. 28, 1814.
971. Jeremiah Hall, born Dec. 21, 1816.
972. Polly Hall, born Dec. 15, 1822; alternated with her sister in teaching school for a number of years. She was married to Jason Farr, as his second wife, Oct. 14, 1875. They lived in Sioux City with his nephew, Jason D. Farr, until his death, Sept. 28, 1884. He had an adopted daughter, but no children of his own. Mrs. Farr is a member of

the Baptist church. She resided (1898) in the same house with her brother and sister, in Frederica, Iowa.

973. Catharine Lois, born March 8, 1827; taught school more or less until her marriage, Nov. 26, 1878, to Oliver C. Ide, in Hamilton, Madison Co., N. Y. They spent a few years, part of the time west and part of the time east. Their housekeeping began in Chapin, Ill. Mr. Ide sold his farm there and removed to another farm, which he owned, in Frederica, Ia., in 1881. There he died Nov. 1, 1885. He left no children. Catharine L. Warriner was his second wife.

MRS. CATHARINE L. IDE.

375 WILLARD WARRINER, son of Willard (182) and Lois, was born Oct. 7, 1795, in Canaan, N. Y.; married Annie Tiffany, in Norwich, N. Y., about the year 1813. He served in the American army in the War of 1812, under Capt. A. F. Hayden, and drew a pension during the last years of his life. His wife died May 3, 1844, and he married, July 31, same year, Lydia Hillman. His creed was Universalism; his occupation farming. He died in Greig, N. Y., Dec. 9, 1881, and is buried there.

CHILDREN OF WILLARD WARRINER (375).

(All born in Martinsburgh, N. Y.; first five were children by first wife.)

980. Jared, born about 1814; died in Greig, N. Y., Nov. 22, 1848.
981. Henry Nelson, born in 1816.
982. William Franklin, born Aug. 1, 1818.
983. Lois, born Nov. 21, 1822; married All Saint Dana; died June 24, 1874. They had seven children.

984. Mary Ann, born about 1825; died at 5 years of age.

985. Willard Sylvester, born Feb. 19, 1827.

986. Alburn, born Aug. 2, 1845; died Aug. 12, 1845.

987. Mary Ann 2d, born Oct. 7, 1846; married John Levi North, Feb. 11, 1865. Children: Ida, dec'd; Laura Amelia; Clara Lenora.

988. Anna Almira, born Oct. 10, 1848; married John A. Morton. Residence (1894), Glendale, N. Y. Children: Addie Louisa, married Wellington Blade; Clarence, died in infancy; Vesta Jane, married Thomas Fuller, of Pittsfield, Otsego Co., N. Y.

989. Alburn C., born May 2, 1851.

990. Emeline, born May 25, 1853; married Wilton Davis; residence 429 West Court st., Rome, N. Y. Children: Hattie Josephine, 1873; Martella, 1876; Sarah Elizabeth, 1877; Geo. Wilton, 1883; Grace Anna, 1887; Ruth Warriner, 1892.

991. Lorinda, born June 4, 1855; died Nov. 29, 1867.

377 CHESTER WARRINER, son of Gad (186) and Lucy, was born in Wilbraham, Mass., Jan. 1, 1784; married, in Vt., 1806, to Drusilla, daughter of Joshua and Hannah Cobb. About 1810 he moved with his father and his two brothers, Willis and Ezra, from Pawlet, Vt., to Genesee Co., N. Y. He was in the War of 1812, rank of major. He was a carpenter by trade. In 1835 he removed to Crawford Co., Pa. He died in Conneaut, Pa., July 10, 1863, and is buried in Conneaut Center. For many years he held the office of deacon in a Presbyterian church. His wife was a native of Pawlet, Vt. She died in Conneaut, Pa., Feb. 5, 1869.

CHESTER WARRINER.

CHILDREN OF CHESTER WARRINER (377).

(The eldest was born in Vt.; the others in Gainsville, N. Y.)

997. Ammoretta, born Feb. 1, 1809; married C. Hamilton, M. D.; died in Newton Falls, O., Jan. 20, 1866. Children: Mary, who married William Penn Gaskill (her husband dec'd; her P. O., 1895, Newton Falls, O.); George Bostwick (died in the army); Gershom Wells (G. A. Hamilton, M. D.), whose P. O., 1895, was Sharon, Pa.

WHEELER R. WARRINER.

998. Wheeler Reed Warriner, born June 12, 1812; married Angeline Wilcox; died in Gainsville, N. Y., Aug. 18, 1887; no children.

999. Mary Ann, born July 7, 1814; married Jared A. Scoville; died in Conneaut, Pa., Feb. 19, 1889; no children.

1000. Chester Warriner, born Feb. 16, 1820, in Gainsville, N. Y.; married Lucy Weeks. He was a druggist in Jackson, Mich.; owned a brick block in that city, and died there Oct. 7, 1886. No children.

1001. Samuel Percival, born Sept. 30, 1823.

CHESTER WARRINER.

378 WILLIS WARRINER, son of Gad (188) and Lucy, was born in Wilbraham, Mass., July 16, 1785. He was married in Vermont, March 3, 1808, to Nancy Armstrong, and moved with his father and brothers to Genesee Co., N. Y., in 1812. His wife was born Jan. 4, 1787. He died in 1830, in Hopkinton, N. Y.

CHILDREN OF WILLIS WARRINER (378).

1002. Elijah R., born Dec. 20, 1808; died Oct. 2, 1810; buried in Vermont.
1003. Elijah R. 2d, born Oct. 9, 1810; died Aug. 21, 1811; buried in Hopkinton, N. Y.
1004. Willis Wait, born Aug. 27, 1812.
1005. Harriet W., born Feb. 20, 1815; married ———— Reeves; died March 7, 1856, aged 41; buried in Salem, Wis.
1006. Mary Ann C., born Aug. 25, 1819; married Orville Kelsey; died Sept. 7, 1856, aged 37; buried in Evans Mills, N. Y.
1007. Mason C., born July 1, 1821; died in Canton, St. Lawrence Co., N. Y., in 1830.
1008. Hiram S., born Dec. 1, 1823.
1009. John S., born June 16, 1827; died May 17, 1848, in Evans Mills, N. Y., aged 20.
1010. Henry L., born Aug. 27, 1833; died Sept. 13, 1847, in Russell, St. Lawrence Co., N. Y., aged 14. He is buried in Russell.

380 EZRA BUSHNELL WARRINER, son of Gad (186) and Lucy, was born in Pawlet, Vt., probably in 1792; moved from Pawlet, Vt., with his father's family, to Genesee Co., N. Y., when 18 years of age. His first wife was Ruth Warriner (403); his second wife was Hepzibah Baldwin, born 1793, died 1861.

CHILDREN OF EZRA BUSHNELL WARRINER (380).

(All born in Gainsville, now Silver Springs, N. Y.)

1011. Laura Ann, born Jan. 31, 1816; married J. Franklin Abbott. P. O., Portageville, N. Y.; no children.
1012. Altie Reed, born Apr. 20, 1820; married Charles B. Briggs; died Jan. 30, 1865, at Silver Springs, N. Y.

Her only son, William Ezra, a soldier in the 5th N. Y. Cavalry, "Ira Harris Guards," died in the hospital at Annapolis, Md. He was a good soldier. The loss of the son hastened the mother's death. One daughter, Maria, is dead. One daughter, Amanda, Mrs. Erwin Wheeler, resided (1895) in Mason City, Ia.; two children.

1013. James Lowing, born Jan. 25, 1824; married Melissa Fuller; died Springs), Gainsville (Silver in Wyoming Co., N. Y.; no children.

1014. Mary Ermina, twin sister of Ruth, born Apr. 18, 1830; married Wm. T. Davis. Two children: Ermina (Mrs. Jones), and Clayton Ezra.

1015. Ruth, twin sister of Mary E., born Apr. 18, 1830; married Lloyd Gibson; no children.

1016. Ezra, date of birth not given; died in infancy.

382 HENRY WARRINER, son of Elijah (187) and Elizabeth, was born in West Durham, N. Y., Nov. 24, 1788; married, 1st, Olive Finnity, and 2d, Betsey Adams; moved from Attica, N. Y., to Battle Creek, Mich., in 1836; died in Flint, Mich., Aug. 21, 1864; buried in Battle Creek. He was a farmer.

CHILDREN OF HENRY WARRINER (382).

1020. Lemuel Castle, born in Genesee Co., N. Y., Aug., 1817.

1021. Elihu Moss, born July 4, 1819.

1022. Chauncey Elijah, born May 6, 1821.

1023. Elizabeth Jane, born Feb. 27, 1823; married Orville Harris. She died in Battle Creek, Mich. Children: Henry, Julius, Helen, Cora, Frank, Stella, Ida, Bella, Alice.

1024. Edwin, born July 5, 1825.

1025. Abigail Cordelia, born June 21, 1827; married Henry Miller; they have one son, Fred. Residence (1898) Battle Creek, Mich.

1026. Olive Helen, born June 11, 1830; married Thomas Dawson Atkinson, Oct. 14, 1850. P. O. (1898)

Fort Worth, Texas. Children: Willhelmina A. (Mrs. M. Scougale), of Fort Worth, Texas; Lelia Z., dec'd; Ellsworth F., of Holland, Mich.

391 ELIJAH WARRINER 2D, son of Elijah (187), was born probably in West Durham, N. Y., March 28, 1809; married Huldah M. Finch.

Children of Elijah Warriner (391) were five in number, but no one could or would furnish their names.

392 WHEELER REED WARRINER, son of Zadok (189) and Mary, was born in Pawlet, Vt., Dec. 18, 1789; married, Feb. 5, 1818, Samantha, daughter of Elisha and Polly Lathrop. Wheeler Reed Warriner moved from Vermont to Unadilla, Otsego county, N. Y. He was a farmer. His wife died Dec. 28, 1865; he died in Franklin, N. Y., Feb. 25, 1876, and is buried in Unadilla.

CHILDREN OF WHEELER REED WAR-
RINER (392).

WHEELER REED WAR-
RINER.

1040. Lyman Morilla, born Dec. 23, 1823; married Hester Ann Hurlburt, Sept. 9, 1862. His post-office (1898) Oneonta, N. Y.; a retired farmer; no children.

1041. Zadok Henry, born Dec. 29, 1830; died in Unadilla, N. Y., June 1, 1833.

1042. Theressa Marinda, born Sept. 4, 1834; deceased.

420 JUSTIN WARRINER, son of Reuben (196) and Sarah, was born about 1785; married, 1st, Cynthia West, who was the mother of his two sons, named below; married, 2d, Lucy McNeil. He was some years a resident of Vershire, Vt. His occupation was farming, and the books of the town of Vershire contain records of his conveyance of land at different times.

CHILDREN OF JUSTIN WARRINER (420).

(Born in Vershire, Vt.)

1050. Chauncey, born Sept. 19, 1812.
1051. Edson, born Dec. 24, 1815; married Martha Darrar. Report says he died in Concord, N. H.

422 REUBEN WARRINER, son of Reuben (196) and Sarah, was born in 1800; married Jemima Lawton in the year 1823. He was the third Reuben in direct descent, and he had a son Reuben Diamond. He was a member of the Methodist church. He was for many years a resident of Vershire, Vt., and the land records mention his name. He died in Hartford, Vt., in 1861, and was buried in North Hartland. His wife died Aug. 10, 1856.

REUBEN WARRINER.

CHILDREN OF REUBEN WARRINER (422),

1060. Sarah Jane, born in Vershire, Vt., Nov., 1824; married, Dec., 1848, George Titus. He died and she married Eben S. Trask. No children. Church, Methodist. P. O. (1898) North Hartland, Vt.
1061. David Lawton, born in Vershire, Vt., July 30, 1827.
1062. Harriet Rowena, born in Vershire, Vt., June, 1831; married Jesse A. Ford, Oct. 5, 1853. Children: Isabel Julia and George Ashby. Her husband died in Hartford, Vt., in 1860. She married John W. Spear in 1878; he died in 1894. Her post-office (1898) Hartland, Vt.; her church, Methodist Episcopal.
1063. Reuben Diamond, born in Piedmont, N. H., Oct., 1832.
1064. Orson Hutchins, born in Thetford, Vt., Sept. 10, 1835.

1065. Jemima, born in Hartford, Vt., Aug., 1838; married Warren T. Griffin, Oct., 1858. P. O. (1898) North Hartland, Vt. Children: Stella, Minnie C., Reuben I., Herbert O., Hattie, Chauncey W., Warren E., Annie L., Lottie M.

1066. Mary Elizabeth, born in Hartford, Vt., Oct., 1841; married James L. Neal in 1858. P. O. (1898) Manchester, N. H. Children: Katie A., Jennie C., Gertie.

451 ELLA WARRINER, son of Israel (202) and Anna C., was born Jan. 15, 1795, in Saratoga Co., N. Y. The mother saw Ella used as a masculine name in a book, and gave that name to her son. The family moved to Erie, Pa., when he was a child, and thence to Zanesville, O. About 1824, at the death of his father, he became the head of the family, and removed to Greensburgh, Ind. He married, in May, 1827, Elizabeth Conde, and then moved to La Porte, Ind., and engaged in mercantile business. His daughter, Mrs. Whiteman, writes: " He was persuaded to become security for some county officers, and was thereby ruined financially. He started for Oregon, overland, located in Portland, and went into the fruit business, in which he was successful. He wrote that he was coming back, but was stricken with pneumonia and died." He was a Universalist in his creed, but not a member of any church. He took great pains to inculcate in his children a love of honesty. His wife was, with her father, among the early settlers of Rush county, Ind. She was a native of Oneida Co., N. Y., a teacher, and a woman of rare intelligence. She died at her daughter's in Columbus, Ind.

CHILDREN OF ELLA WARRINER (451).

1070. Mary Anna, born Aug. 12, 1828; married ———— Tompkins. Residence (1894) Columbus, Ind.

1071. Helen Amanda, born July 6, 1831; died 1834.

1072. Emily Eliza, born May 11, 1834; married Wm. Whiteman, a farmer; resided (1895) near Milroy, Ind. Children: Clarinda E., Horace G., W. H. Seward, Mary E., Martha J., Emily Eliza.

453 ZEBINA WARRINER, son of Israel (202) and Anna, was born in Ohio, probably Nov. 30, 1799; married, Nov. 21, 1824, Esther Potter, who was born July 5, 1801, and died in Greensburgh, Ind., Oct. 22, 1842. He died in Los Angeles, Cal., Dec. 20, 1890. Both he and his wife were members of the Baptist denomination.

ZEBINA WARRINER.

CHILDREN OF ZEBINA WARRINER (453).

1073. Lucy Ann, born Dec. 30, 1825; married Dr. Eben Lewis Mansfield, in Cedar Rapids, Iowa, Apr. 6, 1852; died Aug. 26, 1868. Children: Sylvia (Mrs. Chas. J. Deacon), Elizabeth, Lura, Irene and Lewis Warriner. Dr. Mansfield, after his wife died, married Mary Elizabeth Warriner (476).

1074. Clarinda, twin sister of 1075, born Sept. 8, 1827; died Oct. 20, 1828.

1075. Melinda Eleanor, twin sister of 1074, was born Sept. 8, 1827; married George Zorger, in Greensburgh, Ind., Oct. 11, 1849. He died in Cedar Rapids, Ia. She resided (1896) in Los Angeles, Cal.

1076. Calvin Washington, born Dec. 14, 1830; died Sept. 4, 1831.

1077. Charlotte Emily, born Nov. 26, 1835; married in Cedar Rapids, Ia., to Azariah G. Phelps, and thenceforward lived in California until his death in 1896. Children: Mary Charlotte, born 1870; Lewis Azariah, born 1875, died 1877.

1078. Levinia Josephine, born Sept. 20, 1838; died Oct. 13, 1839.

457 FRANKLIN WARRINER, son of Israel (202) and Anna, was born Dec. 27, 1807; married Jane Heuston in Greensburgh, Ind., May 27, 1831; died there Sept. 13, 1832. His widow lives (1898) with her grandson, Israel F. Warriner, in Greensburgh, Ind, aged 94.

<h3 align="center">Son of Franklin Warriner (457).</h3>

1079. Israel Franklin, born in Greensburgh, Ind., March 15, 1832.

458 Linus Warriner, son of Israel (202) and Anna, was born in Meigs Co., Ohio, Aug. 12, 1809; married, Aug. 16, 1832, Lydia, daughter of John and Rebecca Jacobs. His wife died May 14, 1845; buried in Greensburgh, Ind. He did not keep house after his wife's death. He died in Mattoon, Ill., Apr. 9, 1885.

<h3 align="center">Children of Linus Warriner (458).</h3>

1080. John Jacobs, born May 24, 1833.
1081. Franklin, born June 4, 1835.
1082. Isabel, born Apr. 1, 1837; married James M. Patton, and to them were born three children: Johnson, Lucilla S. and Lydia.
1083. Calvin Prentice, born Feb. 1, 1839.
1084. Julia Ann, born June 2, 1841; married Augustus Dennis, Feb. 20, 1862. Children: Mary Isabella (Mrs. McClure) and Cecil Duane.
1085. Sarah Jane, born Feb. 11, 1843; died young.
1086. James Gageby, born in Greensburgh, Ind., Jan. 18, 1845.

459 Lester Warriner, son of Israel (202) and Anna, was born June 11, 1813; married Julia Jacobs, Feb. 3, 1842. He died Apr. 8, 1844; she died eight days later, Apr. 16.

<h3 align="center">Child of Lester Warriner (459).</h3>

1087. Mary Anna, born Jan. 22, 1843; married Nathan Lewis, Sept. 15, 1870, in Cedar Rapids, Ia. Her husband died, and she resides (1898) in California.

460 ORRIN WARRINER, son of Luther (203) and Eunice, was born in Fairview, Erie Co., Pa., in the year 1803; married, 1st, Zeviah, daughter of Abram and Zeviah (Wallace) Burrell, in Sandy Creek, N. Y., on Jan. 19, 1829. She died Apr. 29, 1834. He married, 2d, Emily Starks, and after her death he married, 3d, Abby Cummings. He lived a long time in North Adams, N. Y.; afterward in Chicago. There he died, April 27, 1876, and is buried in Rose Hill Cemetery. As to denomination he was a Methodist; as to occupation, a fruit merchant.

CHILDREN OF ORRIN WARRINER (460).

1088. Dexter Burrell, born in Belleville, N. Y.; date not given.
1089. Henry, born in Belleville, N. Y.; date not given; his wife's name was Elvira. He died and she married a man named Phillips.
1090. Abraham, born in Sandy Creek, N. Y.; date not given.
1091. Janette, date of birth not given.

468 WALTER WARRINER, son of Reuben (205) and Betsey, was born in Adams, N. Y., Apr. 17, 1807; married, on June 8, 1831, to Eliza, daughter of Col. Henry and Hannah Green. He died in Belleville, N. Y., Jan. 28, 1857, from the effects of a runaway accident. He was a wagon maker by trade. His wife was born in Ellisburgh, N. Y., May 27, 1811, and died March 31, 1891.

CHILDREN OF WALTER WARRINER (468).

1094. Reuben Henry, born Aug. 19, 1833, in Adams, N. Y.
1095. Marietta, born in Adams, N. Y., Feb. 23, 1835; married Nahum C. Houghton, Oct. 12, 1858, in Belleville, N. Y., where they still continued their residence (1896).
1096. Tirzah Janette, born Oct. 31, 1836, in Adams, N. Y.; married Dr. Jerome B. Tamblin, May 12, 1875. P. O. (1895) Greenwood, Neb.

1097. Hannah E., born Jan. 26, 1841, in Ellisburgh, N. Y.; married George P. Reed, Oct. 6, 1864. He died in Anaham, Cal., Dec. 7, 1873. Children: Abby, a teacher in Utica, N. Y.; Walter Warriner, a resident of Denver, Colo.; George Park, dec'd when very young.

473 VIRGIL CHITTENDEN WARRINER, son of Reuben (205) and Betsey, was born Nov. 20, 1819, in Adams, N. Y.; married, Jan. 27, 1845, Ruth A., daughter of Jeremy and Anna Packer, of Ellisburgh, N. Y. His occupation was farming; his church, Presbyterian. He died in Smithville, N. Y., Feb. 16, 1891. He was the only son of Reuben (205), whose descendants of the name Warriner continue to the third generation.

CHILDREN OF VIRGIL C. WARRINER (473).

1100. Virgil Jeremy, born in Depauville, N. Y., July 29, 1846.
1101. Milvern Eddy, born in Ellisburgh, N. Y., Aug. 9, 1856.
1102. Ruth Ann, born in Rural Hill, N. Y., Apr. 16, 1858; married James M. Freeman. P. O. (1898) Adams, N. Y.
1103, William Walter, born in Rural Hill, N. Y., May 5, 1864; married Nellie E. Lewis, of Three Mile Bay, N. Y., May 23, 1889. Both he and his wife attended Adams Collegiate Institute. He was formerly bookkeeper and teller in a bank, and is now (1898) a merchant in Adams, N. Y.

PARLEY E. WARRINER.

475 PARLEY EPHRAIM WARRINER, son of Calvin (206) and Abiah, was born in North Adams,

N. Y., Apr. 27, 1827; married Sarah E. Ward, Dec. 26, 1861. Church, Congregationalist; occupation, farming.

CHILDREN OF PARLEY E. WARRINER (475).

1104. Jennie May, born Jan. 8, 1863. P. O. (1898) Adams, N. Y.
1105. Thomas Reed, born Aug. 11, 1869; graduate of Cornell University, class of 1893. In 1898 civil engineer, Cedar Rapids, Iowa.
1106. Sarah Abiah, born June 4, 1872. P. O. (1898) Adams, N. Y.

477 OLIVER WARRINER, son of Jacob (209) and Sabra, was born Dec. 30, 1795; married Polly Gager, in Claridon, Ohio. He lived for a time in Fort Wayne, Ind., and died at an advanced age in Laporte, Ind., about the year 1878. He was by denomination a Congregationalist; by occupation, a farmer.

CHILDREN OF OLIVER WARRINER (477).

1108. Ora, date of birth not given; married ———— McCoy, who died some years ago.
1109. Norman Lawrence, born in Geauga Co., O., Aug. 7, 1820.
1110. Gilbert, date of birth not given. A Union soldier, killed in the battle of Mission Ridge.
1111. Fidelia, date of birth not given; married Ralph Griffin at Sheboygan Falls, Wis., in 1855, and moved to Grand Rapids, Mich.
1112. Arvilla, a daughter, date of birth not given; years ago was living, unmarried, at Laporte, Ind.

478 REUBEN WARRINER, son of Jacob (209) and Sabra, was born in Mass., Jan. 5, 1797; married Marinda Lindsley. He was a farmer by occupation, and by creed a Congregationalist. Report says that he and his wife started on foot to go to California. She transported her effects in a baby cart. He died after they had crossed the Mississippi river; she then returned, and died in Burton, Ohio.*

CHILD OF REUBEN WARRINER (478).

1114. Augustus,† born in Geauga Co., O.; married and had three daughters. He was killed by gas while working in a well.

480 ELI WARRINER, son of Reuben (478) and Sabra, was born Oct. 23, 1800; married Almada, daughter of Aaron and Polly Farr, in Adams, N. Y., Jan. 3, 1828. He died in Sept., 1868, in Flint, Mich., and is buried there. His widow, aged 94, lives with a daughter in Corunna, Mich (1898).

CHILDREN OF ELI WARRINER (480).

1115. Lydia Melvina, born in Adams, N. Y., Oct. 28, 1828; married Thomas Young. P. O., Corunna, Mich.
1116. Sabra Mary, born in Adams, N. Y., Sept. 21, 1830; married Gideon Mills. P. O. (1898) Stutsboro, O.
1116a. Lorenzo Chauncey, born in Philadelphia, N. Y., Sept. 20, 1832; died in New Orleans, La., about 1863.
1117. Alzina Miranda, born in Philadelphia, N. Y., Nov. 15, 1834; married Jerre C. Webb, May 2, 1861. Children: Addison V., Grace A., Melbert H., Mary L., dec'd. Mr. Webb died Jan. 14, 1890. Residence of Alzina M. Webb, Claridon, O. (1898).
1117a. Rebecca Altheda, born in Philadelphia, N. Y., May 23, 1836; died 1837.
1117b. Loren Riley, born in Philadelphia, N. Y., June 25, 1838.
1117c. Willard Benjamin, born in Rodman, N. Y., Nov. 27, 1840. Residence (1898) Corunna, Mich.

---

* Letter of Grace A. Webb.
† Mrs. Chittenden, of Lenox, Ia., says that this son's name was Justin; Miss Webb gives the name Augustus.

1118. Rebecca Altheda 2d, born in Rodman, N. Y., Jan. 20, 1842; died in infancy.
1119. Mahala Altheda, born in Rodman, N. Y., Apr. 10, 1844; married James Rose. P. O. (1898) Chesamung, Mich.
1119a. Anson Baxter, born in Rodman, N. Y., Dec. 21, 1846; died in infancy.

481 ISAAC WARRINER, son of Jacob (209) and Sabra, was born Feb. 7, 1802.

CHILDREN OF ISAAC WARRINER (481).

1119c. Marcia, date of birth not given.
1119d. Euphemia, date of birth not given.
1119e. Ann, date of birth not given.
1119f. Helen, date of birth not given.

484 WILLARD WARRINER, son of Jacob (209) and Sabra, was born in Rodman, Jefferson Co., N. Y., May 11, 1808; married Emeline A. Bushnell, in Chardon, O.; died Jan. 24, 1884, in Franklin, Neb., and is buried there. He was a mechanic, and a member of the Methodist Episcopal church.

CHILDREN OF WILLARD WARRINER (484).

1120. Henry Martin, born Sept. 28, 1837. P. O. (1896) Riverton, Neb.
1121. Silo Perry, born May 10, 1839.
1122. Edward Willard, date of birth not given. Residence (1896) Riverton, Neb.

485 ORRIN WARRINER, twin brother of Orson, son of Jacob (209) and Sabra, was born in Rodman, N. Y., Apr. 15, 1810; married Pamelia Atkins, Nov. 1, 1843, in Geauga Co., Ohio. She was born in Thompson, O., Aug. 12, 1817; was living (1895) with her daughter, Mrs. Crittenden. Orrin Warriner died in Kent, Union Co., Ia., June 24, 1891; buried in Morgan Cemetery.

CHILDREN OF ORRIN WARRINER (485).

1125. Herman, born Aug. 30, 1844; died in Des Moines, Iowa, March 16, 1884; not married.
1126. Jane, born Apr. 4, 1846; married, Sept. 19, 1866, Samuel W. Rickey. Residence (1895) Winfield, Iowa. Children: Florence E., Minnie M., Joseph H., Louis H., John W., Fay, Cora M., C. Thompson, Jennie M., Bessie M., Edwin O., Ethel P.
1127. Nettie, born Feb. 20, 1852; married, Apr. 3, 1879, Holden Kenyon. He died Nov. 9, 1893. Her residence (1895) was Orient, Ia. Children: G. Wilfred, Clara L., Harry O., Walter L., Lois M., Fannie V.
1128. Cora V., born May 12, 1858; married Herley E. Crittenden, banker. Residence, Lenox, Ia. Son, Louis K., born 1884.

486 ORSON WARRINER, twin brother of Orrin, son of Jacob (209) and Sabra, was born in Rodman, N. Y., Apr. 15, 1810; married Martha Smith, in Painesville, O. She died in 1856, and he married, on June 8, 1859, Clarinda Osborne, daughter of a Congregational minister. He was a farmer, and a member of a Congregational church. His finances were prosperous after his second marriage. Toward his aged and helpless father he was peculiarly tender and dutiful. He was " strictly honest, and his integrity was never questioned." He died in Claridon, O., May 22, 1886.

ORSON WARRINER.

CHILDREN OF ORSON WARRINER (486).

(All born in Claridon, Ohio.)

1130. John Henry, born March 21, 1847.
1131. Elisha, born in 1849; died in Claridon.

1132. Sabra Eliza, born in 1851; died in Claridon.
1133. Emily Amelia, born in 1853. In 1856 she was married to Rev. Holland B. Fry, a Congregational minister. Residence (1896), Oberlin, Ohio. Children: Mary Anna, Margaretta, Clara Emily. The last named died in 1888.

487 HENRY WARRINER, son of Jacob (209) and Sabra, was born in Watertown, N. Y., June 15, 1812; married Olivia Ware. He died in Iowa in 1891; she died in Nebraska. He was by occupation a traveling salesman; by church membership a Congregationalist.

CHILDREN OF HENRY WARRINER (487).

(All born in Geauga Co., Ohio.)

1135. Eunice Boid, date of birth not given; married Roland Goddard; died in Orwell, O.
1136. Ann Melinda, date of birth not given; married A. J. Weston. P. O. (1895) Rialto, Cal.
1137. Isaac, date of birth not given; died in Hampden, O.
1138. Julia, date of birth not given; died in Hampden, O.
1139. Austin Henry, date of birth not given; died in Hampden, O.
1140. Harlan Bush, born Dec. 4, 1852.
1141. Eva, date of birth not given; died in Hampden, O.

488 JACOB WARRINER, son of Jacob (209) and Sabra, was born in Rodman, N. Y., probably March 21, 1814; married Alzadah Atkins, in Chardon, O., Sept. 4, 1850; died in Chardon, Oct. 2, 1869; buried there. From the age of 14 years till his death he was lame, and never walked without crutches. He was a man of genial disposition; a shoemaker by trade.

CHILDREN OF JACOB WARRINER (488).

1145. Erastus Bush, born June 5, 1851; residence (1896), Chardon, O.; unmarried.

1146. Viola Polly, born Dec. 25, 1854; died Sept. 4, 1856.
1147. Dora Ellena, born March 8, 1857; married, Dec. 8, 1884, Wm. D. Bell, who died suddenly, June 30, 1895. Their child was named Wm. Curtis. Her residence in 1896 was Chardon, O.
1148. George Archie, born Jan. 27, 1866. P. O. (1896), Chardon, O. He has traveled much in the west.

491 WILLIAM CHURCH WARRINER, son of Justin (214) and Anna, was born in Springfield, Mass., Feb. 2, 1807; married Julia S. Blackman, in Ansonia, Conn., July 24, 1831, and died there July 8, 1879. His wife, born in Oxford, Conn., Sept. 8, 1807, died in Ansonia, Nov. 26, 1881.

CHILDREN OF WM. CHURCH WARRINER (491).

(All born in Oxford, Conn.)

1150. Mary M., born Sept. 29, 1834; married George C. Allis, of Derby, Conn., Jan. 26, 1860.
1151. Harriet E., born Feb. 21, 1838; married, Jan. 17, 1865, John C. Hotchkiss, of Ansonia, Conn. P. O. (1898), Bridgeport, Conn.
1152. Henry W., born Aug. 17, 1840; died in Ansonia, Conn., July 26, 1864.
1153. Marcus M., born July 30, 1842; enlisted in Co. B., 20th Conn. Vol. Inf., from Derby, Conn., Aug. 7, 1862; mustered into service Sept. 8, 1862; mustered out June 3, 1865; died in Ansonia, Sept. 13, 1871.
1154. Julia A., born Oct. 27, 1848; died in Ansonia, Conn., March 12, 1869.

492 ISAAC FERRE WARRINER, son of Justin (214) and Anna, was born in Springfield, Mass., Nov. 13, 1808; married Hannah W. Cate, Nov. 3, 1831 — "both of Springfield." She died July 15, 1852, aged 40; he died in Hartford, Conn., July 23, 1875. He was a carpenter and joiner.

CHILDREN OF ISAAC FERRE WARRINER (492).

(All born in Springfield, Mass.)

1155. Annie Elizabeth, born Jan. 28, 1833; residence (1896), 40 Holyoke st., Springfield, Mass.; unmarried.
1156. Sarah Eliza, born Aug. 28, 1839; residence (1896), 40 Holyoke st., Springfield, Mass.; unmarried.
1157. Isaac Justin, born Dec. 4, 1842; married Mrs. Mary Sweet; died Feb. 27, 1877; no children.
1158. Hannah Lucinia, born Apr. 4, 1845; died Aug., 1845; buried in Springfield.

493 ISRAEL CHAPIN WARRINER, son of Justin (214) and Anna, was born July 24, 1810; married in Hamburgh, N. Y., Sept. 10, 1835, to Julia Ann Amedon. She died July 24, 1840, aged 29, and on March 27, 1842, he married Olivia S., daughter of Roswell and Betsey Barber. She was born in Windham, N. Y. He was a cabinetmaker, also a lumber dealer. He served as captain in the State militia. He died June 23, 1833, in Buffalo, N. Y., and is buried there. His wife was living in Buffalo in 1893.

CHILDREN OF ISRAEL CHAPIN WARRINER (493).

(All born in Buffalo, N. Y.)

1160. Sophia, born July 19, 1836; died in Lisbon, Mich., in Feb., 1869.
1161. Julia, born June 5, 1838; residence (1898), Buffalo, N. Y.; unmarried; a teacher.
1162. Helen, born Apr. 17, 1840; married Charles Blackall; residence, Lisbon, Mich. Child named Israel.
1163. Frances Olivia, born Aug. 3, 1843; married Joseph Gatley; residence, Buffalo, N. Y. Children: Kate Olivia, George Edward, Henry Stearns, Agnes Frances.
1164. Harriet Lillah, born Apr. 26, 1847. P. O. address, 126 Mohawk st., Buffalo, N. Y.

1165. Kate Gant, born Sept. 26, 1853; died in Buffalo, N. Y., Apr. 26, 1871.
1166. Charles Montgomery, born Nov. 24, 1855.

495 JUSTIN WARRINER, son of Justin (214) and Anna, was born March 8, 1815; married Rebecca D. Roberts, of Hartford, Conn., Sept. 15, 1841. As to denomination he was a Congregationalist; as to trade a cabinetmaker. He died July 19, 1845, aged 30. His widow married George E. Martin. She resided (1893) in Hartford, Conn.

CHILDREN OF JUSTIN WARRINER (495).

1167. Frances, born Jan. 10, 1843; died at the age of 10.
1168. Justin, born July 19, 1845.

496 FRANCIS WARRINER, son of Justin (214) and Anna, was born Feb. 9, 1817, in Hartford, Conn.; married Sarah W. Richards on Jan. 9, 1839. He was a long time a resident of Troy, N. Y. He died March 31, 1889, in Rochester, N. Y. He was a Baptist deacon, and prominent in church and Sunday school work. His employment was in the foundry.

CHILDREN OF FRANCIS WARRINER (496).

1169. Frederick Augustus, born in Hartford, Conn., Nov. 15, 1839.
1170. Sarah Frances, born in Hartford, Conn., Aug. 24, 1845; died in Troy, N. Y., March 16, 1854.
1171. Edward Richard, born in Troy, N. Y., March 20, 1850; died in the same city, Apr. 7, 1852.

498 RALPH WARRINER, son of Justin (214) and Anna, was born in Springfield, Mass., Feb. 15, 1822; married Jane Hight, in Waterford, N. Y., Oct.

RALPH WARRINER.

9, 1844. He died in Saratoga Springs, N. Y., Aug. 23, 1872, and is buried there. He was an iron founder by trade, and an Episcopalian by creed. He was a prominent man in Saratoga Springs, supervisor of the town, president of the village, president of the fire department, etc. His widow resides (1898) in Albany, N. Y., 100 Lark street.

CHILDREN OF RALPH WARRINER (498).

1172. Albert Gunnison, born in Waterford, N. Y., Oct. 27, 1845.
1173. Ella, born in Troy, N. Y., Feb. 3, 1850; married Moses Craver, Jr., of Albany, N. Y.

553 JOHN MCCRAY WARRINER, son of David (219) and Fanny, was born in Wilbraham, Mass., Oct. 24, 1820; married Orpha A. Moses, Nov. 7, 1844. He was a contractor by occupation. His death occurred in Springfield, Mass., Nov. 28, 1886.

CHILDREN OF JOHN MCCRAY WARRINER (553).

(All born in Springfield, Mass.)

1200. James Franklin, born March 18, 1846; died in Springfield, Sept. 25, 1849.
1201. Fanny Jane, born May 16, 1849. P. O. (1894), Springfield, Mass.
1202. Emma Ann, born Apr. 4, 1852; married Russell B. Whitcomb, Aug. 9, 1871. Children: Mabel Rose, Emma Russell, George Warriner Bates, John Howard, Florence Evelyn.

556 CHARLES MOODY WARRINER, son of Charles (221) and Priscilla, was born in Wilbraham, Mass., Oct. 23, 1834; married Elizabeth C. S. Hale, Jan. 15, 1854. The name of Charles N. Warriner is on the Springfield military record, probably intended for Charles Moody Warriner.

CHILDREN OF CHARLES M. WARRINER (556).

1203. Charles H., born in Wilbraham, Mass., Apr. 20, 1855; drowned July 7, 1866, aged 11.
1204. Ella B., born June 6, 1858.

557 GEORGE PADDOCK WARRINER, son of Charles (221) and Priscilla, was born in Wilbraham, Mass., Aug. 10, 1836; married Emma J. Green, Nov. 4, 1857. He enlisted as a Union soldier in the 3d Mass. Heavy Artillery, Sept. 1, 1864.

SON OF GEORGE PADDOCK WARRINER (557).

1206. George H., born Apr. 16, 1859.

625 COL. SOLOMON WARRINER, son of Solomon (228) and Mary, was born in Wilbraham, Mass., March 24, 1778. He married, on March 4, 1801, Eleanor Keep, sister to Rev. John Keep, of Oberlin, O. She died July 8, 1810, aged 33, and on July 4, 1811, he was married to Mary, daughter of Luke and Rachel Bliss, of Springfield. She died Jan. 2, 1859, aged 75. From 1815 to to 1820 Col. Warriner resided in Pittsfield. All the rest of his mature years his home was in Springfield, where he

COL. SOLOMON WARRINER.

died June 14, 1860, aged 82. He ranks as one of the best remembered men of all the generations of Warriners. As farmer, merchant, postmaster, military officer, school visitor, chorister and musical composer, he held an honorable place in the esteem of his fellow citizens.

On the morning after his death the following editorial, doubtless written by Dr. J. G. Holland, a personal friend of Mr. Warriner, appeared in the Springfield Republican: " Our venerable fellow citizen, Col. Solomon Warriner, died on Thursday, at the ripe age of 82 years — a man whose usefulness, modesty, honesty and Christian piety bring a community instead of a single family into the train of his mourners. No old man that has passed out of Springfield within our memory, and shut the gate of life behind him, has turned his face from more friends and fewer enemies. The old men associate his memory with their happiest days, and even the children, over whom his office placed him, will remember to their latest day his benevolent face. . . . His father was a farmer, and it was upon the farm he won the vigor which enabled him to work almost up to the day of his death.

"Very early in life he gave evidence of extraordinary musical powers. At even a tender age he used to sing the old-fashioned " alto " in the village church, and at 12 years of age he was drummer in the Wilbraham military company.

" He served his apprenticeship to a bookbinder in Worcester county, and came to Springfield in 1801, where he was first associated with Dr. Elam Bliss — dealing mostly in drugs and books. Two or three years later he engaged in general merchandise business with two or three others. Subsequently he was in business with his son Solomon, one store on the street, and one at the Upper Water Shops.

" Col. Warriner early manifested fondness for military life, and was chosen lieutenant in a military company about 1802. Subsequently he rose to the rank of colonel, which title he bore through his long life. In the War of 1812 a regiment of artillery, in which he held the rank of major, was ordered to Boston. Col. Edwards, of Northampton, was the commander of the regiment, but the drilling and management of the troops devolved very much upon Major Warriner, who was exceedingly popular with the men. Col. Warriner received from the government a land bounty proportioned to his rank at the time, under the act rewarding the volunteers of 1812. The old men speak with enthusiasm of his gracefulness as a mounted officer, and his fine appearance on field days.

" But that which has made Col. Warriner more widely known than anything else was his devotion to sacred music, and his agency in developing it in this region. He had the direction of the music in the old church of this city, then under the charge of Dr. Osgood, for a great many years, with one intermission. His business interests led him to Pittsfield in 1815, but after remaining there five years, the people of Springfield fairly bought him back. They could not get along without him. He was here in May, 1820, when the First Church was dedicated, and got up the music for that occasion. Col. Warriner took from his business sufficient time to become a somewhat noted compiler of music. The Springfield Collection was the name of a book of sacred music published by him in his younger days. After this, he was associated with the celebrated musician, Thomas Hastings, in the composition and publication of Musica Sacra — a first-class book of sacred music. He maintained a very pleasant correspondence with Dr. Hastings till his closing days. Col. Warriner was the first leader of the first musical society ever formed in Springfield — the old Handel and Haydn Society. Indeed, Col Warriner was the great authority and standard in all musical matters throughout this region, and did more than any other man to elevate the style of sacred music in Western Massachusetts. In the old church his choir numbered from 75 to 100, filled all the singing seats, and ran over.

" His later years were occupied in his garden, and as prudential committee of the city schools. His benevolent face has looked into the school rooms for the last time, and the little stragglers for whom he cared so conscientiously will play truant a good while before his place will be filled by one who will so thoroughly do his duty. The old man's memory

'Smells sweet and blossoms in the dust.' "

He led the choristers in singing Dr. Holland's hymn, " Thou who didst bless the garden land," at a famous national horse exhibition in Springfield in 1853. In 1886, at the celebration of the 250th anniversary of the founding of Springfield, the tunes were selected from Col. Warriner's publications. A memorial of him was printed in the history of the First Church.

CHILDREN OF COL. SOLOMON WARRINER (625).

(Five by first wife, Eleanor; three by second wife, Mary.)

1240. Solomon, born Feb. 10, 1802.
1241. Francis, born Nov. 20, 1804.
1242. William Pitt, born Oct. 29, 1806.
1243. Sophia Eleanor, born June 14, 1808; married Aug.
11, 1835, Charles Merriam, who was afterward
publisher of Webster's Dictionary. She died Apr.
26, 1848, and is buried in Springfield. She had
four children. Her son William was somewhat
eccentric. In his will he gave all his property,
$80,000, to the government. He died on Long
Island, a bachelor. Eleanor Sophia married Col.
Samuel Woods, of the U. S. army, and lived in
California two years. Col. Woods died, and she
returned to Springfield, where she now lives
(1898); no children — an adopted daughter, Edith.
Harriet, another daughter of the Merriams, married Wm. Kirkham, and had two sons, Charles and
Guy. Wm. Kirkham died, and the widow married Chas. D. Hosler, of Springfield. They have
one son, Walter. The youngest child of Sophia
E. Warriner Merriam is Miss Lillian. She has
traveled extensively, has a fine musical education,
and lives in a beautiful home of her own in
Springfield.
1244. Harry, born May 5, 1810.
1245. Lewis, born May 12, 1812.
1246. Mary Bliss, born Feb. 11, 1814; married Judge
Henry Morris, May 16, 1837. Children: Mary,
1839; Edward, 1841; Henry Oliver, 1844, died
1845; Charles Henry, 1846; Frederick William
and Wm. Frederick (twins), 1850. Mary Morris
married Charles Calhoun, son of Wm. B. Calhoun.
They have children named respectively Charles
Morris Calhoun and Margaret Calhoun. Edward
Morris, a lawyer, lives in Springfield, and has his

father's office. Frederick W. Morris is a book-
seller in New York. Helen Morris married W.
W. Gay, a member (1892) of the editorial staff of
the New York World.

1247. Elizabeth Bliss, born Feb. 4, 1816; resides (1898) in
Springfield, Mass., unmarried. The author is
pleased to have made the personal acquaintance
of this elect lady, the last surviving member of her
father's family. Her countenance, her conversa-
tion, her letters, very plainly indicate remarkable
intelligence and kindliness of heart.

JEREMY WARRINER'S U. S. HOTEL, SPRINGFIELD, MASS.

628 JEREMY WARRINER, son of Solomon (228) and Mary,
was born June 10, 1785; married Phebe, daughter of Thomas
Bates, Dec. 4, 1809 — he of Pittsfield, she of Springfield. For
many years he was widely known and popular as keeper of a
tavern or hotel in Springfield, the first ever built in the town.
It was prominently located on the corner of Main and State
streets, was cozy and attractive in appearance, and entertained
the best class of the traveling public. On the opposite corner

was the large brick building, one side of which was occupied
by G. and C. Merriam, publishers of Webster's Dictionary,
the other by Ames & Dwight. On the sign in front of the
tavern was printed, " United States Hotel, J. Warriner."
In the Springfield cemetery are two stones on which are
carved these inscriptions:

JEREMY WARRINER
DIED
MARCH 25, 1859
AGED 74.

PHEBE
WIFE OF
JEREMY WARRINER
DIED APR. 17, 1854
AGED 64 YEARS.

633 JAMES WARRINER, son of Solomon (228) and Betsey,
was born in Wilbraham, Mass., Aug. 5, 1797; married, 1824,
Martha Graves, daughter of John Burgoyne and Martha G.
Root. He was a merchant in Pittsfield, Mass.,* and the first
president of Berkshire County Savings Bank. The church of
his choice was the Congregationalist. He died Aug. 8, 1865,
in Pittsfield, Mass., and is buried there. His wife was born in
Pittsfield, Feb. 26, 1802, and died there Oct. 26, 1866.

CHILDREN OF JAMES WARRINER (633).

(All born in Pittsfield, Mass.)

1248. John Root, born March 22, 1827.
1249. James Lyman, born May 27, 1829.
1250. Maria Root, born Aug. 19, 1831; resides with her
brother James L. in Pittsfield. She is unmarried.
1251. Elizabeth, date of birth not given; died in infancy.
1252. Thomas Hastings, date of birth not given; died in
infancy.
1253. Edward Payson, date of birth not given; died in
infancy.
1254. Martha Cecelia, born June 22, 1839; died Nov. 8,
1869, in Pittsfield.

* Some one wilfully caused an explosion of a gun-powder
magazine in Pittsfield, by which James Warriner's house on
East street was greatly damaged. (History of Pittsfield.)

635 LYMAN WARRINER, son of Solomon (228) and Betsey, was born Jan. 20, 1802; married Maria Center; lived in Pittsfield; had an interest in Berkshire hotel; died about 1865.

CHILD OF LYMAN WARRINER (635).

1255. Helen Maria, born in 1838; married Capt. Moody, of one of the Atlantic steamers. He has been dead some years. Her residence (1892) was Liverpool, England.

642 STEPHEN ORLANDO WARRINER, son of Stephen (230) and Elizabeth, was born in Monson, Mass., Nov. 15, 1793; married, in the same town, Sapphira Flagg, Sept. 29, 1834. Both died and were buried in Monson. The wife died March 14, 1857; the husband, Feb. 13, 1868, aged 74. His occupation was farming; his church, Congregational.

CHILDREN OF STEPHEN ORLANDO WARRINER (642).

(All born in Monson.)

1258. Andrew Austin, born June 9, 1836.
1259. Daphne Sapphira, born Oct. 6, 1837; married Henry L. Naramore; residence (1898), Sharon, Mass.
1260. Stephen Cady, born Aug. 25, 1839.
1261. Elizabeth Ely, born June 14, 1841; died March 11, 1845, aged 3; buried in new cemetery, Monson, Mass.
1262. Joseph Reynolds, born May 7, 1843.
1263. Ellen Elizabeth, born Sept. 27, 1845; married Roland M. Clark. Residence (1898), Winchendon, Mass.
1264. Alfred Ely, born June 26, 1849.

645 ETHAN WARRINER, son of Ethan (231) and Sally, was born Oct. 22, 1802; married Dolly Kent in Wilbraham, Mass.,

Apr. 13, 1826. He was by denomination a Methodist; by trade a carpenter. He died in Palmer, Mass. This cut is a copy of the memorial at the head of his grave in the old burial ground in Wilbraham. His wife was born in Suffield, Conn., Nov. 27, 1806, and died in Indian Orchard, Mass., Jan. 14, 1892.

CHILDREN OF ETHAN WARRINER (645).

(All except the last born in Wilbraham, Mass.)

1268. Ethan, born Jan. 21, 1827.
1269. Cornelia, born July 20, 1828; died in Wilbraham, Dec. 26, 1855, unmarried, aged 27. Tombstone in the old cemetery in Wilbraham.
1270. William, born July 21, 1830.
1271. John, born Oct. 10, 1832.
1272. Mary Elizabeth, born Oct. 2, 1834; married Charles Smith; died in Wilbraham.
1273. George, born Oct. 27, 1837; joined Co. B, 21st Mass. Volunteer Infantry; died in Chicopee, Mass., Aug. 24, 1871; buried in Wilbraham.
1274. Albert Henry, born Apr. 13, 1841.
1275. Harriet Abigail, born June 29, 1843; married Eben Benjamin. Residence (1897), New London, Conn.
1276. Fidelia Miriam, born in Palmer, Mass., June 1, 1847. Residence (1898), Indian Orchard, Mass.

676 WILLIAM BOSTWICK WARRINER, son of William Bostwick (238) and Rebecca, was born Apr., 1811; married Rachel G. Wilson, Apr., 1837; died Oct., 1857, in New York City.

CHILDREN OF WILLIAM BOSTWICK WARRINER (676).

1296. Wilson, date of birth not given; died in childhood.

1297. William, date of birth not given; killed in the War of the Rebellion, at 21 or 22 years of age.

1298. Gertrude, born about 1846; died in New York City, aged about 27.

679 DANIEL CHARLES WARRINER, son of William Bostwick (238) and Rebecca, was born in Charlestown, Mass., May 25, 1818; married Laura Louisa Pitts, Feb. 6, 1848. She was born Feb. 1, 1830. He passed his childhood in Boston. At 18 he went to live in New York, and remained there until 1876, when he moved to Jacksonville, Fla. He was then in poor health, and remained an invalid until his death, March 3, 1894. While in New York he was partner in the firm of Dubois & Warriner, piano manufacturers. In his faith he was a Swedenborgian. A paper in Jacksonville said of him:

DANIEL CHARLES WARRINER.

" He was known to a large and appreciative circle of friends, who attest his sterling integrity, hospitable kindness and great generosity. He was highly literary in his tastes, and distinguished for various accomplishments in this direction." He is buried in Evergreen Cemetery, Jacksonville, Fla.

CHILDREN OF DANIEL CHARLES WARRINER (679).

(All except Florence P. born in New York City.)

1300. May, born Feb. 9, 1849; died in Brooklyn, N. Y., 1874.

1301. Julia Adalaide, born Oct. 11, 1852; married George Hughes, July 12, 1876; died in Florida, Dec. 26, 1883. Children: George Warriner, Florence Longmore, Adalaide Sarah.

1302. Charles Friend, born Jan. 28, 1885.

1303. Florence Plume, born in Brooklyn, N. Y., July 18, 1861. Residence (1898), Jacksonville, Fla.

1304. Laura Emeline, born March 13, 1866. Residence (1898), Jacksonville, Fla.

702 REV. PHANUEL WARRINER, son of Moses (243) and Anne, was born in Wilbraham, Mass., March 17, 1798; married Apphia Gerish, Sept. 28, 1829. She was born in Boscawen, N. H., Apr. 27, 1805, and died in Tyler, Texas, June 22, 1878. One who knew her well describes her as "a good and noble lady."

REV. PHANUEL WARRINER.

Phanuel Warriner studied some years at Yale College, and graduated at Andover Theological Seminary. He became a Presbyterian minister, lived in Michigan several years, did great good in organizing churches in southern Michigan and northern Indiana. It is said that he was the founder of nearly all the Presbyterian churches that existed in the State of Michigan up to 1840. He moved to White Pigeon in that State when the country thereabouts was partly inhabited by Indians. He was a trustee of White Pigeon Academy in 1837. In 1840, on account of a bronchial affection, he moved to Texas, being the second Presbyterian minister in Texas up to that time. He was for many years an active and successful agent of the American Bible Society, prosecuting his work all over southeastern Texas. His memory is cherished in that region. He was a ripe scholar, and a devoted Christian of pure and unostentatious life. "In San Augustine, Sabine, Rusk and Nacogdoches he labored long and successfully as a minister. His whole life was one of faithful service to Christ and His cause." He held slaves when in the south. His health was quite infirm after 1861, and he departed this life in Tyler, Texas, Nov. 3, 1879, and there he and his wife are honored by a memorial in the Presbyterian church.*

* Letter of J. H. Brown.

CHILDREN OF REV. PHANUEL WARRINER (702).

1329. Sarah Ann, born in New York State; married Emory
Clapp, 1852; died 1863; no children.
1330. Emily G., born in Monroe, Mich., 1833; married,
Nov., 1849, J. H. Brown. She died in the city of
Tyler, Tex., Aug. 12, 1897. "She had been a
great sufferer from paralysis of the brain for many
years, but she did well her part in this life." J. H.
Brown is mayor of Tyler, Texas (1898).
1331. Elizabeth Clark, born in White Pigeon, Mich.; married C. N. White. She resides (1898) with her
brother-in-law, J. H. Brown, in Tyler, Tex., and
has one son, Newell W. She is the only living
child of Phanuel Warriner.
1332. Jacob Gerish, born in White Pigeon, Mich.; date
not given; died in Sabine Town, Tex., about 1852.
1333. Joseph Gerish, born in White Pigeon, Mich.; date
not given.

705 ALEXANDER WARRINER 2d, son of Moses (243) and
Anne, was born in Vermont, probably Apr. 10, 1805; married
Harriet Wing, and died in East Gainsville, N. Y.

CHILDREN OF ALEXANDER WARRINER (705).

1337. Pamelia, married ——— Hillman, and died leaving
two children, Alice and Charles.
1338. Ardelia, date of birth not given; died, unmarried.
1339.

707 HARVEY LEWIS WARRINER, son of Moses (243) and
Anne, was born in Vt., Sept. 23, 1809; moved to N. Y. State
with his parents when two or three years old; married Emily,
daughter of Nathan and Sarah Bassett, in Brownhelm, O.,
Apr. 7, 1835. He had moved to Clay township, O., in 1834,
rented 80 acres of land, made a clearing and put up a log house.
After living there one summer he moved out to Portage river,
where a man was building a mill, worked there one year, then

went back to the farm. In 1854 he built a large framed house, and moved into it on Christmas day. His wife, who was a native of Wheatland, Monroe Co., N. Y., died in Clay township, O., Jan. 30, 1864, aged 48; he then moved to Genoa, and married Pamelia Banks, Dec. 11, 1867. He died in Genoa, O., Aug. 29, 1879; buried in Woodville, O.

HARVEY LEWIS WAR-
RINER.

CHILDREN OF HARVEY LEWIS WAR-
RINER (707).

(The first was born in Woodville, O.; the others in Clay township, same State.)

1340. Sarah Anna, born Aug. 22, 1836; married Allen H. Rudes, June 11, 1857. Their residence (1898), is Genoa, O. Their first born daughter died, an infant, in 1858; their second daughter, Cora, was born in 1863, married John F. Cregg, and resides in Rollersville, O. — has several children.

1341. Phanuel, born Jan. 3, 1839.

1342. Charles Elbert, born Aug. 19, 1841.

1343. Walter, born July 9, 1843.

1344. Pamelia, born Sept. 30, 1846; married Hilliard Sloan; died in Detroit, Mich., Jan. 26, 1877. One child was living in 1893, born about 1874, name, Ralph Standish Sloan.

1345. Helen Elizabeth, born March 28, 1851; married Melvin E. Bell; died in Millbury, O., June 14, 1855. She left two children: Wilbur Warren and Edith Ardelia.

1347. Harvey, born May 25, 1856.

709 HIRAM WARRINER 2d, son of Moses (243) and Anne, was born July 17, 1815, in N. Y. State, probably; married,

Sept. 19, 1841, Eliza C. Fish, of Lancaster, Erie Co., N. Y. At the time of his death in Oak Harbor, O., March 27, 1876, he was superintendent of the Poor Farm of Ottawa county. His widow resided (1893) in West Liberty, Iowa.

CHILDREN OF HIRAM WARRINER (709).

1348. Orville Fayette, born Dec. 1, 1842.
1349. Amelia Henrietta, born Feb. 28, 1844; died Jan. 29, 1854, in Ottawa, O.

711 LUCIUS HECTOR WARRINER, son of Dr. William (253) and Lydia Bemis, was born in Hamburgh, Erie Co., N. Y., Aug. 17, 1814; married N. Judith Abbey, Oct. 9, 1836. During his last days his residence was Hull, Sioux Co., Iowa. He died about 1895. One child, a son, died before he was two years old.

713 MARCUS BRUTUS WARRINER, son of Dr. William (253) and Lydia B., was born in Hamburgh, Erie Co., N. Y., June 14, 1819; married Catharine Sayles in 1837; died in Chicago, Ill., about 1890.

SON OF MARCUS BRUTUS WARRINER (713).

1351. William R., date of birth not given; died before 1874, aged about 22.

715 SAMUEL WARRINER, son of Daniel (254) and Mary, was born in Brattleboro, Vt., Feb. 12, 1827; married Anne M., daughter of Asher and Miriam Gilbert Smith, May 5, 1856. He resided until recently in West Brattleboro, Vt., within 100 feet of his birthplace. That was his home continuously after his marriage for nearly forty years. He now lives with his son. While able to work his occupation was farming.

SON OF SAMUEL WARRINER (715).

1354. Chester Gilbert, born Sept. 24, 1862.

716 WILLIAM WARRINER, son of Daniel (254) and Mary, was born in Brattleboro, Vt., Aug. 8, 1829; was married, first, in Boston, Mass., to Ann Clark. She died in Winslow, Me., July 16, 1858. He married, second, Caroline E. Bremner, Sept. 26, 1861, in East Brattleboro, Vt. Residence (1898), Monson, Me.; occupation, farming.

CHILDREN OF WILLIAM WARRINER (716).

1355. Frederick Clifford, born in Winslow, Me., Oct. 5, 1863; died there Jan. 20, 1864.
1356. Henry Allen, born in Winslow, Me., Apr. 16, 1865.
1357. Daniel Lewis, born in Clinton, Me., Feb. 23, 1867.
1358. George Franklin (Frank), born in Monson, Me., July 5, 1872. He spent a year with Rev. E. Warriner in Stepney, Conn.

717 HENRY WARRINER, son of Daniel (254) and Mary, was born in West Brattleboro, Vt., Dec. 28, 1831; married Mary Jane Bangs, Sept. 2, 1868. He resides (1898) in West Brattleboro in the house built by his grandfather, Samuel Warriner (125), in the year 1800.

CHILDREN OF HENRY WARRINER (717).

1359. Emma Luette, born June 15, 1870.
1360. Florence Hadley, born Oct. 16, 1876.

718 CHESTER WARRINER, son of Daniel (254) and Mary, was born Oct. 13, 1833. Judge D. B. Hadley writes: "He came to my house in Akron, O., in the fall of 1851, and left there in the winter following; went to Westport, Mo., made a contract to go to California, overland, but the man broke his contract with him, and he then went to St. Paul, Minn., and taught school till the following summer, when he was drowned in the Mississippi river while bathing. He had read law with me till he went west. He was not married."

722 DANIEL STEWART WARRINER, son of Daniel (267) and Lucy, was born in New York State, Nov. 15, 1805. Some authority states that he married Elizabeth Ellis. He owned a little farm in the town of Clayton, N. Y., near Depauville. Later, it is said, he moved to Iowa.

CHILDREN OF DANIEL STEWART WARRINER (722).

1385. Almedia, date and place of birth not given.
1386. Alzina, date and place of birth not given.

729 HARVEY WARRINER, son of Daniel (267) and Lucy, was born in N. Y. State, Dec. 1, 1821; married Lucy Jane Carley in 1854. He is a farmer (1898), and his residence is in Watertown, Wis.

CHILDREN OF HARVEY WARRINER (729).

1390. Walter Scott, born Jan. 1, 1855. P. O. (1895), Watertown, Wis.
1391. George W., born Jan. 13, 1864. He is a farmer, and his P. O. (1898) is Watertown, Wis.
1392. Lilly Jane, born Sept. 19, 1876.

735 WILLIAM WARRINER, son of Ethni (269) and Rebecca, was born July 23, 1808, probably in Galway, N. Y.; married Leonora, daughter of Willard and Irene Morse, in Rodman, N. Y., Apr. 4, 1832. He died of typhoid fever, in Freedom, Ill., Oct. 18, 1860, and was buried in Harding, Ill. He was a farmer, a member of the Methodist Episcopal church — an honorable and industrious man. His wife was born in Berkshire Co., Mass., and died in Freedom, Ill., Apr. 1, 1861.

WILLIAM WARRINER.

CHILDREN OF WILLIAM WARRINER (735).

(All except the first born in Lorraine, Jefferson Co., N. Y.)
1400. Albert Carlos, born in Ellisburgh, N. Y., May 7, 1833.

1401. Nancy, born Apr. 26, 1836; married Willard M. Taylor. Residence (1894), Jennings, La.

1402. Armelia Lovina, twin sister of 1403, born Dec. 19, 1839; married George French, and lived near Hillsdale, Mich. Their daughter, Lida M., moved to Griswold, Kan. Mr. French died, and his widow married, in Nov., 1891, Augustus Smith. Their residence (1898) is 526 Guthrie st., Ottawa, Ill. Mr. Smith has three children. Mrs. Smith is popular as a writer of poetry.

1403. Armenia Louisa, twin sister of 1402, born Dec. 19, 1839; died in Lorraine, N. Y., May 14, 1844.

1404. Julia Ann, born Oct. 10, 1841; married Latham E. Weaver. Residence (1894), Prairie Center, Ill.

1405. Mary Jane, born Jan. 25, 1844; died May, 1844.

738 Rev. Levi Warriner, son of Ethni (269) and Rebecca, was born March 24, 1814; married Mary Jane Crego, in Michigan. He was for years a member of Michigan Confenence, Methodist Episcopal church. Appointments: 1838, Coldwater; 1839, Lyons Mission; 1840, Mapleton; 1841, Eaton; 1842, Jackson; 1843, Litchfield; 1844, located. He died in 1858, in Moscow, Mich., and was buried in Jonesville, in the same State. His widow married Daniel Wilson, who died not many years after their marriage. She afterwards married David Garlinghouse, and resided in Napoleon, Mich. She was born in 1819, and died March 11, 1896. There is no likeness of Levi Warriner extant.

CHILDREN OF REV. LEVI WARRINER (738).

1407. Henrietta Rebecca, born July 16, 1845; married Daniel A. Wisner; died, leaving one child.

1408. Emma Melinda, born Apr., 1848; married Charles French, her cousin, Nov., 1864, and resides in White Rock, Oklahoma Ter. Children: Arthur E., Minnie L., Clinton E. and Homer L.

1409. Mary Matilda, born in 1850; died in Mosherville, Mich., 1866.

1410. Lester Locy, born about 1853; married Althea Edwards; died from the effects of a runaway accident. He and his wife were members of the Methodist Episcopal church. He was a farmer. No children.

739 SOLOMON JOHNSON WARRINER, son of Ethni (269) and Rebecca, was born in Lorraine, N. Y., Oct. 31, 1816; married Mary Ann Clark, Nov. 6, 1837. He was at different times harness maker, chair maker and farmer. Most of his life was spent in L o r r a i n e, though he resided at various times in Water- town, B l a c k River v i l l a g e and other places in the State of New York. He was a sweet singer, like Col.

SOLOMON J. WARRINER.

MARY ANN WARRINER.

Solomon Warriner, for whom he was named. He was very outspoken and much inclined to express his religious emotions. He held license as a local preacher for a number of years in the Methodist Episcopal church. When about 60 years of age he became a Seventh Day Adventist, the change in his creed being made with evident sincerity. His strong physical constitution bore the shock of many accidents. The kick of a horse caused his sudden death on the 29th day of March, 1888, when he was 71 years of age.

Mary Ann Warriner, his wife, was born in Sacketts Harbor, N. Y., Aug. 15, 1820. She was a woman of delicate constitution, bright intellect, amiable disposition, and recognized by all who knew her as one of the saints. She and her twin sister, Mrs. Maria F. Chandler, were very much alike in their literary tastes, the former writing many poems for various periodicals,* the latter publishing a book of poems (selected and original) entitled The Spirit Harp.

---

* The following is one of her poems which appeared in The Christian Advocate when she was about sixty years of age:

AUTUMN.

Fair Autumn! thou art lovely still;
 For though the rolling year
Has changed the woodlands on the hill,
 More gorgeous they appear.

The sky above is clear and bright,
 As on a Summer's day;
The zephyrs blowing soft and light,
 Make ripples on the bay.

O'er verdant pastures, fresh and fair,
 My eyes are wandering;
And peaceful flocks are feeding there,
 As in the balmy Spring.

But o'er remaining life, grim Death
 Asserts his conquering power;
The leaves are falling in my path —
 I tread on withered flowers.

But Death brings ripeness with decay,
 Nor can we shed a tear,
As in our barns we stow away
 The harvests of the year.

Autumnal days! ye bring to mind
 The man whose death is nigh,
Who looks around him but to find
 He's destined soon to die.

Mary Ann Warriner died on her 74th birthday, Aug. 15, 1894. She was laid to rest by the side of her husband in the ———— cemetery, in Rodman, N. Y.

CHILDREN OF SOLOMON J. WARRINER (739).

1411. Edwin, born in Ellisburgh, N. Y., Jan. 19, 1839.
1412. Oliver, born in Warsaw, N. Y., Jan. 9, 1841; served

He hears men say he's growing old;
  It seems but yesterday
That he was young, and strong and bold —
  'Tis all a mystery!

To him the clear melodious song
  Of birds rings forth as sweet
As when, a boy, he ran along
  With little, swift, bare feet,

The cow-path in the "pasture lot,"
  Or waded in the brooks,
And in his happiness forgot
  His errands and his books.

And yet he knows he's not the same;
  He has felt it many a day;
His vigor's gone, his tottering frame
  Is yielding to decay.

Great changes he has lived to see;
  " The trusted and the true "
Have gone to vast eternity,
  The land " beyond the blue."

Fading, though beautiful is earth!
  We seek a fairer home,
Where all things lovely have their birth,
  Amid *perpetual bloom!*

LORRAINE, N. Y.   MRS. MARY A. WARRINER.

CORPORAL OLIVER WAR-
RINER.

as a soldier in the war for the Union; was a corporal; died in Woodsonville, Ky., in 1868, and is buried there.

1413. Margaret Maria, born in Warsaw, N. Y., Apr. 17, 1843; married Wm. C. Clark, of Mannsville, N. Y., in 1897.

1414. Mary Ann, born in Watertown, N. Y., Aug. 27, 1845; died Sept. 13, 1845; buried in Watertown.

1415. E m m a L o v e, born in Watertown, N. Y., Aug. 31, 1847; married George D. Eaton, of Watertown, N. Y. Children: Ida Florence, John Dempster, Helen Edna, Kate Maud and Edwin Warriner. The two eldest married before 1898.

742 OREL CALVIN WARRINER, son of Ethni (269) and Rebecca, was born in Lorraine, N. Y., Sept. 7, 1822; married Cleantha Park. She died in 1847, and he married Betsey Purdy.

MARGARET M. WARRINER,
AGED 17.

EMMA L. WARRINER,
AGED 12.

After her death, in 1851, he married Margaret Case. She died Jan. 11, 1871. He then married Mary Tuttle. She died the same year, and in 1872 he married Mrs. Mahala Bennett. He served in the war for the Union as a soldier in the Fourth Light Artillery regiment of Michigan volunteers. Residence (1898), Litchfield, Mich.; member of the Methodist Episcopal church.

CHILDREN OF OREL C. WARRINER (742).

(Two by first wife; two by second; five by third; one by fifth.)

1416. Alma Louisa, born Dec. 13, 1844; married Lawrence T. Dale, of Breckenridge, Mo., a native of London, England. They have seven children, namely: Edwin S., William W., Lillian M., Nellie M., George W., Bessie J. and Clifford A.

1417. Myron, born Feb. 28, 1847. Adopted; name changed to Nichols; married Adella Crane. Children: Arthur A., Frank E., Willard C. and Grace Myra Nichols.

OREL C. WARRINER.

1418. Jennie, born Jan. 9, 1849; married Willard F. Cooper. The husband and their only child are dead. Her address (1898) is 1433 Ogden street, Denver, Colo.

1419. Don C., born 1851; died same year.

1420. Theressa Mary, born Aug. 7, 1852; married Case Hocknell. P. O., Litchfield, Mich. Six children: Maud, Madge, Glenn, Bessie, Benjamin and Earl. The last two are dead.

1421. William O., born May 29, 1855; died March 2, 1856.

1422. Lavant Alonzo, born Aug. 13, 1859; married, and lives in Litchfield, Mich.

1423. Annett M., born Jan. 19, 1862.

1424. Minnie Bell, born Jan. 3, 1871.

1425. Emma, born Sept. 4, 1873; married Wm. Mattison. P. O. (1898), Litchfield, Mich.

743 ALFRED WARRINER, son of Ethni (269) and Rebecca, was born in Lorraine, N. Y., Dec. 3, 1827, and was married,

Aug. 14, 1848, to Harriet L. Haynes. He was a soldier in the Mexican War; for some years a cabinet maker; later a druggist. He died in Hillsdale, Mich., Feb. 16, 1875. His wife joined the Woman's Foreign Missionary Society of her church (Methodist Episcopal) at its beginning, and has been an active and useful laborer therein, also in the Woman's Christian Temperance Union. Her residence (1898) is Battle Creek, Mich.

ALFRED WARRINER.

MRS. HARRIET L. WARRINER.

SON OF ALFRED WARRINER (743).

1430. Frank Edgar, born in Litchfield, Mich., July 16, 1849.

746 ORRIN WARRINER, son of Luther (207) and Freelove, was born in New York State in 1808; moved to Michigan and there married. His wife's name was Margaret. About 1864 he moved back to Oriskany Falls, N. Y., his former home. He died there in 1891. He was a tailor by trade, but for a number of years he worked on a farm. His wife, who survived him, is dead. They were both members of the Baptist denomination. They had five children; four died in infancy, and their names are unknown to the writer of this book. One

DAUGHTER OF ORRIN WARRINER (746) is

1436. Laura, date of birth not given; at last account an inmate of the insane asylum in Utica, N. Y.

747 JOHNSON WARRINER, son of Luther (270) and Freelove, was born in Lorraine, Jefferson Co., N. Y., in 1809; married Sally Cole, June 8, 1832. He died in Pitcher, N. Y., in
1886. He and his people were Methodists.

CHILDREN OF JOHNSON WARRINER (747).

1438. Julia A., born Feb. 9, 1834. P. O. (1896), West
Bainbridge, N. Y.; not married.
1439. Emmeline, born Feb. 22, 1836. P. O. (1896), West
Bainbridge, N. Y.; not married.

749 LYMAN WARRINER, son of Luther (270) and Freelove,
was born in Lorraine, N. Y., Jan. 26, 1814; married Laura
Baldwin, in Greenville, Pa., Nov. 28, 1841. He was killed by
the falling of a tree, and was buried in West Franklin, Pa. He
was a farmer, and a member of a Baptist church. His wife
was born Sept. 16, 1825, and died at the home of her son, J. L.
Warriner, in Ballston Spa., N. Y., Feb. 9, 1881.

CHILDREN OF LYMAN WARRINER (749).

(All born in West Franklin, Pa.)

1445. William Allen, born Nov. 11, 1842; died July 11,
1843.
1446. Francis Harvey, born March 15, 1846.
1147. Johnson Horatio, born Feb. 10, 1848.
1448. Justin Lyman, born Nov. 22, 1849.

750 DAVID WARRINER, son of Luther (270) and Freelove,
was born in 1816; married Mary Greene. After he left Jefferson Co., N. Y., his home was in Oriskany Falls, same State.
He died there Dec. 24, 1882. His wife died of consumption
five weeks later.

DAUGHTER OF DAVID WARRINER (750).

1449. Ida Viola, date and place of birth not given; married
Elihu Hewitt; died about 1890.

754 SAMUEL MILLER WARRINER, son of Loren (273) and Hester G., was born in Sherburne, N. Y., about 1821. He was residing in Manlius, N. Y., in the winter of 1844, and, being in poor health, he determined to go to sea. Accordingly he went to Sag Harbor, L. I., and embarked for a three years' voyage on board the whaling ship Silas Richards.

It is said that he sailed round the world. For two years afterward he worked on a farm in N. H. In 1849 he sailed for California in search of gold. Since that time his friends have never heard from him. Mrs. Baldwin, his sister, writes that he was a Methodist exhorter, and that report says he caused the conversion of the ship's crew at sea. In his last letter, dated Keene, N. H., Oct. 17, 1849, and addressed to all his brothers and sisters, he wrote: " I am now on my way to California, and before you will have read these pages I may be the most of the way there, or perhaps in the diggings, if luck be on my side. Are you in Christ? Be faithful. Are you out of Christ? Seek immediately and delay not one moment. Give my love to the church at Manlius.

T. ORLANDO WARRINER.

755 THOMAS ORLANDO WARRINER, commonly called Orlando, son of Loren (273) and Hester G., was born in Sherburne, N. Y., Dec. 9, 1825; married Cynthia Eliza Smith, of Mass., July 3, 1856. She died Dec. 23, 1891, aged 51. After the death of his parents the children were scattered, and unacquainted with each others whereabouts.

He drifted about and finally reached Columbia Co., N. Y. He was eager to obtain a collegiate education, but his poverty and his delicate health made that impossible. He remained for awhile in New Lebanon, N. Y., and divided his time between manual labor and teaching school. He also studied medicine nearly two years with Dr. Robert Worthington, of Lenox, Mass. After his marriage he lived in Canaan, N. Y., till 1876, when he moved to Pittsfield, Mass. He served in the war for the Union as a member of the 21st N. Y. Cavalry. He has held a membership for many years in the Congregational church in Canaan, N. Y.

CHILD OF THOMAS ORLANDO WARRINER (755).

1450. Loren, born about 1868; died about 1876.

756 PHILIP PHILANDER WARRINER, son of Loren (273) and Hester G., was born about 1827; married, Dec., 1849, Frances, daughter of Davis and Anna Jacobs, of Holland Patent, N. Y. He was by trade both a carriage and cabinet maker, and by church association a Methodist. He served as a soldier in the war for the Union; was a prisoner at Andersonville, and died there, shot down by Keeper Woertz, in July, 1864. He wrote the following letter to his wife just after he was taken prisoner:

RICHMOND, June 5th, 1864.

" DEAR WIFE. — I am sorry to state that I am here a prisoner of war. We were taken on the 2d. James Denison and James Stanton are here also. Evan Jones is wounded and prisoner. There were two of our companies taken. We do not know where John Edwards is. We were left out on picket and our forces moved away without calling us in, so we were surrounded before we were aware of it. I think of you and the children always. May God bless you and help you to be cheerful and hopeful. I cannot write more now. From your husband,

P. P. WARRINER."

His widow, born Nov. 23, 1829, died in Holland Patent, N. Y., 1895.

CHILDREN OF PHILIP PHILANDER WARRINER (756).

1451. William Henry, born Oct. 27, 1851; at the age of 14 he went to Kansas, and later to Colorado; wrote regularly to his friends till about 1872, since which time they have not heard from him.

1452. Sarah Frances, born Jan. 15, 1855; married Newton Greenfield. Residence (1898), Saginaw, Mich.
1453. Anna May, born March 30, 1857; married George Barhyte. Residence (1898), Trenton, N. Y.
1454. Charles Loren, born Jan. 21, 1860.
1455. George Frederick, born Sept. 30, 1862.

771 JERE HORTON WARRINER, son of Walter (275) and Betsey, was born March 14, 1811; married Melinda Bicknell. He was a good musician and singer. His trade was that of a mason. He died in the month of June, 1837, in the city of Syracuse, N. Y., aged 26. His widow married John Helm, of Canada. They both died, leaving one child — a son.

SON OF JERE HORTON WARRINER (771).

1470. Francis Dwight, born in 1834.

774 LUCIUS ALBERT WARRINER, son of Walter (275) and Betsey, was born in Frankfort, Herkimer Co., N. Y., Apr. 11, 1816; attended common school; at 14 went to an academy in Utica; taught school three months before he was 16, and succeeded well, though many of his scholars were his seniors; spent two terms in Cazenovia Seminary, and then went to the western part of N. Y. State and taught school in various sections twelve winters. He married one of his scholars, Caroline Mills, on Apr. 26, 1838. She wore at school a wine-colored gown, made of woolen cloth which she had spun and woven herself. He counted that a good recommend. He writes: "We have passed through scenes which pen cannot describe. We have smoothed the dying pillow of the parents of both of us, and of all our children. We are childless, yet the Lord has spared us to one another, and we are trusting in Him whose blood cleanses from all sin."

Leaving the occupation of school teacher, he hired out as clerk in a grocery store, and later as commercial traveler, selling granite and marble, and afterward went into the stone cutting business. His residence (1898) is Sandy Creek, N. Y. He and his wife belong to the Presbyterian church.

CHILDREN OF LUCIUS ALBERT WARRINER (774).

1471. Albert Horton, born in Wethersfield, Wyoming Co.,
N. Y., March 30, 1839; died in Frankfort, N. Y.,
Aug. 9, 1841; buried in Frankfort.
1472. Wallace Horton, born in Frankfort, N. Y., Dec. 12,
1841; died in Sandy Creek, N. Y., July 9, 1865;
buried in Sandy Creek. He was blind from the
age of 10, and many have distinct recollections of
his appearance, led about by his dog. He played
on several musical instruments and became a successful teacher of music. He had a Bible with
raised letters, a book much used and prized.
1473. Helen Maria, born in Frankfort, N. Y., March 27,
1844; married Moreau Salisbury, Jan. 8, 1867;
died in the village of Sandy Creek, Aug. 2, 1891.

779 DR. LORENZO WARRINER, son of Warren (277) and
Catharine, was born in Wilbraham, Mass., Nov. 6, 1807; mar-
ried Emeline R. Burbank. She died, and subsequently, on
March 3, 1847, he married Eliza, daughter of Lyman and
Augusta Day, of Warren, Mass. She was born Apr. 29, 1824.
He died in Warren, Mass., Aug. 17, 1873. He was a member
of the Methodist Episcopal church.

CHILDREN OF DR. LORENZO WARRINER (780).

1490. Alfred Allen, born Dec. 16, 1849.
1491. Alice Eliza, born Aug. 8, 1853; died Aug. 5, 1855.
1492. Myron Anson, born March 30, 1856.

781 ALFORD WARRINER, son of Warren (277) and Catharine, was born in Wilbraham, Mass., June 10, 1811. He married, 1st, March 14, 1837, Emily A., daughter of Leonard and
Electa (Dorman) Owen. She died Oct. 30, 1851, and he married, 2d, a widow named Tower, and after her death he married, 3d, in 1858, Elvira, daughter of Gilbert Bascom, of
Southampton, Mass. He was, in his youth, a Methodist, and
his studies were pursued with the ministry in view. Later he

became a Congregationalist. Soon after his first marriage he moved to Virginia, and had charge of a plantation cultivated by slaves. He returned in 1845, and located in Pelham, Mass. He was engaged while there in some kind of mechanical work. He died in West Springfield, Mass., Oct. 11, 1881, and was buried in the Bascom lot, Southampton cemetery. His widow resides (1898) in Southampton, Mass.

CHILDREN OF ALFORD WARRINER (781).

1494. George Leonard, born in Fredericksburg, Va., Nov. 3, 1842.

1495. Allen Dorman, born in Prescott, Mass., Dec. 14, 1846.

1496. Newton Oscar, born Aug. 14, 1849, in Hatfield, Mass. His mother dying in 1851, he was adopted by his sister and his name changed to Oscar Newton Allen. He died Feb. 5, 1882; left no children.

789 SOLOMON NEWTON WARRINER, son of Alvord (280) and Eliza, was born in Frankfort, N. Y., March 22, 1821; married Harriet Collins, June 14, 1849. He taught common school ten years and was justice of the peace ten years. His residence (1898) is Washington Mills, N. Y.

CHILDREN OF SOLOMON NEWTON WARRINER (789).

SOLOMON N. WARRINER.   (All born in Washington Mills, N. Y.)

1500. Ellen Louisa, born Nov. 13, 1850; died at home, Nov. 21, 1855; buried in New Graefenburg.

1501. Mary Eliza, born Aug. 28, 1852. Residence (1898), Washington Mills, N. Y.

1502. Harriet Maria, born Oct. 11, 1854. Residence (1898), Washington Mills, N. Y.

1503. Arthur Francis, born Sept. 15, 1856.
1504. Linda Marcella, born Aug. 1, 1859.   Residence (1898), Washington Mills, N. Y.
1505. Alice Abbie, born Apr. 15, 1861.   Residence (1898), Washington Mills, N. Y.

795 ABNER EATON WARRINER, son of Theodore (281) and Betsey, was born in Wilbraham, Mass., date not given; married, at Oriskany Falls, N. Y., before 1858, to Marcella B., daughter of Eli Hicks; died in Auburn, N. Y., where the widow and daughter continued to reside after his death.

CHILD OF ABNER EATON WARRINER (795).

1508. Lizzie E., date of birth not given.

796 WILLIAM CHANDLER WARRINER, son of Theodore (281) and Betsey, was born in Wilbraham, Mass., Sept. 10, 1833; married Mary Jane Welton, July 7, 1857. Business, insurance. Previously, from 1861 to 1865, a boot and shoe merchant. From 1859 to Oct. 8, 1894, the date of his death, he was a resident of Davenport, Ia. He was a member of the Masonic fraternity, and a life member of St. Simon of Cyrene Commandery of K. T.

CHILDREN OF WILLIAM CHANDLER WARRINER (796).

(All born in Davenport, Iowa.)

1510. Jean Arvilla, born Jan. 31, 1861; married Walter S. Morse, June 27, 1894.
1511. William Horton, born July 22, 1863.
1512. Charles Theodore, born Jan. 26, 1868.

820 AMOS WARRINER, son of Joseph (301) and Naomi, was born in Monson, Mass., May 16, 1808; married, in Monson, July 4, 1833, Patience Hatch Butler. He died in Pa., March 10, 1860, aged 52. His wife was born in Monson, Dec. 10, 1803, and died in Pa., Sept. 6, 1888, aged 85.

CHILDREN OF AMOS WARRINER (820).

(All born in Monson, Mass.)

1530. Ira, born May 16, 1834.
1531. Joseph, born Dec. 25, 1835; married — name not given. Residence, Stony Fork, Pa. No reply to communications sent.
1532. Elias, born Apr. 1, 1840; married — name not given. He is believed to be the Elias Warriner of Idelwild, Ill. (1883-1891), and later of St. Louis, Mo.
1533. Lumis, born Dec. 10, 1843; died in Monson, July 6, 1848, aged 5.
1534. Caroline, born July 9, 1846; died in Monson, July 8, 1848, aged 2.

824 ELIAS TURNER WARRINER, son of Joseph (301) and Naomi, was born in Monson, Mass., May 31, 1818; married, Oct. 27, 1841, Sarah E. Durkee, who was born Sept. 16, 1822. His P. O. (1898) is North Wilbraham, Mass. His house is in the town of Monson, and his is the only family of the name remaining in the town. The author was pleasantly and kindly entertained by him and his family in the fall of 1893.

ELIAS T. WARRINER.

CHILDREN OF ELIAS TURNER WARRINER (824).

1550. Sanford A., born Oct. 19, 1842; died March 30, 1843.
1551. Josephine H., born March 2, 1845; married, Dec. 18, 1867, Nelson C. Hill, of Warren, Mass.; resided (1894) in Cavendish, Vt. Mr. Hill is a finisher of woolen goods. Their son, Eugene N. Hill, was a clerk in a dry goods store in Springfield in 1893.

1552. Maria Louisa, born June 25, 1849; married Edwin
M. Nichols; died Apr. 14, 1870. Children: Perlin
E., of Mittineague, Mass., and Louise M. (Mrs.
Herbert M. Noble), who died Aug. 4, 1896, and
left an infant son.

1553. Wilson J., born Oct. 30, 1850.

HOME OF ELIAS T. WARRINER, MONSON, MASS.

827 WILLIAM LOMBARD WARRINER, son of William (303)
and Lucy, was born in Monson, Mass., Apr. 8, 1812; married
Naomi Chase, in Wheeler, N. Y., Sept. 4, 1831. She was born
in Wheeler, N. Y., July 13, 1814, and died in Delmar, Pa.,
Feb. 1, 1860. He then married Eleanor Hadley. His death
occurred in Draper, Pa., Apr. 26, 1870. He and his first wife
are buried in Stony Fork. As to denomination, Free Will
Baptist; as to occupation, carpenter.

CHILDREN OF WILLIAM LOMBARD WARRINER (827).

1564. Mary, born in Wheeler, N. Y., June 6, 1832; died in Stony Fork, Pa., Oct. 4, 1834.
1565. Harriet, born in Wheeler, N. Y., Aug. 12, 1833; married, Jan. 1, 1854, John Wesley Ingerick, in Mansfield, Pa. Children: Alfred, Rosella and Frank. She died in 1880, and Mr. Ingerick married again, and, in 1894, was preaching the gospel in South Poultney, N. Y.
1566. Benjamin Howard, born in Delmar, Pa., Dec. 30, 1834.
1567. Ogilva, born in Wheeler, N. Y., Dec. 26, 1836; married Mary Bryant; has charge of the carpenter work on a 95-mile division of Fall Brook Ry. His P. O. is Wellsboro, Pa. He belongs to the Free Will Baptist Church.
1568. Lucy, born Apr. 11, 1836; married B. F. Wheeler. P. O. (1898), Asaph, Pa. Children: Willis F., Mrs. Martha A. Francis, Mrs. Metta E. Brooks, Mrs. Eva E. Beauge.
1569. Hiram, born in Stony Fork, Pa., Sept. 14, 1840.
1570. Asa Chase, born in Stony Fork, Pa., Sept. 28, 1842.
1571. Nathan, born in Stony Fork, Pa., Aug. 16, 1844; died in Jerusalem, N. Y., Oct. 26, 1846.
1572. Abram Melville, born in Stony Fork, Pa., Apr. 11, 1853.

828 HIRAM WARRINER, son of William (303) and Lucy, was born in New Hampshire; married Jane Decker; died in Stony Fork, Pa., in 1893. He was a farmer by occupation, a Free Will Baptist by church membership.

CHILDREN OF HIRAM WARRINER (828).

1574. Mary, date of birth and death not given.
1575. Rachel, date of birth and death not given.

829 SAMUEL BORDEN WARRINER, son of William (503) and Lucy, was born in Delmar township, Pa.; married his cousin, Mary Ann Warriner (850), May 21, 1842; died in Wellsboro, Pa., Feb. 17, 1887, where his widow now resides. He was a member of a Free Will Baptist church; a jeweler by trade.

SAMUEL B. WARRINER.

MRS. MARY ANN WARRINER.

SON OF SAMUEL BORDEN WARRINER (829).

1576. Marshall B., born Sept. 30, 1846.

836 REV. LEVI CLARK WARRINER, son of Nathan (305) and Abigail S., was born in Monson, Mass., May 19, 1819; married Adaline Laura, daughter of Lyman Anderson; died in Parker's Prairie, Minn., May 5, 1871, and is buried there. He was a Baptist preacher, and his ministry covered a period of 30 years. He was a plain, easy, interesting speaker. He moved from Ohio to Minnesota for his health in 1871, but lived only one month after reaching Parker's Prairie. He was the first minister there. His widow resides (1898) in Bloomington, Minn. She is descended from a heroic ancestry. Her father's mother was Irene Jones, whose mother was Irene Bradford, whose grandfather was Gov. Wm. Bradford, of the Plymouth colony.

REV. LEVI C. WARRINER.

CHILDREN OF REV. LEVI CLARK WARRINER (836).

1580. Eliza Marilla, born in Delmar, Pa., May 12, 1844;
married by her father to Azariah Smith, in Addison, N. Y., Oct. 17, 1863. Two children were
born to them in Woodhull, N. Y., namely: Frank,
now deceased, and Herbert A., pharmacist in Min-
neapolis. Mr. Smith was a deacon in the Baptist
church 18 years. He was a widower with three
children when he married Miss Warriner. In
1871 he moved from N. Y. State to Parker's
Prairie, Minn., and was among the first settlers,
having Chippewa Indians for neighbors. The
nearest R. R. station was St. Cloud, 100 miles
away; the nearest P. O. was 25 miles distant. Mr.
Smith organized the first Sunday school, and his
wife taught the first week day school in that
region. The school house, built of logs, was low,
with earth for floor, and was heated by an old cook
stove when the mercury stood at 40 or 46 degrees
below zero. Mr. Smith died Aug. 7, 1889, and
his widow, in 1891, married a Baptist minister,
the Rev. T. H. Sherman, pastor (1898) in
Osage, Ia.
1581. A son, born in Delmar, Pa., Dec. 21, 1845; died
Feb. 4, 1846.
1582. Levi Clark, born in Delmar, Pa., Nov. 27, 1846.
1583. Adaline Betsey, born in Delmar, Pa., Oct. 4, 1848;
married, in 1873, George Nathan McComb, who
has been for many years a missionary of the American Sunday School Union. Their children: Ver-
non Monroe, Daisy Adell, Mary Etta, Wilbur
Levi, Marshall Erwin, Lillian Pearl — all living
in 1894.
1584. Lyman Nathan, born in Brookfield, Pa., Apr. 16,
1850.
1585. Jairus David, born in Brookfield, Pa., Jan. 22, 1852.
1586. Ursula Hattie, born in Brookfield, Pa., June 18,
1856; died Sept. 21, 1861.

1587. Abigail Estella, born in Woodhull, N. Y., Apr. 24, 1858; married Abram T. Palmer. P. O. Bloomington, Minn. Children: Phebe L., Wilbur W., William A., Lucius, Leonard G., Gertrude E.
1588. Jennie Eveline, born in Woodhull, N. Y., Nov. 24, 1860; married George W. Handy. P. O. (1894), Park Rapids, Minn.
1589. James Monroe, born in Woodhull, N. Y., Nov. 15, 1863; died Aug. 9, 1865.

838 PERLIN NATHAN WARRINER, son of Nathan (305) and Abigail S., was born in Monson, Mass., July 24, 1822; married, 1st, Louisa Bunnell. This wife died in Plainville, Conn., Sept. 5, 1845, and he married, 2d, Martha Hart, in Barkhamsted, Conn. She died in Brooklyn, N. Y., Oct. 14, 1858, and he married, 3d, Clarissa T., daughter of Nehemiah and Lucy Hoyt, in New Haven, Conn., Aug. 29, 1859. He was engaged in the steam and gas fitting business in New Haven from 1852 to 1861, and afterward in the steam heating business in New York.

PERLIN N. WARRINER.

He professed conversion when he was 18 years of age, and from the beginning to the end he adorned his profession by a remarkably earnest and consistent life. While in Brooklyn he was a member of Lafayette Avenue Presbyterian Church, Rev. Dr. T. L. Cuyler, pastor. He died in Brooklyn, N. Y., Aug. 30, 1874, and is buried in New Haven, Conn. His widow resides in Brooklyn, 141 So. Elliott Place.

CHILDREN OF PERLIN NATHAN WARRINER (838).

1590. Perlin C., born in Providence, R. I., Nov. 2, 1849; died in the same city, Sept. 28, 1850.
1591. Martha Antoinette, born in Ansonia, Conn., July 21, 1851; died in New Haven, Conn., Jan. 22, 1856.

1592. Addie Cleaveland, born in New Haven, Conn., March 26, 1855; married Oliver Johnston, Jan. 8, 1878, in Brooklyn, N. Y. They have five children, namely: Stella Louise, Olive May, Arthur Warriner, Helen Maude and Harold Lee.

1593. George Edward, born in New Haven, Conn., Feb. 2, 1858.

1594. Jennie Louise, born in Brooklyn, N. Y., Apr. 22, 1861; married James Church, in Brooklyn, June 30, 1886.

1595. Ella Frances, born in Brooklyn, N. Y., Dec. 31, 1862; married Andrew R. Halsey, July 6, 1887.

839 JAMES MONROE WARRINER, son of Nathan (305) and Abigail S., was born in Monson, Mass., July 11, 1825; married Mary Ann Frost, in Springfield, Mass., July 3, 1844. She was three years his senior. He died in Kalamazoo, Mich., Dec. 14, 1886. He was a traveling salesman. His church was the Protestant Episcopal. His widow resides in Detroit, Mich.

CHILDREN OF JAMES MONROE WARRINER (839).

1596. Martha Marilla, born Aug. 9, 1847; married John Taylor on June 1, 1869. Residence, 75 Ash street, Detroit, Mich. Children: Jennie E., Walter G., J. Edith, Charles F., William E.

1597. Henrietta Adaline, born July 13, 1849; unmarried (1893). Residence, Detroit, Mich.

1598. Mary Abbie, born Nov. 20, 1851; married Everett S. Marion. Children: Everett S., David H., Darwin W., James Warriner, Frank A., Lillie M., John T., Ralph E.

1599. Jennie Evelyn, born Apr. 26, 1858; died in Rochester, N. Y., Nov. 2, 1861; buried in Detroit, Mich.

1600. Lillie Agnes, born Sept. 2, 1863; married Wm. A. Gibson, Jan. 2, 1884. Children: William H., John, Arthur M., Charles F., Lottie A.

842 WILLIAM ALLEN WARRINER, son of Benjamin Howard (306) and Matilda, was born July 5, 1820, in Brookfield, Vt.; married, 1st, Cornelia, daughter of William L. Warriner (827), on March 23, 1843. She died in Addison, N. Y., March 18, 1861, and he married, 2d, Bertha J. Thompson, in Addison, Dec. 23, 1861. She died in Vineland, N. J., Feb. 3, 1865. The residence of Wm. A. Warriner (1898) is Vineland, N. J. He is a Baptist by church membership, and a jeweler by trade. He was justice of the peace two terms in Franklin township; for some time postmaster and railroad agent in North Vineland, N. J., and a member of the N. J. N. S. Guards over 20 years. He won three badges consecutively at target practice, at 70, 71 and 72 years of

WM. ALLEN WARRINER.

age. When 72 he was the oldest man and oldest member of Co. K., Sixth Regiment, and won more points than any other man of the company.

CHILDREN OF WILLIAM ALLEN WARRINER (842).

(All except the last two born in Delmar, Pa.)

1605. Stillman Davis, born March 20, 1844.
1606. Louisa Decker, born March 12, 1846; married C. J. Marble, Oct. 7, 1866. Residence (1896), Coudersport, Pa. Children: Charles Warriner, Stillman W., Cornelia, Frank Ferry, Carlton, Arch.
1607. Sarah Sabrina, born Apr. 24, 1849; married Jesse Myers. Residence (1896), Allegheny, Pa.
1608. Emma Jane, born May 9, 1851. Residence (1898), Vineland, N. J.
1609. Laura Cornelia, born June 7, 1853; died in Addison, N. Y., Feb. 10, 1858.
1610. William Anson, born in Addison, N. Y., Apr. 14, 1863; married Kate Lambert. He is professor in Albany Business College (1898).

1611. Bertha May, born in Vineland, N. J., Nov. 20, 1867.
She was a stenographer in 1896 in Schenectady,
N. Y.; married, 1897, Dr. W. L. Woodruff, of
Mobile, Ala. Their son, William Warriner Wood-
ruff, was born Feb. 23, 1898.

843 CHAUNCEY HOWARD WAR-
RINER, son of Benjamin Howard (306)
and Matilda, was born May 25, 1822;
married, Feb. 6, 1842, Lovina M.
Smith; died July 5, 1887, in New Lisbon, Wis.; buried there.

CHILDREN OF CHAUNCEY HOWARD
WARRINER (843).

1613. Joseph O., date and place of birth
not given. He held for some
time an appointment as special
agent for the inspection of
timber depredations in Wis-
consin. His P. O. was Tomah, Wis. Information has been solicited; no reply.
1614. Charles E., date and place of birth not given. His
P. O. was New Lisbon, Wis.

CHAUNCEY HOWARD
WARRINER.

846 IRA MANN WARRINER, son of Benjamin Howard (306)
and Matilda, was born in Roxbury, Vt., March 10, 1837; married, March 26, 1866, H. Elizabeth Carney. P. O. (1896),
Liberty, Tioga Co., Pa.

CHILDREN OF IRA MANN WARRINER (846).

1620. Laura Almira, born June 14, 1867; married, in
March, 1882, Orrin N. Warriner, supposed to be
No. 1638.
1621. Minnie L., born Oct. 26, 1869; married F. K.
Ogden, in July, 1892.
1622. Ida M., born Dec. 31, 1872; married A. W. Dibble,
in the month of March, 1890.

1623. Clara Viola, born Apr. 27, 1876; died May 2, 1886.
1624. Mina Matilda, born May 14, 1878.
1625. Cora V., born March 3, 1881; died Sept. 29, 1881.
1626. Albert Ira, born Oct. 18, 1883.

853 ABEL SILAS WARRINER, son of Abel (309) and Sophia, was born in Monson, Mass., June 18, 1830; married Harriet Stout; died June 5, 1863. He followed farming, and he was a member of the Free Will Baptist church. The P. O. of his widow (1896) was Hornellsville, N. Y.

CHILDREN OF ABEL SILAS WARRINER (863).

1632. Orpha, place and date of birth not given.
1633. Carrie, place and date of birth not given.
1634. Carson A., born 1861; is married; no children. Foreman M. Deutch & Co., Hornellsville, N. Y.

856 JAMES NELSON WARRINER, son of Abel (309) and Sophia, was born in Monson, Mass., Feb. 5, 1835; married Adaline Decker. P. O. (1898), Stony Fork, Pa.

CHILDREN OF JAMES NELSON WARRINER (856).

(All born in Stony Fork, Pa.)

1636. Clarence, date of birth asked for but not given.
1637. Bertha, date of birth not given.
1638. Orrin N., date of birth not given.

858 CHARLES ROYCE WARRINER, son of Abel (309) and Sophia, was born in Delmar township, Pa., Jan. 26, 1841; married Elizabeth Miller for his first wife and Elizabeth Plumley for his second wife.

CHILDREN OF CHARLES ROYCE WARRINER (858).

1640. George, date of birth not given.
1641. Charles, date of birth not given.

859 JOHN FERRY WARRINER, son of Abel (309) and Sophia, was born in Delmar township, Tioga Co., Pa., March 10, 1844; married Delana Backus. He died June 3, 1890. His widow resides in Stony Fork, Pa. (1898).

CHILDREN OF JOHN FERRY WARRINER (859).

1643. Lewis Abel, date of birth not given.
1644. George Luther, date of birth and death not given.
1645. Nettie Jane, date of birth and death not given.
1646. Mabel Sophronia, date of birth not given.
1647. Edith Anne, date of birth not given.

862 JAMES WILSON WARRINER, son of James (310) and Cretey, was born March 11, 1828; married Polly Ann Demill. P. O. (1898), Greenwood, N. Y.

CHILDREN OF JAMES W. WARRINER (862).

1650. Charles Scott, killed by railroad cars in Steuben Co., N. Y., at the age of 18.

867 VOLARUS B. WARRINER, son of James (310) and Lucretia (often called Cretey), was born Jan. 15, 1839, in Tioga Co., Pa.; married Huldah M., daughter of Bradshaw and Nellie White, in West Union, Steuben Co., N. Y. Residence (1896), Greenwood, N. Y. Farmer; member of the Methodist Episcopal church.

CHILDREN OF VOLARUS B. WARRINER (867).

1655. William V., born about 1862.
1656. Amelia, born about 1864; married Curtis Mattison.
1657. Bradshaw, born about 1868.
1658. Ephraim, born about 1870.
1659. Nellie, born about 1872.
1660. Charles, born about 1873.
1661. Carrie, born about 1879.
1662. May, born about 1886.

868 NATHAN ALLEN WARRINER, son of James (310) and Cretey, was born Nov. 7, 1842, in Delmar, Pa.; married Mary P. White, at West Union, N. Y., Jan. 1, 1863; class leader and exhorter in Wesleyan Methodist Church; has held offices in the towns of Jasper and Greenwood, N. Y.

CHILDREN OF NATHAN A. WARRINER (868).

1670. Effie Isadore, born May 27, 1864; died Apr. 17, 1880.
1671. Francis Lazelle, born Jan. 17, 1866.

875 MOSES WARRINER, son of Capt. Walter (313) and Sophia, was born in Springfield, Mass., Aug. 1, 1817; married Jane, daughter of George and Susanna Hale, in Waterford, N. Y., in Jan., 1839. He was a farmer. He died in Springfield, July 28, 1896.

CHILDREN OF MOSES WARRINER (875).

(Born in Springfield, Mass.)

1680. Walter B., born Dec. 1, 1850.
1681. Sarah, born Jan. 29, 1853; married, Sept. 28, 1871, Albert B. Crosby, wire worker, of Springfield, Mass. They have a son named Charles.

890 WILLIAM D. WARRINER, son of Daniel (313) and Rebecca (Darling), was born in Springfield, Mass., May 6, 1826; married, in Springfield, Dec. 25, 1848, Elizabeth, daughter of Chauncey Belknap, who was born Feb. 28, 1826. He was for many years a resident of East Windsor, Conn., and from that town, on Nov. 1, 1861, he enlisted in the 11th Vol. Infantry of Conn.; mustered Nov. 14, 1861; promoted May 28, 1862; wounded at Antietam Sept. 17, 1862; died Oct. 5, 1862, in East Windsor, Conn. His widow married Daniel Warner.

910 JUSTIN BLISS WARRINER, M. D., son of Hezekiah (320) and Hannah, was born in Hawley, Mass., March 15, 1818;

married Laura Alfreda Grout. He went to Philadelphia when young, graduated at the College of Pharmacy, later at the Medical College; practiced medicine in Burlington, N. J., and died there July 13, 1849. His widow married Christopher Stebbins. She writes concerning her former husband: " As a physician he was devoted to his profession, and really sacrificed his life for his patients during the cholera season of 1849. He had forty cases a day to look after, and every one recovered. His last day's work, when he was going from 3 o'clock in the morning till 10 at night was too much for him; and so rapidly did the deadly disease do its work that, although he prescribed for his patients till 10 A. M., he had gone to his reward before 5 P. M." No children.

911 EDWIN WARRINER, son of Hezekiah (320) and Hannah, was born in Agawam, Mass., May 10, 1819. He was married on Jan. 27, 1848, to Elizabeth, daughter of Edward and Apphia Crowell. She was born in Hadley, Mass., June 16, 1823, and was living there in 1894. He died June 15, 1882, in Hawley, Mass., and is buried there. He was a farmer and a deacon in the Congregational church. He served in Co. E., 52d Regiment, Mass. Volunteers, in the war for the Union.

CHILDREN OF EDWIN WARRINER (911).

(All born in Hawley, Mass.)

1695. Hezekiah Edward, born March 10, 1849; died in Hawley while very young.
1696. Justin Bliss, born Oct. 21, 1851.
1697. William Henry, born Feb. 27, 1855.
1698. Henry Augustus, born Nov. 3, 1866.

912 JUDGE BENJAMIN LEONARD WARRINER, son of Hezekiah (320) and Hannah, was born in Hawley, Mass., Sept. 15, 1820. He married, 1st, Laura Eldridge. She died in Springfield, and he was married again to Lucina Kinney. He learned the carpenter's trade while young. He moved to California in 1849, and thence to Idaho about 1863. On going west he became a lawyer; was a member of the Legislature of Idaho Ter. in 1876 and 1877, and was judge of probate of Boise Co. at the time of his death in Idaho City in June, 1889. He was buried with Masonic honors, being at the head of the order in Idaho, and having been a Mason nearly 50 years. No children. His widow, Lucina, died May 29, 1895.

913 HEZEKIAH RYLAND WARRINER, son of Hezekiah (320) and Hannah, was born in Hawley, Mass., July 23, 1822. He married Olive Longby. He engaged in teaching in Philadelphia for a number of years, and was remarkably successful and popular. When he left his school in Philadelphia to take charge of Deerfield Academy in Massachusetts, several of his pupils followed him. He returned after awhile to Philadelphia, studied law, and practiced there his profession until he died, Jan. 31, 1873. Some of his old students in Deerfield erected a monument there to his memory. " None knew him but to praise." No children.

PROF. H. RYLAND WARRINER.

HENRY A. WARRINER, M. D.

914 HENRY AUGUSTUS WARRINER, M. D., son of Hezekiah (320) and Hannah, was born Sept. 21, 1824, in Hawley, Mass. In Yellow Springs, O., he married Fanny Swan. She died in less than a year after their marriage, and in May, 1865, he married Sarah Pope Shepard. He studied medicine and received his degree in a Cincinnati medical school, but never practiced, as he preferred teaching. So he went to Cambridge and studied a year with Agassiz at Harvard previous to taking a professorship in comparative anatomy at Antioch College,

Yellow Springs, Ohio. At the breaking out of the Civil War he gave up his chair and offered himself as a soldier, but his friends knew that he was capable of doing a greater service, and were gratified when he was induced to take the superintendency of the distribution of supplies in the western department of the Sanitary Commission. His health failed, and he had to abandon that work. After recruiting he edited a daily newspaper in Louisville, Ky., but the Union sentiment there was not strong enough to sustain it long. He was then appointed to write the history of the Sanitary Commission, but his health utterly failed before he had completed his task, and he died in Plymouth, Mass., Nov. 17, 1871. No children.

926 SAMUEL DEXTER WARRINER, son of Reuel (327) and Anna, was born in Agawam, Mass., Feb. 11, 1817, and was a farmer at the old homestead before his marriage. He married the widow of Capt. Strong Holt, a popular and wealthy master of a whaling vessel for many years, who, after surviving many perils by sea, was drowned in New London harbor by the capsizing of a small pleasure boat. Mr. Warriner still owns the homestead in Agawam (1898), but since his marriage has had no business except to manage his own and his wife's property. No children.

932 REV. EDWARD AUGUSTUS WARRINER, son of Reuel (327) and Anna, was born in Agawam, Mass., Feb. 19, 1829; married, in Lancaster, Pa., July 5, 1865, to Louisa Voorhis. She died in 1874, in Bridgeport, Pa., and he was married to Esther Bolles, June 30, 1881. He prepared for college in a classical school in Springfield, boarding at home and crossing the river daily. He entered Yale University in 1850; was laid by a year on account of ill health; graduated at Union University in 1855; in the following year was admitted to the bar in Springfield, Mass.; practiced three years; health failed; went south; taught an academy in Washington, Ga.; during a period of enforced seclusion on account of the war studied the Bible systematically and determined to enter the ministry.

Since 1867, with the exception of two years when he was in charge of Christ Church, Philadelphia, he has been rector of St. Paul's Church, Montrose, Pa., and "has won enviable distinction for his literary attainments and pulpit ability." He has written several poetical works which show real talent. They deal largely with speculative and moral philosophies. His latest literary production is a prose volume, published in 1898, entitled: "The Gate Called Beautiful; an Institute of Christian Sociology." He is described in the Magazine of Poetry as "fond of athletic sports, . . . utterly without pretension, and though socially and professionally a successful man, yet seemingly indifferent to prominence or promotion."

REV. EDWARD A. WAR-RINER.

MRS. LOUISA VOORHIS WARRINER.

CHILDREN OF REV. EDWARD AUGUSTUS WARRINER (932).

(The eldest was born in Lancaster, Pa.; the others in Montrose, Pa.)

1710. Samuel Dexter, born Feb. 24, 1867; graduated from Springfield, Mass., High School, Amherst College and Lehigh Valley University School of Mines — from each with high honors; has the degrees of A. B.,

SAMUEL DEXTER WAR-RINER.

PHILIP BOLLES WARRINER.   JESSE BOLLES WARRINER.
MRS. ESTHER BOLLES WARRINER.
PAUL SHERMAN WARRINER.   ANNA CHAFFEE WARRINER.

A. M., B. S. and E. M. For a time he was engaged in the engineering department of the

EDWARD VOORHIS WARRINER.　　LOUISE VOORHIS WARRINER.

Lehigh Valley Coal Co., and is now (1898) super-intendent of Calumet and Hecla Copper Mine, Calumet, Mich. He was married to Stella Mercer Farnham, of Wilkesbarre, Pa., May 18, 1898.

1711. Edward Voorhis, born Sept. 12, 1869; residence (1898), 143 Cedar street, Springfield, Mass.

1712. Reuel Chaffee, born Jan. 11, 1872; graduated from Springfield High School and Lehigh University School of Mines, and has the degrees of B. S. and

REUEL CHAFFEE WAR-RINER.

E. M. He was mining engineer for Lehigh Valley Coal Co., and is now (1898) acting in the same capacity for the Rand Gold Mining Co. at Johannesburg, South African Republic.

1713. Louise Voorhis, born June 24, 1882.
1714. Jesse Bolles, born March 18, 1885.
1715. Paul Sherman, born Nov. 11, 1886.
1716. Anna Chaffee, born May 22, 1888.

942 EDWIN BALDWIN WARRINER, son of Lewis (341) and Fannie, was born Jan. 25, 1826, in West Springfield, Mass. (now Agawam); married Charlotte W., daughter of Wm. H. McNutt, in Yellowhead, Will Co., Ill., Oct. 21, 1851. He removed with his father to Lake Co., Ind., in 1837; moved thence to Kankakee, Ill., in 1855, and resided there to the time of his death, July 29, 1893. He held many positions of public trust, and was always looked upon as one of the foremost men in that section of the State. He was a member of the Baptist church in Kankakee for more than 30 years. He was deputy county clerk four years; county treasurer one term; justice of the peace a number of years. He was buried with honors by the Masonic fraternity, of which he was a prominent member. His wife was born in Nova Scotia, Jan. 13, 1828.

CHILDREN OF EDWIN BALDWIN WARRINER (942).

1720. Lewis Henry, born in Tinkersville, Lake Co., Ind., Nov. 8, 1852.
1721. Sissy, born March 4, 1855; died March 5, 1856.
1722. Sylvester William, born in Otto township, Ill., Dec. 10, 1856; died in Kankakee, Nov. 2, 1864.
1723. Robert Lincoln, born in Otto, Ill., May 22, 1860; died Nov. 13, 1888.
1724. Edwin Baldwin, born in Kankakee, Ill., Jan. 30, 1864. He succeeds his father in insurance and real estate business. P. O. (1898), Kankakee, Ill.
1725. Lottie Ellen, born in Kankakee, Ill., Dec. 24, 1866.
1726. Lucy Amelia, born in Kankakee, Ill., Oct. 19, 1869.

946 OLIVER FOWLER WARRINER, son of Norman (342) and Mirilla, was born in West Springfield, Mass., Nov. 11, 1825; married, 1849, Fanny M., daughter of Nathan and Lydia Warren, in Harding, Ill. He moved with his father to Ohio in 1837; subsequently moved to Indiana; then to Illinois, and finally to Kansas in 1854. He died Sept. 23, 1890, in Fort Scott, Kan., and is buried there. He was postmaster in Warrenton, Kan., in 1887; he was by occupation a merchant; by church membership a Baptist. His wife was born in Cazenovia, N. Y., Nov. 10, 1830. Her home (1898) is Ottawa, Ill.

CHILDREN OF OLIVER FOWLER WARRINER (946).

(All, excepting possibly the first two, born in Amboy, Ill.)

1730. Lydia, born Oct. 19, 1851; died Sept. 18, 1852.
1731. Carrie, born Feb. 13, 1853; died Oct. 28, 1854.
1732. Martha Caroline, born Feb. 17, 1855; married F. D. Miller; died in Murray, Neb., Feb. 17, 1894. Children: Ethel S.; Ina E.; Elsie W., dec'd; Ross M.
1733. Janette, born Aug. 17, 1858; died in Amboy, Ill., Dec. 10, 1874.
1734. Norman, born Nov. 17, 1860; married Ida Johnson; residence (1898), Argenta, Arkansas.
1735. William Lucian, born Sept. 23, 1872.
1736. Fanny, born 1871; died in Amboy, Ill., 1872.
1737. Oliver Fowler, born Sept. 5, 1873; residence (1898), Baker, Ill.

948 REMINGTON WARRINER, son of Norman (341) and Mirilla, was born July 17, 1833, in West Springfield, Mass., probably; married Sarah Ellen, daughter of B. P. and Maria F. Gilbert, at Onarga, Ill., on July 2, 1864. He died July 2, 1882, in Paw Paw, Ill., and is buried there. His wife was born near Laporte, Ind., in 1840, and died at Ann Arbor, Mich., June 22, 1892.

CHILDREN OF REMINGTON WARRINER (948).

1739. Eugene Clarence, born in Earlville, Ind., Dec. 7, 1866.
1740. Samuel Hills, born in Dixon, Ill., Apr. 13, 1877. P. O. (1894), Ann Arbor, Mich.

963 CHESTER WARRINER, son of Hiram (364) and Lucinda, was born in Bennington, N. Y., June 29, 1831; married Delana A. Doty, July 6, 1856. He was a member of Co. H., 136th N. Y. Vols., in the Civil War, and orderly sergeant in signal corps. He is a member of the Methodist church and resides (1898) in Cedar Falls, Ia.

CHILDREN OF CHESTER WARRINER (963).

1760. Blanche Estelle, born in Bennington, N. Y., Apr. 18, 1858; died in Bennington, Aug. 11, 1861.
1761. Myrtie Odell, born in Bennington, N. Y., March 27, 1863; married Henry Edward Hunt, Dec. 24, 1891; resided (1894) in Cedar Falls, Iowa.
1762. Millicent M., born in Richland, Ia., Aug. 31, 1871; resided (1894) in Cedar Falls, Ia.

REV. REUBEN L. WARRINER.

970 REV. REUBEN LYON WARRINER, son of Jeremiah (371) and Eunice, was born in Sherburne, N. Y., Feb. 28, 1814; married, Dec. 24, 1835, Clarissa Benedict, in Smyrna, N. Y. He was a Baptist minister, ordained in Smyrna, N. Y., in 1844. He spent his last days in Deposit, N. Y., with his son, Edwin R., and died there Apr. 4, 1874. He was an " earnest, devoted, self-sacrificing minister, poor in this world's goods, but rich in heavenly treasures." His wife was born in Sherburne, N. Y., Feb. 3, 1819, and died in Greene, N. Y., Aug. 16, 1871.

CHILDREN OF REV. REUBEN L. WARRINER (970).

1780. Edwin Reuben, born in Smyrna, N. Y., July 22, 1838.

1781. Ella Seretta, born in Smyrna, N. Y., Sept. 10, 1840; died in South Valley, N. Y., in June, 1864.

1782. Cyrus Waldo, born in Lebanon, N. Y., Oct. 8, 1842; enlisted as a Union soldier; killed at Fredericksburg, Va., in May, 1863.

1783. Eunice Esther, born in Georgetown, N. Y., July 28, 1844; died in Preston, N. Y., Apr. 22, 1852.

1784. Jeremiah Eugene, born in Smithville, N. Y., March 24, 1848.

1785. Willifred Sidney, born in Preston, N. Y., March 2, 1856.

1786. Frank Ralph, born in West Burlington, N. Y., June 1, 1861; not married; became a school teacher.

1787. Carey Judson, born in Chaseville, N. Y., Jan. 3, 1863; lives (1898) on a farm in Harpersville, N. Y.; not married.

971 JEREMIAH HALL WARRINER, son of Jeremiah (371) and Eunice, was born in Sherburne, N. Y., Dec. 21, 1816. He was married, Oct. 7, 1841, to Jane E. Livingston, who was born in Hebron, Washington Co., N. Y., July 28, 1818. They were married in Lebanon, N. Y., and lived there till their removal to Hamilton, Madison Co., N. Y., in 1866.

JEREMIAH H. WARRINER.

MRS. JEREMIAH H. WARRINER.

While at Lebanon he was colonel in the State militia and justice of the peace for a number of years. While residing in Hamilton he worked at the cabinet maker's trade. He moved to Frederica, Ia., in 1885, where he and his wife celebrated their golden wedding in 1891. In 1896 they visited the scenes of their earlier years in the State of N. Y. The church they attend is the Methodist Episcopal.

981 HENRY NELSON WARRINER, son of Willard (375) and Annie, was born in Martinsburgh, N. Y., in 1816; married, Nov. 29, 1840, Caroline Bradley. She died in Plover, Wis., Nov. 27, 1864, and he was married again to Elizabeth Beau, in Plover, Wis., Dec. 17, 1865. He was painter and paperer in New Haven, Conn., and afterward mill owner and farmer in Plover, Wis. In the last-named place he died in January, 1882. His widow resided in Spokane Falls, Wash., in 1890.

CHILDREN OF HENRY NELSON WARRINER (981).

1800. William Nelson, born in New Haven, Conn., Sept. 2, 1841.
1801. Mary Ann, born in New Haven, Conn., Nov. 3, 1842; died May 6, 1845.
1802. Ellen Eugenia, born in New Haven, Conn., Oct. 1, 1844; died in Plover, Wis., Jan. 3, 1862.
1803. Mary Frances, born in New Haven, Conn., Dec. 7, 1846; married Benjamin L. Roe, Dec. 21, 1865; residence (1895), Waukesha, Wis.
1804. Jane Augusta, born in Neptune, Wis., Aug. 17, 1849; married Wm. J. Roe; residence (1895), Kingman, Arizona.
1805. Alida Ann., born in Neptune, Wis., July 4, 1853; married John W. Dolloff, May 24, 1874; residence (1895), Denver, Colo.
1806. Charles Henry, born in Neptune, Wis., Nov. 1, 1856.
1807. Willard Sterling, born in Plover, Wis., March 5, 1861.

1808. Caroline Bradley, born in Plover, Wis., Jan. 9, 1868; married Frank M. C. Chase. Was teacher in Spokane Falls, Wash., in 1890; residence (1895), Portland, Oregon. Children: Fontenelle and Aldyth.

1809. Horace Sylvester, born in Plover, Wis., Sept. 25, 1873; was clerk in Spokane Falls, Wash., in 1890; post-office (1895), Portland, Oreg.

982 WILLIAM FRANKLIN WARRINER, son of Willard (375) and Annie, was born in Martinsburgh, N. Y., Aug. 1, 1818; married Augusta Wells Harrington, May 6, 1848; died in Derby, Conn., Aug 6, 1856. His church was the Congregational. He was proprietor of a stage route between Derby and New Haven. His widow and their daughter Caroline lived in Ansonia for a time. The widow died in Derby, Conn., Sept. 12, 1892.

CHILDREN OF WILLIAM F. WARRINER (982).

(All born in Derby, Conn.)

1812. William Franklin, born May 16, 1849. He is clerk in the Patent Office, Washington, D. C. (1898).

1813. Estelle, born Sept. 24, 1851. P. O. (1898), Derby, Conn.

1814. Caroline Elizabeth, born Jan. 11, 1854. P. O. (1898), Derby, Conn.

985 WILLARD SYLVESTER WARRINER, son of Willard (375) and Annie, was born in Martinsburgh, N. Y., Feb. 19, 1827; married Laura Jane, daughter of Salmon and Annie Osborne. She was born in Stepney, Conn., Oct. 29, 1828, and married there Apr. 6, 1847. They are Congregationalists. He is a manufacturer of cattle stanchions. Residence (1898), Forestville, Conn.

CHILDREN OF WILLARD S. WARRINER (985).

(All born in Birmingham (now Derby), Conn.)

1815. Frances Almira, born May 26, 1848; residence (1898), Forestville, Conn.

1816. Catharine Jane, born Oct. 14, 1852; married Eliezer Holmes, Nov. 12, 1881. Post-office, Plainville, Conn. Children: Grace Warriner, dec'd; Charles Willard, dec'd.

1817. Willard Fitchroy, born Jan. 1, 1855.

1818. Charles Henry, born Dec. 20, 1856.

989 ALBURN C. WARRINER, son of Willard (375) and Annie, was born in Martinsburgh, N. Y., May 2, 1851. He is married. P. O. (1898), Glendale, N. Y.

CHILDREN OF ALBURN C. WARRINER (989).

1819. Edith Adalaide, born Apr. 27, 1878.

1819a. William Willard, born Oct. 28, 1881.

1819b. Harold C., born July 6, 1887.

SAMUEL P. WARRINER.

1001 SAMUEL PERCIVAL WARRINER, son of Chester (377) and Drusilla, was born Sept. 30, 1823; married, in 1847, Keziah Kennedy, granddaughter of Samuel Warriner (193). He studied at Kingsville, O., Academy. His occupation is farming; his church Congregational. He has held the office of justice of the peace. He is owner (1898) of the old homestead his father settled on when he moved to the State of Pennsylvania in 1835.

CHILDREN OF SAMUEL P. WARRINER (1001).

1820. Hattie Ellen, born in Conneaut, Pa., Aug. 28, 1855. P. O. (1898), Center Road, Pa.

1821. Sadie L. D., born in Conneaut, Pa., March 10, 1859; married, 1878, J. A. Potter; died in Center Road, Pa., July 4, 1887.

HOME OF SAMUEL P. WARRINER, CENTER ROAD, PA.

1004 WILLIS WAIT WARRINER, son of Willis (378) and Nancy, was born Aug. 27, 1812; married Pamelia B. Curtis, of Sacketts Harbor, N. Y., on the 6th day of Sept., 1836. She was born July 5, 1814. He was by trade a carpenter. He moved from Russell, N. Y., to Canton in the same State, and thence to Racine, Wis., where he died Aug. 5, 1864. His wife died in Bristol, Wis., Jan. 8, 1874.

CHILDREN OF WILLIS WAIT WARRINER (1004).

1824. Mary Jane, born Nov. 22, 1837.
1825. Roswell H., born Aug. 6, 1839; joined Co. K., 6th N. Y. Cavalry, and was reported killed.

1826. Harriet Ermina, born Dec. 30, 1840; married in Pennsylvania.
1827. Lucius Smith, born Sept. 7, 1842.
1828. Mary Ann B., born March 6, 1844; married a man named Williams. P. O. (1897), Rockford, Ill.
1829. Florentine Kelsey, born May 3, 1850; married W. H. Will. P. O. (1897), Rockford, Ill.
1830. Henry Cyrus, twin brother to John Silas, born Oct. 3, 1854.
1831. John Silas, twin brother to Henry Cyrus, born Oct. 3, 1854.

1008 HIRAM S. WARRINER, son of Willis (378) and Nancy, was born Dec. 1, 1823; married Mary Goodell, May 20, 1845; died about 1896 in Nicholsville, N. Y.

CHILDREN OF HIRAM S. WARRINER (1008).

1840. Orville S., born July 20, 1846.
1841. Sarah A., born Sept. 10, 1850; married Myron Morgan, Sept. 28, 1852.
1842. Henry, born June 10, 1852; married Elizabeth Wilsey, June 10, 1876.

1020 LEMUEL CASTLE WARRINER, son of Henry (382), was born in Genesee Co., N. Y., Aug. 7, 1817; married Ann, daughter of Thomas and Ann Beadle. He died in Battle Creek, Mich., in Nov., 1850.

CHILDREN OF LEMUEL CASTLE WARRINER (1020).

1852. Annie, born in Battle Creek, Mich.; married William Aldrich Winfield.
1853. Elsie, born in Battle Creek, Mich.; married a man named Flick.

1021 ELIHU MOSS WARRINER, son of Henry (382), was born in Genesee county, N. Y., about 1819; married Deborah, daughter of Thomas and Rebecca Atkinson. She died June 5, 1879. He died in Battle Creek, Mich., Sept. 28, 1888.

CHILD OF ELIHU MOSS WARRINER (1021).

1858. I. Eugene, date of birth not given; died in 1877.

1022 CHAUNCEY ELIJAH WARRINER, son of Henry (382), was born May 6, 1821; married Feb. 14, 1847, Elizabeth, daughter of Thomas and Rebecca Atkinson. P. O. (1898), Battle Creek, Mich.

DAUGHTER OF CHAUNCEY ELIJAH WARRINER (1022).

1860. Lenna D., born in Battle Creek, Mich., Dec. 11, 1854; teacher (1895) in her native town.

1024 EDWIN WARRINER, son of Henry (382), was born in Genesee county, N. Y., about 1825; married Ann Hoag. P. O. (1894), Battle Creek, Mich.

CHILDREN OF EDWIN WARRINER (1024).

1862. Eva, date of birth not given. She graduated at 19, and has been engaged in teaching ever since.

1863. Charles E., date of birth not given; married Clara E. Skillman in Sparta, Wis., Aug. 18, 1887. He is a machinist. P. O. (1896), St. Paul, Minn.

1050 CHAUNCEY WARRINER, son of Justin (420), was born Sept. 19, 1812, in Vershire, Vt.; married Abbie C., daughter of Ira and Sarah C., Towle, in Freyburgh, Me., Sept. 10, 1855. He died Feb. 6, 1884, in Freyburgh, and is buried there. He was a jeweler by trade, and a Swedenborgian by church membership. He is described as " a worthy, industrious citizen."

CHILDREN OF CHAUNCEY WARRINER (1050).

1865. Mary, born in Washington, D. C., in May, 1856; married Charles F. Lord; post office (1894), Portland, Me.

1866. Edson, born in Washington, D. C., in Apr., 1858. He resided in Seattle, Wash., in 1894; was a watch-

maker, also a musician in the 1st Reg't band. His
church is Swedenborgian.

1867. Ira Justin, born in Freyburgh, Me., in March, 1868.

1061 DAVID LAWTON WARRINER, son of Reuben (422) and
Jennie L., was born in Vershire, Vt., July 30, 1827; married
Sophia T., daughter of Harlin L. and Adaline Gilman, in
Hooksett, N. H., Dec. 13, 1849. She was a native of Marsh-
field, Vt. He was a grocer. He died Aug. 3, 1892, in West
Springfield, Mass., and is buried there.

CHILDREN OF DAVID LAWTON WARRINER (1061).

1875. Clarence Allison, born in Manchester, N. H., Nov.
16, 1851.
1876. Herbert Edson, born in West Lebanon, N. H., May
13, 1856; married, in W. Springfield, Mass., March
3, 1886, Anne E. Bartlett, a native of Knoxville,
Tenn. Residence (1896), West Springfield, Mass.
1877. Addie May, born in St. Albans, Vt., March 11, 1858;
died May 10, 1872.
1878. Ella Augusta, born in Brandon, Vt., Nov. 12, 1867.

1063 REUBEN DIAMOND WARRINER, son of Reuben (422)
and Jemima L., was born in Piedmont, N. H., Oct., 1832;
married Eliza Davis. P. O. (1894), Hooksett, N. H. He is
a farmer and railroad employee.

CHILDREN OF REUBEN DIAMOND WARRINER (1063).

1880. George M., born 1857; married, 1891, Sarah Maria
Tilton.
1881. Perley Edson, born 1858; married, 1890, Blanche
May McGillers.
1882. Mark Eugene, born 1860; married, 1881, Frances
Murray.

1064 ORSON HUTCHINS WARRINER, son of Reuben (422)
and Jemima L., was born in Thetford, Vt., Oct., 1841; married

Marion R. Rosenkrans, July 9, 1873. Church, Presbyterian; business, locomotive engineer; postoffice (1894), Portage, Wis.

CHILDREN OF ORSON HUTCHINS WARRINER (1064).

1884. Richard Orson, born Dec. 18, 1876; died May 24, 1878; buried in Columbus, Wis.
1885. Haskell, born March 9, 1879; postoffice (1894), Portage, Wis.

1079 ISRAEL FRANKLIN WARRINER, son of Franklin (457) and Jane, was born in Greensburgh, Ind., March 15, 1832; married Lucinda, daughter of Harvey and Louisa Lathrop, March 11, 1851; died in Greensburgh, Ind., July 14, 1851. Business, harness making; church, Presbyterian.

SON OF ISRAEL FRANKLIN WARRINER (1079).

1900. Israel Franklin, born in Greensburgh, Ind., Feb. 28, 1852.

1080 JOHN JACOBS WARRINER, son of Linus (458) and Lydia, was born May 24, 1833; married, 1st, Caroline Paul; married, 2d, Caroline Perine. P. O. (1898), Goodland, Kan.

CHILDREN OF JOHN J. WARRINER (1080).

1901. Charles F., date and place of birth not given.
1902. Clarinda, date and place of birth not given.
1903. William, date and place of birth not given.
1904. George F., date and place of birth not given.
1905. Walter, date and place of birth not given.
1906. Fred, date and place of birth not given.

1081 FRANKLIN WARRINER, son of Linus (458) and Lydia, was born in Greensburgh, Ind., June 4, 1835; married Margaret Ownby, Apr. 16, 1856. His wife died in Mattoon, Ill., Oct. 9, 1884. He is a member of the Christian church, as are most of his children. He is a harness maker, and resides at Mattoon, Ill.

CHILDREN OF FRANKLIN WARRINER (1081).

1907. Mary Lida, born in Greensburgh, Ind., June 8, 1857; married John R. Black, March 1, 1881; residence, Marshall, Ill.

1908. Ida, born in Greensburgh, Ind., Dec. 25, 1859; married Albert Mounts, Aug. 20, 1885; residence, Mattoon, Ill.

1909. William, born in Crawfordsville, Ind., March 4, 1862; married Bridget O'Connor, June 28, 1887; died in Muncie, Ind., Jan. 23, 1893.

1910. Lillie Bell, born in Shelbyville, Ill., Feb. 22, 1864; married Edgar Griffith, May 1, 1895.

1911. Jabez, born in Mattoon, Ill., Dec. 20, 1866, and died there Sept. 20, 1890.

FRANKLIN WARRINER.

1912. Robert Linus, born in Mattoon, Ill., Jan. 11, 1867; married Margaret Dempster, March 24, 1889.

1913. George, born in Mattoon, Ill., Jan. 4, 1873; married Effie Hawkins, Sept. 30, 1894.

1914. Harry, born in Mattoon, Ill., Dec. 31, 1877.

1915. Claude, born in Mattoon, Ill., Apr. 1, 1882.

1083 CALVIN PRENTICE WARRINER, son of Linus (458) and Lydia, was born in Decatur Co., Ind., Feb. 1, 1839; married Sarah F. Carper, Jan. 31, 1862; was a private in Co. F., 7th Indiana Vol. Inf. — one of the first 75,000 to enlist. By occupation, farmer; by denomination, Baptist. Residence (1898), Belknap, Ia.

CHILDREN OF CALVIN P. WARRINER (1083).

1921. John Franklin, born in Ind., 1862; married Lizzie E. Krewzon, 1894.

1922. Elsie F., born in Ind., 1864.

1923. Mary Lydia, born in Iowa, 1872; married Orville T. Swinney, 1897.

1924. Sylvia Grace, born in Mo., 1877.

1086 JAMES GAGEBY WARRINER, son of Linus (458) and Lydia, was born in Greensburgh, Decatur Co., Ind., Jan. 18, 1845; after his mother's death brought up in a family named Jones; came to Iowa; married Elizabeth C. Bunten, Jan. 9, 1870. He served the Union cause in the 8th Iowa Vol. Inf.; took part in Bank's Red River expedition in 1864. He is a farmer. His entire family belong to the Christian church. His P. O. (1898) is Likens, Ia.

CHILD OF JAMES GAGEBY WARRINER (1086).

1925. Clara Bell, born Oct. 6, 1874; a school teacher.

1088 DEXTER BURRELL WARRINER, son of Orrin (460) and Zeriah, was born in Belleville, Jeff. Co., N. Y.; married, Oct. 9, 1863, Sarah Blanche Botkin. Business, contractor in caulking; church, Presbyterian; residence (1898), Chicago, Ill.

CHILDREN OF DEXTER B. WARRINER (1088).

1927. Carrie Antoinette, born in Rochester, N. Y., Aug. 22, 1864; married Benj. R. Gibson; residence, Chicago, Ill. Children: Kate Olive Blanch, dec'd, and John Warriner.

1928. Georgiana Dexter, born in Chicago, Ill., Apr. 13, 1866; married Wm. Seward Reed; residence, Chicago, Ill. Children: Wm. Dexter; Roy Raymond, dec'd.

1930. William Henry, born Nov. 21, 1871; died in Chicago, Apr. 29, 1872.

1931. Zeriah Blanche, born Jan. 31, 1873; residence (1896), Chicago, Ill.

1094 REUBEN HENRY WARRINER, son of Walter (468) and Eliza, was born Aug. 19, 1833; married, Aug. 23, 1854, Lydia, or Lucy, Woolley; died in Toledo, O., Feb. 12, 1886. His wife died Feb. 17, 1888.

CHILDREN OF REUBEN HENRY WARRINER (1074).

1955. Elijah J., born June, 1856; died when 8 months old.
1956. Lillian M., born in Henderson, N. Y., March 30, 1858; married Charles Russell, Dec. 10, 1878, in Toledo, O.

1100 VIRGIL JEREMY WARRINER, son of Virgil Chittenden (473) and Ruth, was born in Depauville, N. Y., July 29, 1846; married Clarie Barnie, Feb. 23, 1869. Traveling salesman. Baptist. P. O. (1896), Smithville, N. Y.

CHILDREN OF VIRGIL J. WARRINER (1100).

1965. Virgil C., born in Rural Hill, N. Y., Jan. 5, 1870.
1966. Minnie E., born in New Castle, Neb., Feb. 3, 1872; died in Rural Hill, N. Y., March 19, 1882; buried in Woodside Cemetery.
1967. Albert C., born in New Castle, Neb., Apr. 11, 1874.
1968. Mabel M., born in Smithville, N. Y., March 11, 1877.
1969. Ruth Ann, born in Smithville, N. Y., Nov. 5, 1883.

1101 MILVERN EDDY WARRINER, son of Virgil Chittenden (473) and Ruth A., was born in Ellisburgh, Jeff. Co., N. Y., Aug. 9, 1856; married, March, 1880, Dell Freeman. Residence, Adams, N. Y. Traveling salesman.

CHILDREN OF MILVERN E. WARRINER (1101).

1972. Blanche Mahala, born Aug. 3, 1885.
1973. Bertha Anna, born Oct. 6, 1890.

1109 NORMAN LAWRENCE WARRINER, son of Oliver (477) and Polly, was born in Geauga Co., O., Aug. 7, 1820; married Rebecca M'Keon in 1842, in Greenville, Pa.
In 1846 he moved from Pa. to Milwaukee, Wis., and was well known as a first-class wheelwright in that region for 20 years. He died in Crab Orchard, Neb., Apr. 7, 1889. He was a Methodist class leader and local preacher. The text of his funeral sermon was Ps. 37:37, and seemed appropriate to his case. His wife died in Tecumseh, Neb., Nov. 15, 1878. Both are buried in Tecumseh.

NORMAN L. WARRINER.

CHILDREN OF NORMAN L. WARRINER (1109).

1983. Sylvester Clark, born in New Castle, Pa., May 27, 1846.
1984. Clara May, born in Sheboygan Falls, Wis., May 13, 1853; married Thomas Knight. P. O., Badger, Wis.
1985. Charles Clarence, born in Point Bluff, Wis., Apr. 25, 1866; married B. F. Gaylord.

1117b LOREN RILEY WARRINER, son of Eli (480) and Almeda, was born in Philadelphia, N. Y., June 25, 1838; married, Aug. 23, 1871, Eliza J. Tift. His wife died in Corunna, Mich., May 14, 1886. He served one year in the 7th Ohio Inf., and 3 years in the 10th Ohio Cav. He is a painter by trade. Residence (1898), Corunna, Mich.

CHILDREN OF LOREN R. WARRINER (1117b).

1989. Frederick G., born in Elyria, O., Aug. 1, 1874; married, Jan. 18, 1897, Lydia Wager.
1990. Phebe L., born in Elyria, O., July 23, 1877.

1121 SILO PERRY WARRINER, son of Willard (484) and Emeline A., was born in Chardon, O., May 10, 1839; married Sarah M. Brainerd, Oct. 14, 1868. Enlisted, Sept. 10, 1861, as private in Co. G., 41st Ohio Vol. Inf.; discharged Nov. 27, 1865, as first lieut. in command of company. He has been a long time active in public life as road commissioner, sheriff two terms, councilman, commander Reed Post, G. A. R., member of National Union Royal Arcanum, and 32° Mason. His P. O. (1898) is Chardon, O.

CHILDREN OF SILO PERRY WARRINER (1121).

(All born in Chardon, O.)

1995. Edwin Perry, born Apr. 2, 1875.
1996. Frank Garfield, born Dec. 12, 1879.

1130 JOHN HENRY WARRINER, son of Orson (486) and Martha, was born in Claridon, O., March 21, 1847; married Caroline Wells, Jan. 1, 1873. Residence (1898), Claridon, O.

CHILDREN OF JOHN HENRY WARRINER (1130).

2000. Lottie C., born Dec., 1873.
2001. Alfred E., born Nov., 1875.
2002. Della, born March, 1882.

1140 HARLAN BUSH WARRINER, son of Henry (487) and Olivia, was born in Hampden, Geauga Co., O., Dec. 4, 1852; married Lucy A. Ware, Apr. 13, 1873. Business, merchant. Church, Congregational. P. O. (1895), Rialto, Cal.

CHILDREN OF HARLAN BUSH WARRINER (1140).

2080. Jennie Olivia, born in Red Oak, Ia., Nov. 15, 1874. P. O. (1894), Utica, Neb.
2081. Harry Hastings, born in Naponee, Neb., Apr., 1881. P. O. (1894), Utica, Neb.
2082. Bessie Clare, born in Milford, Neb., March 20, 1887. P. O. (1894), Utica, Neb.

1166 CHARLES MONTGOMERY WARRINER, son of Israel
Chapin (493) and Olivia S., was born in Buffalo, N. Y., Nov.
24, 1855; married Olivia M. Dean, Nov. 3, 1884. His education was obtained in the public schools of Buffalo. He is an
Episcopalian.

CHILDREN OF CHARLES M. WARRINER (1166).

2120. Lucy Stevens, born in Buffalo, N. Y., Nov. 5, 1885.
2121. Edna Dean, born in Kalamazoo, Mich., July 20,
1887.
2122. Frank Chapin, born in Kalamazoo, Mich., Dec. 29,
1892.

1168 JUSTIN WARRINER, son of Justin (495) and Rebecca,
was born July 19, 1845; married Mrs. Adalaide Holmes. He
died May 15, 1876.

SON OF JUSTIN WARRINER (1168).

2124. Charles J., born Apr. 15, 1873; residence (1893),
Hartford, Conn.; clerk.

1169 FREDERICK AUGUSTUS WARRINER, son of Francis
(496) and Sarah W., was born in Hartford, Conn., Nov. 15,
1839; married Josephine, daughter of Richard and Martha D.
Ferguson, in Troy, N. Y., June 18, 1861. She was born in
Greenbush, N. Y., March 27, 1842. He died in Troy, N. Y.,
Nov. 19, 1879; buried in Troy. He was by occupation an
electrician; by church membership a Baptist. His widow's
residence in 1894 was Troy, N. Y.

CHILDREN OF FREDERICK A. WARRINER (1169).

(All born in Troy, N. Y.)

2126. Frances Anna, born June 6, 1862; teacher in Troy,
N. Y.
2127. Edward Shavor, born May, 1865.
2128 Sarah Shavor, born Nov. 8, 1869.
2129. Herbert Richard, born Aug. 22, 1872.

1172 ALBERT GUNNISON WARRINER, son of Ralph (498) and Jane, was born in Waterford, N. Y., Oct. 27, 1845; married Emma C. Mills, Jan. 5, 1870. Business, fruit and commission merchant. Residence, Kansas City, Mo.

CHILDREN OF ALBERT G. WARRINER (1172).

2130. Eva Mills, born in Saratoga Springs, N. Y., Nov. 9, 1871; married Edward L. Marty, Sept. 20, 1893; residence (1895), Kansas City, Mo.

1240 SOLOMON WARRINER, son of Col. Solomon (625) and Eleanor, was born in Springfield, Mass., Feb. 10, 1802; married Sarah B. Olmstead, Jan. 21, 1836. After the death of this wife he married Harriet Ball. Shortly after their marriage he died, Oct. 21, 1860, aged 56. His widow died at the home of her sister in Pittsfield, Mass., Nov. 27, 1893. This Solomon Warriner was a merchant in New York. A great fire destroyed his business, and he was afterwards employed as bookkeeper. Though brought up a Congregationalist, he became an Episcopalian, and was employed as a singer in St. George's Church and Sunday school, New York City, under the rectorship of Dr. Milner and the elder Dr. Tyng. He died of brain fever at Northampton, Mass. He is spoken of as a very estimable man.

CHILDREN OF SOLOMON WARRINER (1240).

2135. Solomon, born May 28, 1837. He is an Episcopalian; a music teacher in New York City; not married.

2136. William Henry, born July 15, 1839; was clerk in New York City; enlisted in the Union army; supposed to be dead.

2137. Sarah Beaumont, born July 27, 1841; married H. A. Hamman. P. O. (1898), Springfield, Mass. They have two children.

2138. Mary Bliss, born Apr. 23, 1844; married Emil H.

Weber; residence (1898), 363 Carlton ave., Brooklyn, N. Y.

2139. James Olmstead, born Feb. 8, 1847; died Dec. 12, 1848.

2140. Edward Brewster, born Mar. 20, 1849; died Dec. 18, 1849.

1241 REV. FRANCIS WARRINER, A. M., son of Col. Solomon (625) and Eleanor, was born in Springfield, Mass., Nov. 20, 1804; married Sarah A. Hamilton, Nov. 25, 1842. He became an active and devoted Christian in 1821; prepared for college at the academy in Homer, N. Y.; graduated at Amherst College in 1830; studied theology in New Haven, Conn., under Dr. Taylor, also at Union Theological Seminary, New York. Both his college and theological courses were somewhat interrupted by ill health. He made a voyage around the world on board the U. S. frigate Potomac. This occupied three years, and then, as at all times, he manifested a deep interest in the religious welfare of those about him, and it is said that he gained the confidence and respect of the sailors in a remarkable degree. After his return he wrote a book entitled: "Cruise of the United States Frigate Potomac Round the World, During the Years 1831-1834." The book was published in New York, also in Boston in 1835. After preaching more or less in New Jersey, in Saybrook and Essex, Conn., and elsewhere, he was ordained pastor of the First Congregational Church in Chester, Mass., in 1840. After remaining there six years and witnessing one great revival, he removed to Waterford, Vt., where he remained twelve years. His ministry there was very successful, but not being robust enough to endure the severe climate, he returned to Chester and resumed his pastorate there. He died in the midst of his work, Apr. 22, 1866, aged

REV. FRANCIS WARRINER, A.M.

61. His brother Lewis wrote a sketch of him for the Congregational Quarterly. The centennial of the church in Chester was celebrated in 1894. During the exercises honorable and touching mention was made of Pastor Warriner and his labors. A gentleman from New York sent the following testimonial: " Chester Hill was our summer home for many years, and I learned to know and to love Mr. Warriner, whose name must of necessity be prominent in your celebration. Socially Mr. Warriner was most gentle and lovable, full of life and fun, but he never for a moment lost his dignity as a minister and public teacher. All who knew him loved him."

His widow, Sarah A. Warriner, resides (1898) in Hinsdale, Mass. She is a daughter of John Hamilton, of Chester, Mass., whose grandfather was Duke Hamilton, of Scotland. She is sister of Rev. John Hamilton, D. D., of Boston, and of Rev. B. F. Hamilton, D. D., of Boston, also of Rev. H. H. Hamilton, of Hinsdale, N. H.

CHILDREN OF REV. FRANCIS WARRINER (1241).

2142. Helen Hamilton, born in Chester, Mass., in 1846; married Wm. Ambrose Taylor, of Hinsdale, Mass., in 1866. Mr. Taylor is connected (1898) with the Byron Weston Paper Co., of Dalton, Mass. Their children: Charles P., born 1869; Sarah P., born 1864; Mabel E., born 1875. Charles P. Taylor is connected (1898) with the Stanley Electric Co., of Pittsfield, Mass. Sarah P. Taylor was married Nov. 25, 1896, to John Henry Roache. Principal (1898) of High school in Millbury, Mass. Their son, Frederick Ambrose Roache, was born in Hinsdale, Mass., Sept. 13, 1897.

2143. Sophia Merriam, born in Waterford, Vt., in 1854; married Moody Harrington, of Amherst, Mass., in 1869. They have a daughter, Helen Warriner Harrington, born 1893.

1242 WILLIAM PITT WARRINER, son of Col. Solomon (625) and Eleanor, was born in Springfield, Mass., Oct. 29, 1806; married Elizabeth E. Fessenden in 1842. He was a merchant in New York; afterwards moved to Pittsfield, Mass., where he engaged in mercantile business with James Warriner (633), and where he died May 25, 1863. His widow, cousin of Hon. Wm. Pitt Fessenden, resided in Portland, Me., with some of the Fessenden family. They had no children. Dr. Todd's book, " The Model Superintendent," was based on W. P. Warriner's example as a Sunday school superintendent. Dr. Todd was his pastor.

WM. PITT WARRINER.

1244 HENRY WARRINER, son of Col. Solomon (625) and Eleanor, was born in Springfield, Mass., May 5, 1810; married, in 1837, Eliza A., daughter of Nathaniel and Elizabeth (White) Frank. After spending some time on the sea, he removed to Peoria, Ill., and lived on a farm. He died May 25, 1838, in Hadley, Will Co., Ill. His wife was born in Granville, N. Y., Apr. 17, 1816, and died Aug. 23, 1892. She is buried in Evergreen Cemetery, Cazenovia, N. Y.

DAUGHTER OF HENRY WARRINER (1244).

2144. Sophia Elizabeth, born in Hadley, Ill., Dec. 1, 1838; married Theodore J. Parkinson. Her husband died May 9, 1892, leaving her a home and a country store, also the office of postmaster in Chittenango Falls, N. Y., which was transferred to her — all of which she has carried on since his death.

1245 LEWIS WARRINER, son of Col. Solomon (625) and Mary, was born May 12, 1812; married Elizabeth L. Whittlesey, Nov. 9, 1836. He was clerk and cashier in the old Springfield bank. He was chosen as one of the selectmen of Springfield, was a member of the Massachusetts Legislature, and held the office of deacon in the Congregational church. He died March 14, 1883. His widow, a native of Saybrook, Conn., resides (1898) in Springfield, Mass.

LEWIS WARRINER.

CHILDREN OF LEWIS WARRINER (245),

2157. Thomas Hastings, born 1838; died Jan. 25, 1839.
2158. Lewis Bliss, born 1840; died March 26, 1841.
2159. John Hampden, born in 1842; killed by a fall on board ship at sea — the ship " Dashing Wave " — Oct. 2, 1860, aged 18.
2160. Charles W., born June 11, 1845; enlisted in 13th Regt., Mass. Inf., in 1862; was discharged on account of ill health; entered the navy and was drowned at the mouth of the Rio Grande while landing troops from Gen. Banks' expedition.
2161. Francis Henry, born July 25, 1850; died July 5, 1851.
2162. Elizabeth Lynde, born May 29, 1853; died of typhoid fever, Nov. 19, 1869, aged 16.

1248 JOHN ROOT WARRINER, son of James (633) and Martha, was born in Pittsfield, Mass., March 22, 1827; died, unmarried, in Pittsfield, June 19, 1889. He was cashier and afterwards president of Agricultural Bank in his native city. The church to which he belonged is Congregational.

1249 JAMES LYMAN WARRINER, son of James (633) and Martha, was born in Pittsfield, Mass., May 27, 1829. Residence (1898), Pittsfield, Mass.; not married. He succeeded his brother John as president of Agricultural Bank. He has held the position a long time, and he shares largely the respect and confidence of his fellow-citizens. He is a member of the Congregational church.

1258 ANDREW AUSTIN WARRINER, son of Stephen Orlando (642) and Sapphira, was born in Monson, Mass., June 9, 1836; married Sarah Jane Wood, Dec. 28, 1859. Residence (1898), Palmer, Mass. His wife is a native of Monson, born Aug. 2, 1839. Mr. Warriner was elected and served as assessor for his native town in 1865, and four successive years thereafter, and he served the same town on the school committee for the four years previous to 1876. In 1896 and 1897 he was elected one of the assessors of the town of Palmer, in '97 receiving a larger vote than any other candidate on the ticket.

CHILDREN OF ANDREW A. WARRINER (1258).

(All born in Monson, Mass.)

2236. Walter Andrew, born March 18, 1861; died Apr. 28, 1867.

2237. Homer Wood, born Oct. 22, 1862; died Jan. 6, 1863.

2238. Fred Homer, born Oct. 9, 1863; died March 9, 1887.

2239. Elsie Maria, twin sister to 2240, born July 5, 1865; married Edward B. Milliken. P. O. (1898), Nashua, N. H.

2240. Ella Mary, twin sister to Elsie Maria, born July 5, 1865. P. O. (1898), Palmer, Mass.

2241. Andrew Louis, born July 1, 1867; married Amanda Korff. P. O. (1898), Three Rivers, Mass.

2242. Arthur Warren, born Jan. 17, 1869.

2243. George Lincoln, born Apr. 9, 1871.

2244. Alvin Smith, born May 14, 1874.

2245. Hattie Lulu, born Feb. 14, 1876. P. O., Palmer, Mass. (1898).

2246. Lena Josephine, born Aug. 28, 1878. P. O. (1898), Palmer, Mass.

ELSIE M.   FRED H.   ELLA M.

MR & MRS. A. A. WARRINER
& FAMILY

A. LOUIS

LENA J.

GEORGE L.   HATTIE L.   ALVAN S.

1260 COL. STEPHEN CADY WARRINER, son of Stephen Orlando (624) and Sapphira, was born in Monson, Mass., Aug. 22, 1839; educated at Monson Academy; mustered, June 21, 1861, as a soldier in the 10th Mass. Infantry. He was in battle at Williamsburgh, Fair Oaks, Charles City, Cross Roads, White Oak Swamp and Malvern Hill. He was promoted to captain in 36th Mass. Inf. by special order from the War Department for meritorious conduct. He performed active service, also, at Fredericksburg, Vicksburg, Jackson, Blue Spring, Campbell Station and at the siege of Knoxville. He resigned Apr. 22, 1864. His name is on the marble tablet in Memorial Hall, Monson, Mass.

COL. STEPHEN C. WARRINER.

Col. Warriner was married, Sept. 19, 1865, to Mary Warren Lincoln, and after her death he was married to Ida Marion Lincoln, both daughters of William Lincoln, who was one of the prominent and wealthy men of Western Massachusetts, very extensively engaged in the fire insurance business. He was the eldest son of Col. Warren Lincoln and Dolly Warriner (263).

Col. Warriner was a member of Gov. Thomas Talbott's staff in 1879. He has been a member of the Republican State and city committees, served as councilman and alderman, and he received the nomination for mayor of the city of Springfield in 1887. He was Republican representative to the General Court in 1893, and received the election in 1894. He conducts an extensive business in fire insurance. He is a member of First Congregational Church of Springfield.

SON OF COL. STEPHEN CADY WARRINER (1260).

2249. William Stephen, born in Warren, Mass., July 15, 1866. He was chosen a member of the Republican committee of Springfield, and an officer in the United States navy reserves. Capt. Co. K., 2d

Mass. U. S. V., in war with Spain; wounded July
1, 1898, before Santiago.

1262 JOSEPH REYNOLDS WARRINER, son of Stephen
Orlando (642) and Sapphira, was born in Monson, Mass., May
7, 1843; married Mary E. Fiske. His residence (1898),
Worcester, Mass. He received his education at the common
school and academy of his native town and at Wilbraham
Academy. During vacation from school, on July 14, 1863, he
enlisted at Springfield in the 2d Mass. heavy artillery as a
private for three years, or during the war. He served in Co.
B., a detachment under Gen. Schofield in North Carolina,
most of the time; was discharged Sept. 3, 1865. His name is
on the marble tablet in Memorial Hall, Monson, Mass.

1264 ALFRED ELY WARRINER, son of Stephen Orlando
(624) and Sapphira, was born in Monson, Mass., June 26, 1849;
married, in San Francisco, Cal., Aug. 21, 1866, Elizabeth
Sarah, daughter of Lorin and Elizabeth Whiting, of Hender-
son, Ky. He was educated at Monson Academy; enlisted in
Co. E., 36th Mass. Vol. Inf., in March, 1864; transferred to
Co. B, 56th Reg't of Mass., in the spring of 1865; discharged
at Alexandria, July 12, 1865, and returned to Monson. His
name is on the marble tablet in Memorial Hall, Monson, Mass.
After residing for a time in Williamsport and Philadelphia,
Pa., and graduating from Bryant, Stratton and Kimberley's
Business College in 1866, he took steerage passage from New
York to San Francisco, Cal., via Isthmus of Panama in 1875;
spent some months in 1881 in Honolulu, H. I. After his marriage he settled in El Verano, Cal. He was elected in 1896
trustee of Harvey school district, which office he still holds
(1898). Mr. Warriner became a member of Napa Lodge No.
18, I. O. O. F., in 1876, and later a member of Oriental
Encampment No. 57, I. O. O. F. His business is that of carpenter and builder. P. O., El. Verano, Cal.

CHILD OF ALFRED ELY WARRINER (1264).

2250. Alfred Ely, born in San Francisco, Cal., June 8, 1890.

FAMILY OF ALFRED ELY WARRINER.

1268 ETHAN WARRINER, son of Ethan (645) and Dolly, was born in Wilbraham, Mass., Jan. 21, 1827; married, Nov. 23, 1851, Emily F. Dimmock; lived many years in Palmer, Mass.; was a carpenter and builder; was a member of Thames Lodge of Masons in Palmer; died in Providence, R. I., Dec. 28, 1896; buried in Palmer. His wife, a native of New Suffolk, Conn., died in Indian Orchard, Mass., Jan. 14, 1892.

CHILDREN OF ETHAN WARRINER (1268).

(All born in Palmer, Mass.)

2265. Ida Emily, born Nov. 26, 1854; only surviving member of the family (1898). P. O., New London, Conn.

2266. Annie Frances, born July 27, 1856; died in Palmer, Mass., July 19, 1885.
2267. Mae Louise, born Nov. 3, 1860; died in Palmer, Mass., Apr. 8, 1882.

1270 WILLIAM WARRINER, son of Ethan (645) and Dolly, was born in Wilbraham, Mass., July 21, 1830. His wife Elizabeth was born in East Windsor, Conn. He was by trade a moulder.

CHILDREN OF WILLIAM WARRINER (1270).

2268. Charles H., born in Springfield, Mass., Jan. 11, 1851.
2269. Gilbert F., born in Springfield, Mass., Oct. 20, 1854.

1271 JOHN WARRINER, son of Ethan (645), and Dolly, was born in Wilbraham, Mass., Oct. 10, 1832; married, in Springfield, Dec. 23, 1863, Frances H. Worthen, of Boston. His occupation was at one time recorded overseer, at another time grocer. His P. O. in 1895 was Indian Orchard, Mass.

CHILDREN OF JOHN WARRINER (1271).

(All born in Springfield, Mass.)

2272. John H., born Feb. 3, 1864.
2273. John E., born Feb. 3, 1867.
2274. Frank K., born July 23, 1870. Bookkeeper in Springfield, Mass., 1893.

1274 ALBERT HENRY WARRINER, son of Ethan (645) and Dolly, was born in Wilbraham, Mass., Apr. 13, 1841; married Jennie, or "Jane," Marion Sanders. He was a grocer and a livery keeper in Springfield; died in Amherst, Mass., Aug. 20, 1873; buried in Wilbraham.

SON OF ALBERT HENRY WARRINER (1274).

2286. Albert, born in Springfield, Nov. 14, 1864, or, according to another record, in Chicopee, Aug. 19, 1865.

1302 CHARLES FRIEND WARRINER, son of Daniel Charles (679) and Laura L., was born in New York City, Jan. 28, 1855; married Nathalie R. King, Feb. 9, 1888. Residence (1898), Jacksonville, Fla. Manager Tropical Fibre Company in that city.

CHILDREN OF CHARLES FRIEND WARRINER (1274).

2285. Olga, born Jan. 14, 1889.
2286. Nathalie, born Jan. 17, 1890.
2287. Mabel, born March 6, 1891.
2287. Laura Salome, born 1893.

1333 JOSEPH GERISH WARRINER, son of Rev. Phanuel (702) and Apphia, was born in White Pigeon, Mich.; married Susie Boggs; died in Kaufmann, Tex., about 1880.

CHILDREN OF JOSEPH GERISH WARRINER (1333).

2295. Willie J., date of birth not given.
2296. Apphia, date of birth not given; married L. A. Perkins; they have a son.
2297. Mary, date of birth not given; died.
2298. Joseph, date of birth not given.

1341 PHANUEL WARRINER, son of Harvey Lewis (707) and Emily, was born in Clay township, O., Jan. 3, 1839; married Lucy Rudes. He was a soldier in the Union army; died in Genoa, O., March 18, 1876.

SON OF PHANUEL WARRINER (1341).

2305. Charles Hilliard, date of birth not given.

1342 CHARLES ELBERT WARRINER, son of Harvey Lewis (707) and Emily, was born in Clay township, O., Aug. 19, 1845; married Julia A. Johnson, Nov. 6, 1866; died Nov. 1, 1868, in Wichita, Kan. He enlisted in an Ohio regiment July

21, 1862, aged 20; was honorably discharged at Greensboro, N. C., June 20, 1865; went to Wichita, Kan., in 1872 where he filled many positions of honor and trust. He was a man of high moral worth. Those who knew him best spoke of his " beautiful character and life." He was a member of Garfield Post, G. A. R., in Wichita, Kan. The Warriner Post in Valley Center was named for him. His widow lived, in 1895, in Wichita, Kan. She gave the Warriner Post a life-size portrait of her husband. He was a bookkeeper. No children.

CHARLES ELBERT WAR-
RINER.

1343 WALTER WARRINER, son of Harvey Lewis (707) and Emily, was born in Clay township, O., July 9, 1843; married Hannah Bowland in Elenora, O.; died in Genoa, O. He was a private soldier in the Union army, a farmer, and a member of the Christian denomination.

CHILDREN OF WALTER WARRINER (1343).

(All born in Genoa, O.)

2308. Emily May, born Apr. 30, 1866; died, unmarried, in Oak Harbor, O., June 18, 1883.
2309. Verne Standish, born March 29, 1869; attended public schools in his native town and in Oak Harbor, O.; cadet in U. S. Military Academy, West Point, N. Y.; admitted June, 1890; discharged May, 1891; cause, tuberculosis in both lungs. For some years reporter in Denver, Colo.
2310. Bertha, born June, 1872; died in Genoa, O., about 1873.

1347 HARVEY WARRINER, son of Harvey Lewis (707) and Emily, was born in Clay township, O., May 25, 1856; married

Pamelia Banks. She was granddaughter of second wife of Harvey Lewis Warriner (707), and lived (1895) in his old home.

CHILD OF HARVEY WARRINER (1347).

2315 Walter, born about 1887.

1348 ORVILLE FAYETTE WARRINER, son of Hiram (709) and Eliza C., was born Dec. 1, 1842; enlisted, 1861, in Co. B., 21st N. Y. Infantry, when the first call was made for three months' men. He was accidentally wounded and died of lockjaw the next day after he was discharged. His mother never knew till thirty years afterward what became of him. About 1894 she wrote to the author of this book: " I could learn nothing whether he was living or dead after his discharge from the hospital. It was a great trial. Sometimes it seemed more than I could bear. I had one thing to comfort me, he was a Christian. Often when writing to me while he was in the army he told of his trust in his Heavenly Father." He was not married.

1354 CHESTER GILBERT WARRINER, son of Samuel (715) and Anne, was born in West Brattleboro, Vt., Sept. 24, 1862; married Mary Ellen Campbell, Nov. 18, 1884. He attended Brattleboro Academy; became a resident of New York City in 1883; was secretary of Mix National R. R. before English capitalists obtained control. He has a good position as stenographer in the Custom House in New York City. He was brought up a Congregationalist, but is now a member of the Presbyterian church. No children. He has recently discovered that on his mother's side he can lay claim to an Irish king as an ancestor — through the Mr. Fox who wrote " Fox's Book of Martyrs."

1400 ALBERT CARLOS WARRINER, son of William (735) and Lorena, was born in Ellisburgh, N. Y., May 7, 1833; married Harriet Cooley, Jan. 22, 1855. He was eight months a

Union soldier, and was honorably discharged for disability. He is a gardener; his church is the Methodist Episcopal; his residence (1898) is Ottawa, Ill.

CHILDREN OF ALBERT C. WARRINER (1400).

2325. Florence Amelia, born in Freedom, Ill., June 3, 1859; married Joseph E. Todd, Feb. 13, 1878. Residence (1898), Ottawa, Ill. Their children: Louis A., Charles A., Harry H.

2326. Carrie Adora, born in Freedom, Ill., Dec. 13, 1860; married, Aug., 1878, Richard A. Clifford. Residence (1896), Chicago. Children: Guy and Arthur.

2327. Jessie Anita, born in Ottawa, Ill., March 6, 1865; married W. S. McEwing, Nov. 24, 1888. Residence, Ottawa, Ill. Children: Frank Albert, Hazel Constance, Mildred Irene.

EDWIN WARRINER (at 15.)

1411 REV. EDWIN WARRINER, son of Solomon J. (739) and Mary Ann, was born in Ellisburgh, Jeffereson Co., N. Y., Jan. 19, 1839; married Laura Ann, daughter of Winsor and Eliza Whipple, June 20, 1862. While yet a child he became a member of the Methodist Episcopal church, and was licensed to exhort at the age of 15, and received local preacher's license at 18. He taught a district school when 15 years of age; attended Fairfield Seminary in Herkimer county, N. Y.; graduated in 1858; finished a three years' course at the Concord, N. H., Biblical Institute (now Boston University School of Theology) in 1861. He proposed to complete a college course at Wesleyan University after graduating in theology, but being invited to serve the First Battalion, Conn. Cavalry, as chaplain, he went to war and

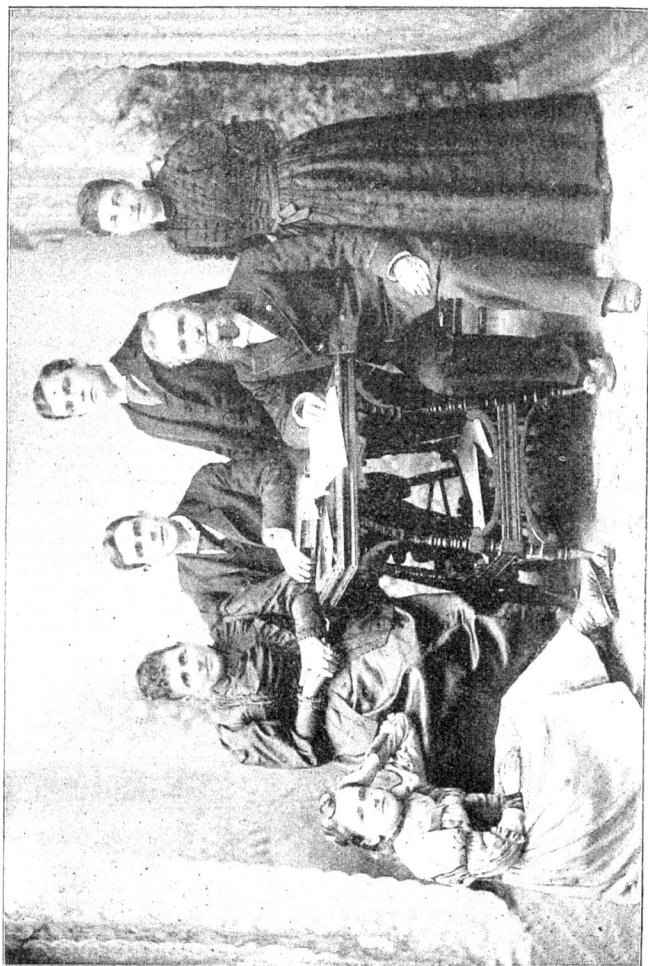

FAMILY OF REV. EDWIN WARRINER — 1892.

WILLARD IVES WARRINER.   MRS. LIZZIE WARRINER THOMAS.
MRS. LAURA A. WARRINER.   WINSOR WHIPPLE WARRINER.
EDNA LAURA WARRINER.   REV. EDWIN WARRINER.

[223]

sacrificed the college course. Resigning in March, 1864, he joined New York East Conference, and has preached without intermission up to this date, 1898, his appointments having been about equally divided between Connecticut and Long Island. He is the author of this work. He has written and published a large volume entitled, " Old Sands Street Methodist Episcopal Church of Brooklyn, N. Y.," and has in course of preparation a " Cyclopedia of Long Island Methodism."

[The subject of this sketch died in Stepney, Ct. His death came as a result of disease contracted while serving his country as chaplain in the Civil War — chronic diarrhœa, which developed cancer in the bowels. He was an indefatigable worker, and toiled on in his last illness, sometimes when in much pain. He was gratified to see the manuscript of this book ready for the printer before he passed away. He made friends everywhere and left an enviable record — "having served his generation by the will of God." Eaton & Mains, of New York, have published a volume entitled, "A Story of Life-long Consecration," memorial of Rev. Edwin Warriner, which they would send to any purchaser on receipt of 50 cents.

LAURA W. WARRINER.]

(See obituary at end of volume.)

CHILDREN OF REV. EDWIN WARRINER (1411).

2330. Emma Eliza, born in Durham, Conn., Apr. 21, 1864; took the prize in elocution at the Morgan High School, Clinton, Conn.; traveled in Europe in 1886; taught music in Hartford College, Ky.; married, Sept. 2, 1890, D. Ellis Thomas, of Hartford, Ky. Their daughter, Laura Warriner, was born Feb. 27, 1894. Mr. Thomas has two daughters by his first wife, namely: Mary Caroline and Kate Elizabeth.

2331. Willard Ives, born in Forestville, Conn., Apr. 5, 1866.

2332. Edwin D'Orsay, born in Sag Harbor, N. Y., Oct. 19, 1870; died in Glen Cove, N. Y., Jan. 24, 1877; buried in Huntington, L. I.

2333. Winsor Whipple, born in Southold, L. I., March 24, 1874; studied at Hackettstown, N. J., Collegiate Institute and Wesleyan University, Middletown, Conn.

2334. Walter Lindsay, born in Huntington, L. I., Apr. 18, 1876; died in Glen Cove, L. I., Dec. 23, 1878; buried in Huntington, L. I.

2335. Edna Laura, born in Great Neck, L. I., Nov. 27, 1880. She has been a student at Wesleyan Academy, Wilbraham, Mass., amid scenes which commemorate her early ancestors.

1430 FRANK EDGAR WARRINER, son of Alfred (743) and Harriet, was born in Litchfield, Mich., July 16, 1849; married, Feb. 25, 1880, Sarah A. McKee.

SON OF FRANK E. WARRINER (1430).

2337. Alfred James, born June 21, 1882.

1446 FRANCIS HARVEY WARRINER, son of Lyman (749) and Laura, was born in Franklin, Pa., March 15, 1846; married Helen E. Rockwell, Feb. 10, 1869. When a boy 4 years old, his father having died, he was adopted into a family by the name of Smiley, and lived there until he was nearly 18, when he enlisted in the regular U. S. army. He remained in the service until 7 months after the close of the war. He has been engaged in the foundry and machine shop business, and the mercantile business, and was, in 1895, bookkeeper for Towanda Iron Works, Towanda, Pa.

CHILDREN OF FRANCIS HARVEY WARRINER (1446).

2345. Mary Alice, born Feb. 6, 1870.
2346. Harry Lyman, born May 16, 1872.
2347. Fred, born May 24, 1875; died Feb. 29, 1876.
2348. Charles Harvey, born Dec. 29, 1876.
2349. Genevieve, born March 21, 1882.

226

1447 JOHNSON HORATIO WARRINER, son of Lyman (749) and Laura, was born in Franklin, Pa., Feb. 10, 1848. Being left fatherless at two years of age he was brought up by his uncle, Johnson Warriner; married Ann Eliza Seeley, May 1, 1872. His church is Baptist; his postoffice, West Bainbridge, N. Y.

CHILD OF JOHNSON HORATIO WARRINER (1447).

2352. Alice May, born in Sidney Center, N. Y., Apr. 11, 1881.

1448 JUSTIN LYMAN WARRINER, son of Lyman (749) and Laura, was born in West Franklin, Pa., Nov. 22, 1849; married Agnes A. Groom. He enlisted in 1st N. Y. Mounted Rifles (7th Cavalry), Aug. 31, 1864; was injured at Suffolk, Va., Apr. 8, 1865; took part in 5 general engagements and numerous small fights in the Army of the James, under Gen. B. F. Butler; performed the same service as other soldiers, though 80 days less than 15 years old when he enlisted. He is a furniture finisher, and his P. O. address in 1894 was 69 Park ave., Binghamton, N. Y.

SON OF JUSTIN LYMAN WARRINER (1498).

2354. William Henry, born in Ballston Spa., N. Y., March 31, 1883.

1454 CHARLES LOREN WARRINER, son of Philip Philander (756) and Frances, was born in Holland Patent, N. Y., Jan. 21, 1860; married Nellie Palmer, Oct. 17, 1883. He has been for some years asst. treas. C. C. C. & St. Louis Ry. Co. Residence (1896), Wyoming, O.

CHILDREN OF CHARLES LOREN WARRINER (1454).

(All born in Cleveland, O.)

2360. Willard Palmer, born Dec. 11, 1885.
2361. Ella Emeline, born Aug. 3, 1888.
2362. Charles Harold, born Jan. 31, 1892.

1455 GEORGE FREDERICK WARRINER, son of Philip Philander (756) and Frances, was born Sept. 30, 1862; married Addie Eugenia Duly, June 30, 1883. Residence (1896), 135 Genesee st., Utica, N. Y.

CHILDREN OF GEORGE FREDERICK WARRINER (1455).

2370. Mary Frances, born in North Gage, N. Y., May 19, 1884.
2371. Tessa Floy, born in Trenton, N. Y., Sept. 15, 1885.
2372. William Frank, born in Hinckley, N. Y., Nov. 21, 1892.
2373. George Frederick, born in Grant, N. Y., Apr. 28, 1894.

1470 FRANCIS DWIGHT WARRINER, son of Jesse Horton (771) and Melinda, was born in the year 1834; married about 1859; died in 1878, of consumption. His widow married Daniel J. Hagan, and resided (1895) in Syracuse, N. Y.

CHILDREN OF FRANCIS DWIGHT WARRINER (1470).

2400. Jennie D., born in Syracuse, N. Y., Apr. 20, 1861; married Charles F. Kast. P. O. (1895), Palmyra, N. Y.
2401. Henry Horton, born in Mexico, N. Y., March 28, 1864; his wife's name was Kate G. He died of consumption in Syracuse, N. Y., Dec. 24, 1891.

1490 ALFRED ALLEN WARRINER, son of Lorenzo (770) and Eliza A., was born Dec. 16, 1849; married Charlotte L. Beebe, Feb. 13, 1878. He is a fruit and dairy farmer; studied one year in Amherst Agricultural College; is a member of Worcester South Agricultural Society, and of ex-com. in West Brookfield Farmers' Club; secretary of Warren Grange; agent and reporter four years for New England Homestead; author of several essays read before farmers' clubs. P. O. (1898), Warren, Mass.

CHILDREN OF ALFRED ALLEN WARRINER (1490).

(All born in Warren, Mass.)

2420. Alice Maud, born Nov. 22, 1880.
2421. Florence May, born Nov. 23, 1883.
2422. Grace Ethel, born July 3, 1894.

1492 MYRON ANSON WARRINER, M. D., son of Lorenzo (779) and Eliza A., was born in Warren, Mass., March 30, 1856; married, Nov. 3, 1887, Flora C. Pepper, of North Brookfield, Mass.; medical practitioner in North Brookfield, Mass., and for the last few years in Bridgeport, Conn.

1494 GEORGE LEONARD WARRINER, son of Alford (781) and Emily, was born in Fredericksburg, Va., Nov. 3, 1842; married, in Springfield, Mass., June 19, 1867, Aratine, daughter of Alanson and Elizabeth Bugbee. He engaged some time in the grocery business, and, since 1881, has been city messenger of Springfield. He is very genial and popular, the right man for the office he holds.

CHILD OF GEORGE L. WARRINER (1494).

2430. Lillian E., born in Springfield, Mass., Dec. 7, 1868; married, Nov. 20, 1882, James H. Lay. Children: Florence Warriner, Lillian Mildred.

1495 ALLEN DORMAN WARRINER, son of Alford (781) and Emily A., was born in Prescott, Mass., Dec. 14, 1846; married Charlotte Loomis; died in Merrick, Mass., June 10, 1898. " He was an honest, upright, Christian man."

CHILDREN OF ALLEN DORMAN WARRINER (1495).

(All born in West Springfield, Mass.)

2432. A daughter, born Nov. 6, 1873.
2433. A son, born Nov. 24, 1875.
2434. Alford, born March 20, 1881.

1503 ARTHUR FRANCIS WARRINER, son of Solomon Newton (789) and Harriet, was born in Washington Mills, N. Y., Sept. 15, 1856; attended Utica Academy, Utica, N. Y.; married, first, Virginia Embry, Sept. 27, 1883. She died in Cleveland, O., Aug. 9, 1884, and he married, second, Edith May Embry, Dec. 24, 1891. His residence is Fort Wayne, Ind., and his occupation, bookkeeper.

CHILDREN OF ARTHUR FRANCIS WARRINER (1503).

2436. Lewis Erastus, born in Cleveland, O., Aug. 8, 1884; died in infancy.

ARTHUR FRANCIS WARRINER.

2437. Arthur Philip, born in Fort Wayne, Ind., Sept. 27, 1895. The likeness represents the child at one year of age.

ARTHUR PHILIP WARRINER.

1511 WILLIAM HORTON WARRINER, son of William Chandler (796) and Mary Jane, was born in Davenport, Ia., July 22, 1863; married, March 10, 1889, Elizabeth Rice.

CHILD OF WILLIAM HORTON WARRINER (1511).

2440. Marguerite, born in Chicago, Jan. 12, 1891.

1512 CHARLES THEODORE WARRINER, son of William Chandler (796) and Mary Jane, was born in Davenport, Ia., Jan. 26, 1868; married, Sept. 23, 1889, Leonora Bowen. He is an architect in St. Louis, Mo.

DAUGHTER OF CHARLES T. WARRINER (1512).

2444. Jean, date of birth not given.

1566 BENJAMIN HOWARD WARRINER, son of William Lombard (827) and Naomi, was born in Delmar, Pa., Dec. 30, 1834; married Rachel A. Sabin, July 2, 1854; captain Co. A., 149th Pa. volunteers. He was postmaster in Teadaghton, Pa., from 1882 to 1889. His trade is that of carpenter; his church, Free Will Baptist; his P. O. (1898), Draper, Pa.

CHILDREN OF BENJAMIN HOWARD WARRINER (1566).

(All born in Delmar, Pa.)

2510. George Salem, born March 27, 1855 died Sept. 3, 1858.
2511. Stephen Lombard, born Dec. 20, 1856.
2512. Burt Alvin, born Feb. 12, 1859.
2513. Sarah Naomi, born Apr. 23, 1861.

1569 HIRAM WARRINER, son of William Lombard (827) and Naomi, was born in Stony Fork, Pa., Sept. 14, 1840; married Emma Johnson. P. O. (1898), Petersburg, Va.

CHILDREN OF HIRAM WARRINER (1569).

2516. Nellie, date of birth not given.
2517. Harry, date of birth not given.
2518. Sarah, date of birth not given.
2519. Ralph, date of birth not given.

1570 ASA CHASE WARRINER, son of Wm. Lombard (827) and Naomi, was born in Stony Fork, Pa., Sept. 28, 1842; married Josephine Hoadley, March 14, 1866. He enlisted in 1861 in Co. H, 6th Pa. Vol. Cav.; transferred, 1862, to Co. A, 1st Pa. Lt. Art.; wounded Oct. 27, 1864, at Fair Oaks; discharged May 30, 1865, and returned to his home in Tioga Co., Pa. He is a Republican in politics; a member of Cook Post No. 315, G. A. R., of Wellsboro, Pa. P. O., Asaph, Pa.

CHILDREN OF ASA CHASE WARRINER (1570).

2521. Edith D., born in Delmar, Pa., July 2, 1868; married Arthur E. Hawk, Aug. 26, 1885. Residence, Asaph, Pa. Children: Hazel D. and Lora M.

2522. Ina M., born in Delmar, Pa., June 24, 1872; married
    Clarence B. Bradley, March 2, 1893. Residence
    (1898), Asaph, Pa., Child: Lyle I., born 1894, died
    1895.

1572 ABRAM MELVILLE WARRINER, son of Wm. Lombard (827) and Naomi, was born in Stony Fork, Pa., July 11, 1848; married Lida Ann Penn, a descendant of William Penn. P. O. (1894), Petersburg, Va.

CHILDREN OF ABRAM M. WARRINER (1572).

2525. William, date of birth not given.
2526. Jessie, date of birth not given.
2527. Name unknown.
2528. Name unknown.

1574 ORRIN ADELBERT WARRINER, son of Wm. Lombard (827) and Naomi, was born in Stony Fork, Pa., Apr. 11, 1853; married Adele Butler. P. O. (1894), Morris, Pa.

DAUGHTER OF ORRIN ADELBERT WARRINER (1574).

2529. Grace, date of birth not given.

1576 MARSHALL BISHOP WARRINER, son of Samuel B. (829) and Mary Ann (850), was born Sept. 30, 1846; married Helen Spicer, Dec. 31, 1868. Occupation, jeweler; denomination, Methodist. P. O., Wellsboro, Pa.

CHILDREN OF MARSHALL B. WARRINER (1576).

(The first born in Stony Fork, the others in Wellsboro, Pa.)

2531. Menora Blanche, born Oct. 6, 1869.
2532. Walter Roy, born July 5, 1871.
2533. Mary Christina, born June 7, 1876.
2534. Katharine, born Aug. 20, 1878.
2535. Fred Verner, born Apr. 17, 1882.
2536. Robert Rex, born Aug. 13, 1889.

1582 LEVI CHURCH WARRINER, son of Rev. Levi C. (836) and Adaline L., was born in Delmar, Pa., Nov. 27, 1846; married, 1st, Sept. 22, 1872, Ettie Baker, of Fremont, N. Y., who died Apr. 22, 1877. He married, 2d, Mrs. Priscilla Hardee, of Rathboneville, N. Y. His church is the Methodist Episcopal; his occupation that of gardener; his P. O., Wadena, Minn.

CHILDREN OF LEVI C. WARRINER (1582).

2538. Bertha Mary, born Sept. 1, 1873; married, 1896, Charles Wilcox, of Freemont, Steuben Co., N. Y.
2539. Ettie May, born Feb. 26, 1877; died Oct. 7, 1877.

1584 LYMAN NATHAN WARRINER, son of Rev. Levi C. (836) and Adaline L., was born in Brookfield, Pa., Apr. 16, 1850; married Grace Allyn, Sept. 19, 1887. P. O. (1895), Parker's Prairie, Minn. His church is Baptist; his occupation, farming.

CHILDREN OF LYMAN N. WARRINER (1584).

2540. Laura Lina, born in Meltana, Minn., Dec. 5, 1889.
2541. Altie Jessie, born in Parker's Prairie, Minn., Oct. 1, 1891.
2542. Larva Irene, born in Parker's Prairie, Minn., July 14, 1893.

1585 JAIRUS DAVID WARRINER, son of Rev. Levi C. (836) and Adaline L., was born in Brookfield, Pa., Jan. 22, 1852; married Tillie Merring, May 22, 1886. He is a carpenter and a farmer, and a member of the Baptist church. P. O. (1895), Parker's Prairie, Minn.

SON OF JAIRUS D. WARRINER (1585).

2545. Raymond J., born in Parker's Prairie, Minn., May 29, 1887.

1605 STILLMAN DAVIS WARRINER, son of William A. (842)

and Cornelia N., was born in Delmar, Pa., March 20, 1844;
married Hope Eliza Graham, Apr. 16, 1864. She was born in
Plymouth, N. Y., Sept. 1, 1842. He died in Vineland, N. J.,
March 28, 1881.

CHILDREN OF STILLMAN D. WARRINER (1605).

2570. Clara Cornelia, born in Watkins, N. Y., Nov. 3,
1865.
2571. Emma Birdella, born in North Vineland, N. J., Feb.,
1868.

1655 WILLIAM V. WARRINER, son of Volarus B. (867) and
Huldah M., was born in West Union, N. Y., about 1862; mar-
ried, March 21, 1886, Mary A. Cornwell. Residence (1895),
Hornellsville, N. Y.

CHILDREN OF WM. V. WARRINER (1655).

2600. Lawrence A., born in Greenwood, N. Y., Dec. 27,
1887.
2601. Robert A., born in Hornellsville, N. Y., June 11,
1890.

1671 FRANCIS LAZELLE WARRINER, son of Nathan A.
(868) and Mary P., was born in Delmar, Pa., Jan. 17, 1866;
married Susan Barnard, Feb. 13, 1889. He is a farmer in
Greenwood, N. Y.

CHILDREN OF FRANCIS L. WARRINER (1671).

2605. Marshall Francis, born in Jasper, 1889.
2606. Minnie Marie, born in Greenwood, N. Y., 1897.

1696 JUSTIN BLISS WARRINER, son of Edwin (911) and
Apphia, was born in Hawley, Mass., Oct. 21, 1851; married
Alice G. Leonard, Sept. 29, 1878. His wife died in Hawley,
Mass., Apr. 29, 1891, and is buried there.

CHILDREN OF JUSTIN BLISS WARRINER (1696).

(Born in Hawley, Mass.)

2620. Edward L., born June 24, 1881.
2621. Jessie Elizabeth, born Dec. 29, 1885.

1697 WILLIAM HENRY WARRINER, son of Edwin (911) and Apphia, was born in Hawley, Mass., Feb. 27, 1855; married at 17; wife died in one year and one month. He belonged to Capt. J. V. R. Wills' company during the Bannock wars. He is a member of the Salvation Army. His P. O. in 1894 was Boise City, Idaho. In his letters he dwells somewhat at length on his affliction. " My mental trouble," he says, " was caused by exposure in trying to save the life of a friend who was injured in a prospecting trip in the mountains, and I somehow can't get right again."

1720 LEWIS HENRY WARRINER, son of Edwin Baldwin (942) and Charlotte W., was born in Tinkersville, Lake Co., Ind., Nov. 8, 1852; married Ida Ella Burns, Feb. 8, 1879. He was postal clerk in railway service from 1889 to 1891. He and his wife and four of his children are members of the Baptist denomination. He has been for some years superintendent of the Sunday school and chorister of his church. His P. O. (1898) is Kankakee, Ill.

CHILDREN OF LEWIS HENRY WARRINER (1720).

(All except the youngest born in Kankakee, Ill.)

2630. Lewis Henry, born Nov. 24, 1879.
2631. Alvah Edwin, born Aug. 27, 1881.
2632. Mabel Ethelyn, twin sister of 2633, born Dec. 30, 1883.
2633. Maud Evelyn, twin sister of 2632, born Dec. 30, 1883.
2634. Frederick Earl, born Sept. 26, 1886.
2635. Howard Burns, born March 20, 1890.

2636. Ida Ella, born Oct. 26, 1892.

2637. Charlotte Ann, born in Chicago, Ill., Sept. 8, 1895.

1735 WILLIAM LUCIEN WARRINER, M. D., son of Oliver Fowler (946) and Fanny M., was born in Amboy, Ill., Sept. 23, 1862; married Jennie Mansfield Lyon, May 16, 1888. He graduated with the degree of M. D. at Northwestern Medical School, Chicago; has been coroner Bourbon county; city physician, Fort Scott, Kan., and surgeon for the Kansas City and Memphis R. R. He wrote from his home in La Cygne, Kan., in January, 1894: "A few years will find me in New York or Berlin perhaps, pursuing some specialty in my chosen profession, as I have great aspirations." In January, 1898, he writes: "My address after May 1 will be Topeka, Kan., where we will locate. Mrs. Warriner's brother is there — a prominent dentist."

CHILD OF DR. WM. LUCIEN WARRINER (1735).

2640. Charles William, born in Fort Scott, Kan., Aug. 22, 1889.

1780 EDWIN REUBEN WARRINER, A. M., son of Rev. Reuben L. (970) and Clarissa, was born in Smyrna, N. Y., July 22, 1838; was married, Apr. 30, 1865, to Mary J. Dargavel, of Guilford, N. Y., who died in Deposit, N. Y., Dec. 21, 1875; married again, Dec. 1, 1876, to Elizabeth Speak, of Binghamton, N. Y., a teacher, and graduate of Oswego Training School. He was educated at Norwich (N. Y.) Academy, and Madison (now Colgate) University; became principal of schools in New Berlin, N. Y., Deposit, N. Y., Hackettstown, N. J., and Brooksville, Fla. His present home (1898) is 25 Q street, N. W., Washington, D. C.

PROF. S. R. WARRINER, A.M

CHILDREN OF PROF. E. R. WARRINER (1780).

ELLEN WARRINER.   ARTHUR B. WARRINER.   CLARA WARRINER.
ANNA WARRINER.   MARY J. WARRINER.

2649. Edward Sylvester, born in Guilford, N. Y., Sept. 18, 1866; died in Philadelphia, Pa., Jan. 13, 1889.
2650. Anna, born in New London, N. Y., July 20, 1868; present home (1898), Guilford, N. Y.
2651. Ellen, born in Deposit, N. Y., Feb. 3, 1870; typewriter and graphophone, Washington, D. C.
2652. Clara, born in Deposit, N. Y., Sept. 12, 1871; stenographer and typewriter, Washington, D. C.
2653. Arthur Bateman, born in Deposit, N. Y., May 13, 1873; printer, Washington, D. C.
2654. Mary Janette, born in Deposit, N. Y., May 11, 1875; stenographer and typewriter, Washington, D. C.

1784 JEREMIAH EUGENE WARRINER, son of Rev. Reuben L. (970) and Clarissa, was born in Smithville, N. Y., March 24, 1848; married Fannie M. Thompson, of Hamilton, N. Y., Aug. 8, 1867. He was a student in Madison (now Colgate) University; served in 3d N. Y. Cavalry, 1864 and 1865. His business is house and bridge builder; his home is in Hamilton, N. Y.

CHILDREN OF EUGENE J. WARRINER (1784).

2656. Eugene F., born in Hamilton, N. Y., May 22, 1868.
2657. Ralph T., born in Norwich, N. Y., May 29, 1870.

1785 WILLIFRED SIDNEY WAR-
RINER, son of Rev. Reuben L. (1790)
and Clarissa, was born in Preston, N.
Y., March 2, 1856. He attended New
Berlin Academy and Harpersville
Academy in N. Y. State, and was a
sergeant in U. S. A. He married, June
9, 1878, Olive L. Truesdale. He is a
farmer, and has been justice of the
peace. His home (1898) is in Creighton, Knox Co., Neb.

WILLIFRED S. WAR-
RINER.

CHILD OF WILLIFRED S. WARRINER
(1785).

2659. Waldo Stirling, born in Clum Valley, Neb., Sept.
18, 1881.

1800 WILLIAM NELSON WARRINER, son of Henry Nelson
(981) and Caroline, was born in New Haven, Conn., Sept. 2,
1841; married Almeda L. Reynolds, Dec. 23, 1860; died in the
service of the United States, a member of Co. E., 32d Wis.
Vol. Infantry, in Memphis, Tenn., March 25, 1863.

CHILD OF WM. NELSON WARRINER (1800).

2665. Dellie, date of birth not given; died young.

1806 CHARLES HENRY WARRINER, son of Henry Nelson
(981) and Caroline, was born in Notomon, Wis., Nov. 1, 1856;
married Emma Frances Winslow, Dec. 19, 1877. Residence
(1895), Sheriden, Wyoming.

CHILDREN OF CHARLES HENRY WARRINER (1806).

2668. Ethel Effie, born 1878.
2669. Albert Henry, born 1880; died 1880.
2670. Lillie May, born 1882.
2671. Fred Leroy, born 1883.
2672. Pearl Clarinda, born 1886.
2673. Charles Harold, born 1890.
2674. Alger, born 1891.

1807 WILLARD STERLING WARRINER, son of Henry Nelson (981) and Caroline, was born in Plover, Wis., March 5, 1861; married Edith L. Sutter, Feb. 22, 1888. Residence (1895), Big Horn, Wyoming.

CHILDREN OF WILLARD S. WARRINER (1807).

2677. Nellie May, born 1888.
2678. Henry Willard, born 1891.

1817 WILLARD FITCHROY WARRINER, son of Willard S. (985) and Laura J., was born in Birmingham (now Derby), Conn., Jan. 1, 1855; married Mary Griswold, Sept. 11, 1884. Residence, 2054 South ave., New York.

SON OF WILLARD F. WARRINER (1817).

2680. Frederick Willard, born July 26, 1887.

1818 CHARLES HENRY WARRINER, son of Willard S. (985) and Laura J., was born in Birmingham (now Derby), Conn., Dec. 20, 1856; married Lillian J. Martin, Dec. 25, 1888. Residence, Lansingburgh, N. Y.

DAUGHTER OF CHARLES HENRY WARRINER (1818).

2682. Lillian Jane, born in Forestville, Conn., Sept. 30, 1889.

1827 LUCIUS SMITH WARRINER, son of Willis Wait (1004) and Pamelia B., was born in Russell, N. Y., Sept. 7, 1842; married Elizabeth Beardsley in Conn. He was a railroad engineer and farmer. He died in Etna, N. Y., Jan. 8, 1874. His wife died a few years later.

CHILDREN OF LUCIUS SMITH WARRINER (1827).

2686. Lucius Smith, born Aug. 8, 1865. He is conductor of a passenger train on the N. Y., N. H. & H. R. R. He has a family, but does not respond to inquiries concerning the record.

2687. Willis Wait, born May 12, 1867. He has been a brakeman on a railroad. He was clerk in Ithaca, N. Y., a few years ago. (Named William in directory by mistake.) His post-office address in 1894 was Little Rock, Ark.; not married.

1830 HENRY CYRUS WARRINER, son of Willis Wait (1004) and Pamelia B., twin brother of 1831, was born in Russell, N. Y., Oct. 3, 1854; married Eva L. Weaver in Ithaca, N. Y. He is by occupation a salesman, and his P. O. (1898) is Etna, N. Y.

CHILDREN OF HENRY CYRUS WARRINER (1830).

(Born in Etna, N. Y.)

2691. Maude L., born Oct. 26, 1877; died Apr. 1, 1888.
2692. Fred Garfield, born Nov. 2, 1880.

1840 ORVILLE S. WARRINER, son of Hiram S. (1008) and Mary, was born July 20, 1846; married Ellen Shelley; she died Nov. 26, 1892, and he married Lorice B. Mahan, from Kentucky. P. O. (1898), North Stockholm, N. Y.

1842 HENRY WARRINER, son of Hiram S. (1008) and Mary, was born June 10, 1852; married Elizabeth Wilsey, June 10, 1876. He died May 1, 1885.

CHILDREN OF HENRY WARRINER (1842).

2710. Orville S., born Dec. 23, 1878.

2711. Fred, born Apr. 20, 1882.

1875 CLARENCE ALLISON WARRINER, son of David Lawton (1061) and Sophia T., was born in Manchester, N. H., Nov. 16, 1851; married Minnie A. Hendry, June 13, 1877. She is a native of Troy, N. Y. He is a railroad engineer. P. O., West Springfield, Mass.

CHILD OF CLARENCE A. WARRINER (1875).

2730. Ella Augusta, born in West Springfield, Mass., July 1, 1878.

1900 ISRAEL FRANKLIN WARRINER, son of Israel F. (1079) and Lucinda, was born in Greensburgh, Ind., Feb. 28, 1852; married, Aug. 8, 1872, Euphemia Belle Caskey.

CHILDREN OF ISRAEL FRANKLIN WARRINER (1900).

2740. Lucinda C., born in Andersonville, Ind., Feb. 23, 1874; married, Jan. 27, 1890, James E. McCracken. A son, Franklin T., was born to them in 1891.

2741. Charles Harvey, born in Greensburgh, Ind., Jan. 20, 1876.

2742. Lucy Gageby, born in Greensburgh, Ind., Dec. 2, 1877.

2743. Hazel Lucretia, born in Greensburgh, Ind., Nov. 24, 1879.

1983 SYLVESTER CLARK WARRINER, son of Norman Lawrence (1109) and Rebecca, was born in Newcastle, Pa., May 27, 1845; enlisted Dec. 12, 1863, as a private in the 4th Wis. Cavalry; received his discharge Sept. 15, 1865; married Martha Jane Hinds, Dec. 29, 1866. His wife died in Nebraska in 1890, and he married, on Dec. 31, of that year, Mary Alice, daughter of Wm. H. Van Slyke, of Crawfordsville, Ind. He is a member of the Methodist Episcopal church. He was a wagon and carriage maker, and later (1897) a grain and coal merchant at 618 North 12th st., Lincoln, Neb.

CHILDREN OF SYLVESTER C. WARRINER (1983).

2755. Sylvester Carroll, born in Royalton, Wis., Nov. 28, 1867. P. O. (1896), Superior, Neb.
2756. Carrie May, born in Waupaca, Wis., Oct. 7, 1869; married, July 4, 1888, Joseph Bosick. P. O. (1895), Carlysle, Iowa.
2757. Guy Fritz, born in Waupaca, Wis., Nov. 26, 1871; a member of U. S. Infantry in 1895.
2758. Norman Lawrence, born Aug. 2, 1874; married Anna May Ward, Aug. 30, 1894.

1985 CHARLES CLARENCE WARRINER, son of Norman L. (1112) and Rebecca, was born in Point Bluff, Wis., Oct. 2, 1859; married Mary F. Dorsey. His occupation, school teacher and farmer; his church, Methodist Episcopal; his P. O. (1896), Crab Orchard, Neb.

CHILDREN OF CHARLES CLARENCE WARRINER (1985).

(All born in Tecumseh, Neb.)

2760. Edwin Ernest, born Aug. 2, 1883.
2761. Jennie May, born Feb. 11, 1886.
2762. Ben Franklin, born June 15, 1888.
2763. Goldie, born Dec. 9, 1890.

2127 EDWARD SHAVOR WARRINER, son of Frederick A. (1169) and Josephine, was born in Troy, N. Y., May 27, 1865; studied in Troy public schools, served two years and six months in the 4th N. Y. Cavalry and 14th U. S. Infantry; was discharged as sergeant, Apr. 27, 1894. In less than a month after his enlistment he was put on extra duty in the adjutant's office as clerk, and proved himself a very competent clerk and

post school teacher. He was detached at Boise Barracks,
Idaho, as post sergeant-major. As a member of the Order of
Good Templars he has passed the chairs, and was a representa-
tive to the Grand Lodge in 1894. He is also a member of
I. O. O. F. and the " Regular Army and Navy Union," which
denotes honorable service. Supt. shirt factory, Fair Haven,
Vt., in 1896.

2129 HERBERT R. WARRINER, son of Frederick A. (1169)
and Josephine, was born in Troy, N. Y., Aug. 21, 1872; married Mae Belle Reynolds, Nov. 21, 1892; drowned at Fort Lee,
N. J., June 23, 1894; buried in Oakwood Cemetery, Troy,
N. Y., near the graves of his father and grandfather. Residence of his widow (1898), Rochester, N. Y.

CHILD OF HERBERT R. WARRINER (2129).

2765. Florence Matilda, date of birth not given.

2242 ARTHUR WARREN WARRINER, son of Andrew Austin
(1258) and Sarah Jane, was born in Monson, Mass., Jan. 17,
1869; married Catharine Webb, Jan. 17, 1890. His occupation (1898) is acting paymaster; his P. O., Three Rivers, Mass.

CHILDREN OF ARTHUR WARREN WARRINER (2242).

(Born in Three Rivers, Mass.)

2767. Raymond Rudolph, born Nov. 6, 1891.
2768. Ralph Terrett, born Oct. 31, 1896.

2305 CHARLES HILLIARD WARRINER, son of Phanuel
(1341) and Lucy, was born — date not given. He resided in
Liberty Center, Henry Co., O., and later (1896) in Genoa, O.

CHILDREN OF CHARLES H. WARRINER (2305).

2800. Ralph, date of birth not given.
2801. Cecil, date of birth not given.

2331 WILLARD IVES WARRINER, Ph. B., son of Rev. Edwin (1411) and Laura A., was born in Forestville, Conn., Apr. 5, 1866. He was named after a friend of his father, Hon. Willard Ives, of Watertown, N. Y. He gained the prize for oratory in the Morgan School, Clinton, Conn. In 1889 he graduated at Wesleyan University, Middletown, Conn. In June, 1893, he married Laura Buel, daughter of Howland and Anna (Hempstead) Harris, of New London, Conn. Since leaving college he has been engaged in the electric light business in Honolulu, H. I., and in Los Angeles, Cal. He had charge of vocal music at the inauguration of the Hawaiian Republic, and was a member of the home guards at the time of the insurrection. He and his wife are members of a Presbyterian church in Los Angeles. They are both musicians, and of much service in Y. M. C. A. and " Christian Endeavor " work. For portrait of W. I. Warriner, see No. 1411.

CHILD OF WILLARD IVES WARRINER (2331).

2825. Douglas Whipple, born in Honolulu, H. I., March 25, 1894; died Oct. 28, 1894.

2511 STEPHEN LOMBARD WARRINER, son of Benj. Howard (1566) and Rachel, was born in Stony Fork, Pa., Dec. 20, 1856; married, March 5, 1882, to Nettie Barrett. He was some time postmaster in Tiadaghton, Pa. His residence in 1894 was Delmar, Pa.

2512 BURT ALVIN WARRINER, son of Benj. Howard (1566) and Rachel, was born in Delmar, Pa., Feb. 12, 1859; married, June 10, 1883, to Alice May Townsend. His P. O. in 1894 was Delmar, Pa.

CHILDREN OF BURT ALVIN WARRINER (2512).

(All born in Delmar, Pa.)

2850. George Howard, born July 28, 1884.
2851. Flora Ethel, born Sept. 2, 1886.
2852. Elsa Albina, born Sept. 28, 1889.

2656 EUGENE F. WARRINER, son of Eugene J. (1784) and Fannie M., was born in Hamilton, N. Y., May 5, 1868; married, 1889, Jennie Andrews.

CHILDREN OF EUGENE F. WARRINER (2656).

2875. Ralph, born June 20, 1891.
2876. Frank, born June 12, 1893.

2657 RALPH T. WARRINER, son of Eugene J. (1784) and Fannie M., was born in Norwich, N. Y., May 29, 1869; married Frederica Burns, May, 1891.

CHILD OF RALPH T. WARRINER (2657).

2880. Florence, born May, 1892.

APPENDIX.

Concerning persons in America of the name Warriner, Warrener or Warinner, not known to be of New England stock.

RALPH WARRENER, PIONEER SETTLER IN VIRGINIA, AND HIS TWO CHILDREN.

In a volume of records of the old county of Rappahannock, Va., which included the present counties of Essex and Richmond, is recorded the will of Ralph Warrener. The copy from which the extract was made is from old and frequently mutilated originals at the courthouse of Essex, and in this case it is believed that the copyist has run together the will of Ralph Warrener and the choice of a guardian for his son.

The will of Ralph Warrener gives his son, Ralph, his whole estate in " lands, chattles, hoggs and household stuff," he paying unto Mary Warrener

3000 lbs of good tobacco and
six   delivered to her when she
attains the age of seventeen: Thos Gouldman [who was later a magistrate] to have the care of the estate during the children's minority, to keep said children, provide for them such education as to teach them to write and to teach " the girl to sow." [Then follows, written in the copy as if a part of the will, but evidently it is not]: " Know &c all men by these presents that I Ralph Warrener, of the age of sixteen years but under the age of one and twenty, son of Ralph Warrener of the county of Rappa. deceased hereby elect and choose

Thomas Gouldman of the aforesaid county, now resident upon my father's plantation my curator or guardian;" the 21 day of ———

Recd Feb. 3, 1669."

. RALPH WARRENER.

Following is an abstract of the will of Ralph Warrener the younger, recorded in the books of Old Rappahannock [now Essex] county, Va.

"I Ralph Warrener, sick in body, but in perfect mind and memory, Desire to be buried at home near my father and mother. To Francis Freger my cow, squired at Col. Vassell's old plantation. My horse to Col. Dyer. All my tobacco to my guardian Thos. Gouldman he to lay out the same for my sister's particular use. To my sister three young black cows, a steer, one bull & two sows."

Dated March 7, 1673-4. Proved in Rappahannock May 31, 1674.

In the tax list of Lancaster Co., 1754, which then included Rappahannock, Ralph Warrener was assessed with three tithables.

Another Rappahannock county record is as follows:

"Samuel Thacher and wife Mary, only daughter and heir of Ralph Warrener, late of Essex, made due Rappahannock Co., Va. May 7, 1698."

The elder Ralph Warrener, mentioned above, was in all probability the "Ralfe Warriner" reported in Old Colony, Massachusetts, records in 1639, and not named in any subsequent records in New England, so far as ascertained. See page 16 of this volume. Tradition says he was brother of the New England forefather, William Warriner.

The foregoing extracts show that Ralph Warrener's only son died without issue, and the question is still unanswered, Who was the original ancestor of the Warriner's of Virginia?

DANIEL WARRENER, OF VIRGINIA.

The Henries Co., Va., records report Daniel Warrener defendant in a suit, 1721. Daniel Warrener was a freeholder and voted in Henries in 1751.

JOHN WARRINER, OF VIRGINIA.

The Henries Co., Va., records contain a copy of a deed dated Oct., 1770, to John Warriner, of Henries.

DAVID WARINNER, OF VIRGINIA, AND SOME OF HIS DESCENDANTS.

David Warinner is believed to have married Elizabeth Murphy, of Buckingham Co., Va. He had five sons, named David, William, Reuben, Thomas and James, and four daughters, Mary, Agnes, Elizabeth, and one other.

William Warinner, son of David, married Elizabeth Edwards, of Henries Co., Va. They had three children, namely: William M., John W. and Augusta. Only the first of these was living in 1895.

William M. Warinner, son of David, was born in Rappahannock Co., Va.; married Fannie Harris, of Powhattan Co., Va., and she died leaving two children, namely: Cornelia E., who married Wm. Grover, of Henries Co., Va., and Willie Patrick, who died young. After his first wife's death Wm. M. Warinner married Louisa W. Fussell, of Henries Co., Va. They had five children, namely: (1) John M., who married Lucy Glover, and is an undertaker in Fair Haven, Wash.; (2) Dr. Jairus E., who practices his profession in a place five miles from Richmond; (3) Mattie S., who married C. E. Nance, of Charles City, Va., and who died about 1888; (4) William F., druggist in Richmond; (5) Loula C., who married G. E. Dunkum, of 60 Duke street, Norfolk, Va.

ROBERT WARRENER, OF VIRGINIA, SOLDIER.

R. A. Brock, secretary of the Southern Historical Society, looked up the following record:

"Warrener, Robert No. 667

100 a   Warrant No. 5769

Robert Warrener is entitled to the proportion of land allowed a private of the Continental Line for three years service

Colonial Chamber

Dec. 10, 1809

JOHN TYLER."

"Warrant No. 5769 for 100 acres issued to Robert Warrener the 20th Dec. 1809, and delivered to Archibald Rutherford."

Mr. Brock wrote that he had no means of locating the residence of the soldier. Quite likely this man's pedigree could be traced. In a book entitled Ancient Windsor, a history of Windsor, Conn., is the following:

"John Rockwell married Sarah, daughter of James R. Ensign 6 May, 1651. He died and his widow married (2) Robert Warrener of Middletown, Ct., 2 Feb. 1674 — children."

The town clerk of Middletown writes that there is no such name in the town records, that is, no Robert Warrener. If Robert Warrener was of Middletown in 1674, he probably left soon afterwards, and perhaps went to Virginia. It is not unlikely that Robert Warrener who enlisted was a descendant of his.

JAMES WARINNER, OF VIRGINIA, AND SOME OF HIS DESCENDANTS.

This man's father was probably David Warinner, sketched in the foregoing pages, who had a son James; but of this identity we have no absolute proof. Robert D. Warriner, of Carterville, Mo., says the family came from England at an early day. James was born in Va., and was a young man at the close of the Revolution. He married Annie Pollard. They had four sons and two daughters, named respectively, James, Iverson, William, Elizabeth, Mary and Jacob, all born in Virginia. The elder James Warinner, of Va., accompanied by his son Jacob, emigrated to Kentucky in the early part of this century.

Jacob Warinner, youngest son of James, was born in Rockingham Co., Va., May 3, 1783. He married Mary Riffe, who was born in Md., May 13, 1790. Her father migrated to Ky. when she was quite young, and at Boone's Station she was tomahawked and left for dead. Jacob Warinner was a farmer and a preacher, first a Baptist and later connected with the Disciples or Christian Church. He moved from the frontier of Kentucky to the frontier of Missouri, and died in Ray Co., Mo., Sept. 12, 1845. His widow died Aug. 1, 1848. Both were buried in South Point, Mo. They had nine children that lived to maturity. Their names were Willis, Hiram, Eliza, William T., Robert D., Richard C., Sarah J., Mary F. and Nathan P. In 1894 Robert D., Sarah J., Mary F. and Nathan P. were yet alive.

Willis Warinner, son of Jacob, was the first of a family of six sons and three daughters. He was a merchant about forty years, and died in Memphis, Tenn.

Lee Harrison Warinner, eldest son of Willis, married Gussie Menefee in 1864, and two children were the result of this marriage, namely: Frank, who died in 1891, aged 26, and Jessie Lee, wife of a young Baptist minister in Kansas City, Mo.

Hiram C. Warriner, another son of Willis, is a lawyer of large practice in Memphis, Tenn.

A daughter of Willis Warinner, Mrs. Annie Warinner Smith, resides in Excelsior Springs, Mo.

Robert D. Warinner, of Carterville, Mo., a son of Jacob, was born in Casey Co., Ky., Sept. 16, 1819, and moved with his father to Ray Co., Mo., in 1837; married Mary Blain, Dec. 23, 1841. She died in 1891, and he was married again in 1892 to Lavinia J. Ball. His religious denomination is Christadelphian; his trade that of jeweler.

SAMUEL WARRINER, OF BUCKINGHAM, OR HENRIES COUNTY, VIRGINIA, AND SOME OF HIS DESCENDANTS.

Samuel Warriner was born in Buckingham Co., Va., in 1767, and died in the same county in 1847. He was a farmer and a member of the Methodist church. His parents had eight children, and one authority states that they were all born in Henries Co., Va. Their names were: William, John, Isaac, Joseph, Joshua, Thomas, Samuel and Rebecca. These all died in Henries Co. except William, who died in Prince Edward county.

John Warriner, a son of Samuel, was born in Henries Co., Va., Apr. 8, 1801; married Mildred B. Rock, in Charles City, Va., and died in the same place, Nov. 25, 1866. His children were born in Henries county, and their names were as follows: Elizabeth W., who married Zack Pearman; Andrew T., who was born in 1832, married Belle Falcon, and is supposed to have died at Port Delaware in 1863; John William, a blacksmith and a Methodist, residing in Glendale, Va., who was born in 1837; Josiah C., who was born in 1839, and was killed at Welden, N. C., in 1864; Julia A., who was born in 1841, married Robert J. Warriner, and died in Henries Co., Va., in 1873.

The children of John William Warriner were all living in 1893. They are as follows:

(1) Josiah C. Warriner, who was born in Henries Co., Va., Sept. 8, 1867, and who married Mary E. Sned in 1892. Their daughter's name is Lannie. He is a Methodist, a drygoods clerk of 820 West Main street, Richmond, Va.

(2) Araella E. Warriner, of Glendale, Va., born 1869.

(3) Emma Turner Warriner, who was born in 1871, and who married Wm. J. Osborne, of Richmond, Va.

(4) Lelia Virginia Warriner, of Richmond, born 1878.

(5) John William Warriner, of Glendale, Va., who was born in 1880.

Joshua Warriner, a son of Samuel, was born in Henries Co., Va., in November, 1806. He was married, first, to Susan Smith, second to Fanny Tuqua, third to Susan Monson. By denomination, Baptist; by occupation, farmer.

MATTHEW WARRENER, OF LINCOLNSHIRE, ENG., AND HIS
DESCENDANTS IN AMERICA.

(1) Matthew Warrener and his wife Mary Warrener.
(2) John Warrener, son of (1), who was born March 2,
1749, at St. Swithin's parish, Lincoln, Eng. He was a freeman of the city.
(3) Dr. Charles Warrener, son of (2) and Sarah (Metham)
Warrener, was born Nov. 2, 1775, at St. Peters, at Arches,
Lincoln, Eng. He was a well educated man, a physician and
surgeon, and is said to have served in the English royal navy.
He was married at Penn, Buckinghamshire, Eng., about 1811,
to Shelome Morton. Of this marriage there were three children, all born at Penn, namely; Sally, Charles Metham and
John Metham. He left England with his daughter a few
months before the birth of the youngest child, staid in Ireland
about one year, then came to the United States and purchased
160 acres of land in March, 1818, and afterward 80 acres
adjoining. This land is in what is now (1898) Ames township, Athens Co., O. He was very successful in his profession here, and invested a considerable sum in the U. S. bank,
all of which was lost. He died Feb. 17, 1851, and in accordance with his request, was buried in an " Indian Mound " on
the farm.
(4) John Metham Warrener, son of Dr. Charles (3) and
Shelome (Morton) Warrener, was born at Penn, Buckinghamshire, Eng., July 3, 1817. He was a carpenter and builder.
He went to London, where, in 1844, he married Martha Verry,
who was born in 1824. He visited the United States in 1858,
and again with his wife in 1867 and 1878. He died in 1879.
He was father of eight children: William John, Jane Mary,
Charles Morton Verry, Emily Shalomy, Martha Maria, Samuel Verry, John Metham, Walter Thomas.
(5) Rev. William John Warrener, son of John Metham (4),
was born in London, Aug. 23, 1845. He was well trained by
his mother, who was a woman of unusual piety and intelligence.
Experiencing conversion at the age of 19, he became an active
member of a Congregational church, and soon began preaching in the open air in the northwest suburbs of the city of

Harrison Percy.   John Mason.   Sydney Kelly.
     Emily Wilhelmina.   Annie Alice.
Mrs. Rachel Amelia.   Rev. William John
     Rose Katrina.   Mary Estella.

London. In 1869 he came to the United States, and settled about three miles from the city of Amesville, O., upon land bought in the early part of the century by his grandfather. He had been a carpenter in England, and came to America intending to spend the rest of his days in the pursuit of agriculture. But his mind had been trained to great activity, and he seems, though diligent as a farmer, to have been almost as laborious and successful as Elihu Burritt, "the learned blacksmith," in acquiring a liberal education. His school was what some one has called "the college of the small hours."

During the seven years of his farm life he accumulated an exceptionally large and choice library.

On Sept. 23, 1871, he was married to Miss Rosabell Kelley. They had been associated as teachers in the same Sunday school in London

Mr. Warrener united with the Christian church in 1876. He entered at once upon the active work of the ministry, and has served almost continuously as secretary of the Conference and Assembly of which he is a member. His work as an organizer and revivalist has borne large fruit in several counties within easy reach of his home, and notably in his own neighborhood. In the summer of 1876 he began holding Sunday school and other religious services in his barn. From this beginning a church was organized, and the society now own a fine building known as Mound Hill Church. It is built on an elevation overlooking the Federal valley. Four acres of land have been deeded to it from the Warrener estate.

The Rev. Wm. J. Warrener excels as a pulpit orator and as a writer. In controversy he is remarkably able, and "his poems exhibit considerable constructive imagination and express pure and refined sentiment." L. W. H., to whose biography of Mr. Warrener we are indebted for the above facts, says further concerning him: "Besides being a poet, an orator, a singer and a versatile prose writer, he is something of an artist, having acquired a thorough mastery of the draughtsman's art, and having some considerable knowledge of colors. He has used this knowledge to good purpose in his Sunday school works, where his ready and versatile use of the crayon has been a source of delight to both old and young alike. Some way or other the subject of our sketch has never been able to keep entirely out of politics. In local affairs he has held several important elective offices, which have, however, come unsought. As a member of the Prohibition party he has been frequently called to take the stump, and has done effective work there. He was one year the Prohibition candidate for State senator, and had the satisfaction of running ahead of his ticket. Among his friends, Elder Warrener is known as a whole-souled, companionable gentleman, full of jokes and good stories, and ever ready to give and take in repartee. Above all he is a devout, consecrated Christian man, who feels that the greatest work he can engage in is to win souls to Christ."

MATTHEW WARRINER, OF YORKSHIRE, ENG., AND SOME OF HIS DESCENDANTS IN AMERICA.

There is a large family of Warriners which sprang from Redmire, a small village in York, Riding of Yorkshire, situated in the beautiful dale called Wensleydale, which John Wesley mentions in his journals as the most charming of all the dales.

One of these was Matthew Warriner, several of whose descendants reside in Liverpool, and several in different parts of America. He was a farmer and a member of the Established Church. He died in Redmire in 1838.

William Warriner, son of Matthew, was born in Redmire, Yorkshire, Eng., and died there about 1860. He was a farmer and a Weslevan Methodist. He married Mary, daughter of Isaiah and Mary Row, and their children were: Matthew, Isaiah, John, twin sisters Mary and Ellen, William, David, Edward, Joseph and Roger (twins), Roger 2d, Robert, Ellen 2d. All of these, except David, of New Orleans, La. Mary and Ellen 2d died prior to 1893.

David Warriner, Sen., fifth son of William of Yorkshire, was born in Redmire, County of Yorkshire, Eng., Dec. 4, 1827; married Isabella, daughter of William and Ann Arundale, of Liverpool, in 1855. Some years ago they moved to New Orleans, La. Their children, all of whom, except the eldest, grew to maturity, are named John, William, David, Matthew, Robert A., Isabella, George, John 2d, Annie Adaline. All these were born in Liverpool.

David Warriner, Jr., son of David, Sen., was born in 1859; married Annie Mercer; resides in New Orleans, La.

Matthew Warriner, another son of David, Sen., was born in Liverpool, Eng., in 1860; married Emily Vogeville; resides in New Orleans, La.

Robert Arundale Warriner, fifth son of David, Sen., was born in Liverpool, Eng., in 1863; married Margaret Johnston; resides (1898) in New Orleans, La. He is a ship broker by occupation. His eldest son, George Douglas, was born in Minn. in 1888. Another, Alfred Louis, was born in New Orleans, La., in 1893.

Isabella Warriner, daughter of David, Sen., was born in 1865; married John Foss; resides in White Rock, Dakota.

George Warriner, sixth son of David, Sen., was born in 1867; married Eva Morgan; resides in White Rock, Dakota.

Annie Adaline Warriner, daughter of David, Sen., was born in 1871; married Charles F. Lewis; resides in White Rock, Dakota.

Robert Warriner, youngest son of William, and grandson of Matthew of Yorkshire, was born in Redmire, Yorkshire, Eng., in 1843, and died in Liverpool in 1891. He married Ellen Foster, and they had seven children, of whom the following are in America:

(1) Robert Henry Warriner, son of Robert, resides in New Orleans, La. He was born in 1869, in Liverpool, Eng.; prepared for Cambridge University at Wood's Academy, Everton, near Liverpool, and was prevented by severe sickness from pursuing a course at Cambridge. He was, when reported in 1893, chief clerk of West India & Pacific Steamship Co. He is a Wesleyan Methodist. Not married, 1893.

Ernest Christopher Warriner, another son of Robert, was

born in Liverpool, Eng., in 1871. His P. O., 1895, Carlyle Asso. N. W. T. His occupation is farming. His Christian denomination, Methodist. Not married in 1895.

John Foster Warriner, a son of Robert, was born in Liverpool, Eng., in 1875; came to America; resided, 1895, in White Rock, Dakota.

THOMAS WARRINER, OF ENGLAND, AND HIS DESCENDANTS IN AMERICA.

Thomas Warriner, a weaver; a Wesleyan Methodist; born in England; married Jane Aton; came to America; died near Colborne Harbor, Ont., Can., Oct. 20, 1852. His wife died at Haldemond, near Colborne Harbor, in 1839. Their three elder children, and perhaps the other three, were born in England.

(1) Sarah, the eldest, was born in Dockley, Yorkshire, Aug. 23, 1812; married Wm. Lobb, in Colborne, Ont., Aug. 3, 1830; died in Hastings, Ont., Nov. 27, 1888. She had four sons and four daughters. One of the sons is the Rev. R. J. Lobb, a Baptist minister of Allen, Mich. His only child, Lottie Luella (Mrs. Julius S. Nichols), died soon after her marriage. Sarah Warriner Lobb's daughter Mary (Mrs. C. Wilson) resides in "Vine Villa," Gault, Ont. She is the only living daughter. Two sons of Sarah Warriner Lobb, John Lobb and Thomas Lobb, reside in Hastings, Peterboro Co., Ont.

(2) Mary Warriner, second child of Thomas, married Hamlin Ives, and they had three sons and two daughters. She died in 1866.

(3) William Willis Warriner, third child of Thomas, was born Dec. 12, 1815; married Tryphena P., daughter of Sabin and Abigail Bailey, in Brasher Iron Works, N. Y., Sept. 1, 1839; went to Colborne Harbor, Ont., and died there Jan. 1, 1865. He was by occupation a moulder. His wife was born June 15, 1823, and died at Louisville Landing, St. Lawrence Co., N. Y. The children of Wm. Willis Warriner are as follows:

1. George Albert, first child of Wm. Willis Warriner, died young at Brasher Iron Works, N. Y.

2. William Willis, second child of Wm. Willis Warriner,

born in Montinette, Ont., Dec. 2, 1840. He left home in 1859; married, 1st, Rhoda C. Moore, May 3, 1864. She died May 15, 1880, and he married, 2d, Emily C. Calkins, Feb. 4, 1881. His residence is Monmouth, Ia. He was employed some time in U. S. mail service. His denomination is Methodist Episcopal. His 13 children (6 by the first wife and 7 by the second) were all born in Iowa, and all were living in 1894. They are as follows: (1) William Willis, born 1865, married Lizzie Gibson, and they have a daughter Marjorie; (2) Horace Clinton, born 1866, married Lizzie Piquot, and they have a son Howard; (3) Roscoe Henry, born 1869; (4) Evora Tryphena, born 1871; (5) Guy Amos, born 1873; (6) Arthur Owen, born 1875; (7) George Levi, born 1881; (8) Alvira Honore, born 1882; (9) Howard Elmer, born 1884; (10) Bertha Belle, born 1885; (11) Minnie Frances, born 1887; (12) Ruba Ella, born 1889; (13) Jessie Edith, born 1891.

3. Sarah Tryphena, third child of William Willis Warriner, was born May 2, 1843, and died at Alborne, Harborne Harbor, Ont., in 1846.

4. Thomas Henry, fourth child of Wm. Willis Warriner, was born in Brockville, Ont., Apr. 7, 1846; married Josephine Stone, and resided in Bay City, Mich. He was by occupation a marine engineer. He died at Gretna, La., Apr. 20, 1897. He was a soldier in one of the Ohio volunteer regiments in the Civil War. His two children were born in Bay City, Mich. (1) William Henry, born in 1878; married Jessie Quick, of Terry, Huron Co., Mich., Aug. 16, 1897; P. O., Bay City, Mich. (2) Elizabeth, born 1880; P. O., Bay City, Mich.

5. Ida Louisa, daughter of Wm. Willis Warriner, born in N. Y. State, Aug. 25, 1850; married, Dec. 8, 1869, to an English Canadian, Robert Smith. Her P. O., Monmouth, Ia. Children: George Albert, Charles Wesley, Anna Ida.

6. Albert Bailey, son of Wm. Willis Warriner, was born in Canada in 1854; married Emma Willard, and resides in the State of Nebraska.

7. Ada Abigail, daughter of Wm. Willis Warriner, was born in Colborne, Ont., Can.; married and lives in Grafton, Can.

8. Levi Sabin, son of William Willis Warriner

9. Anna M., daughter of Wm. Willis Warriner, was born in Colborne, Can., in 1862. P. O. address, Mrs. Anna M. McGee, Louisville Landing, St. Lawrence Co., N. Y.

10. Arthur Owen, son of Wm. Willis Warriner, was born in Colborne, Can., in 1864. P. O. Schaller, Ia.

Richard Warriner, a son of Thomas, of England, was born in Yorkshire; married Betsey Brown; died in Port Perry, Ont., in 1890, aged 71. Children of Richard Warriner: Wm. Wallace, Nettie, Sarah and Victoria.

William Wallace Warriner, son of Richard, resides in Port Perry, Ont. His daughter married Ephraim Card, of Wicklow, Ont.

Thomas Warriner, son of Thomas, of England, married but left no issue. He died in Colborne Harbor, Ont.

Elizabeth Warriner, daughter of Thomas, of England, married David Baker; died in Port Perry, Ont., Jan. 20, 1888, aged 64.

Thomas Warriner, 2d, of England, and His Descendants in America.

Three children of Thomas Warriner, of England (deceased), and Mary, his wife, are in America (1898): (1) James Warriner, machinist, Peacedale, R. I. His family consists of his wife, Elizabeth, and his son, Ernest Edward. (2) John William Warriner, of Providence, R. I. His family consists of wife, Mary Anne, and son, Thomas. (3) Mary Jane (Mrs. Gaskill).

William Warriner, of Canada, and Some of His Descendants.

William Warriner, a farmer, was born in England, probably. He died in Roaches Point, Ont., and is buried in Keswick. His children are as follows:

(1) Martha, married Richard Marvin. P. O., Keswick, Ont.

(2) William, married Anna Jilson. P. O., Keswick, Ont.
(3) Robert. P. O., Chicago, Ill.
(4) John, born in Ont. Can.; married Mary Amy Morton. He is a carpenter. His P. O. is Keswick, Ont. There his children were born. They are as follows: 1. Harty, born 1862; married M. Connell. 2. David Henry, married Mary A. Booiyton, Feb. 2, 1892; he is a civil engineer; his P. O. is Walkerville, Montana. 3. Mary Arvetia, born 1866. 4. John Wilmot, born 1870; P. O. Keswick, Ont. 5. Russell Fred, born 1879. 6. Hugh Ernest, born 1884.

FRANK TERRY WARRINER has been for years 2d mate on sail and steam ships. He was born in Cork, Ireland, and his last known address was 205 East street, San Francisco, Cal. He is a member of the Presbyterian church. His father, of St. Marysville, Cork, Ireland, a Presbyterian, and for a long time of the Cork, Black Rock and Passage Railway, was born in Birmingham, Eng., and was, before going to Ireland, a member of the Established Church. He married Susan Redman. They have seven children, of whom Frank Terry alone resides in the United States. He began going to sea when 14 years of age, and came to San Francisco in 1889.

A List of Persons Bearing the Family Name, Whose Lineage Has Not Been Ascertained.

Rev. Wm. Henry Warriner, A. B., B. D., 7 Shuter st., Montreal, Can., pastor of a Presbyterian church. He is a native of England.

Robert C. Warriner, Toronto, Can.

Thomas Warriner, Cleveland, O.

Robert J. Warriner, Richmond, Va.

John T. Warriner, Lynchburg, Va.

Miss Ruth Warriner, Lynchburg, Va.

Miss Maud S. Warriner, Lynchburg, Va.

Warren Warriner, Omaha, Neb.

George W. Warriner, Manchester, Va.

Wm. W. Warriner, Pittsburg, Pa.

E. P. Warriner, New York City, 1891.

M. J. Warriner, Richmond, Va.

R. C. Warriner, Portland, Ore.

Wm. A. Warriner, Richmond, Va.

Edward H. Warriner, Richmond, Va.

Eppy Warriner, Fort Worth, Tex.

Miss Laura A. Warriner, Fort Worth, Tex.

Miss Leona M. Warriner, Fort Worth, Tex.

Charles Warriner, Fall River, Mass.

James Warriner, Fall River, Mass.

James F. Warriner, Fall River, Mass.

Benjamin Howard Warriner, Dalesboro, Manitoba, Can.

William Thomas Warriner, M. D., Creeve, Va.

Charles Warriner, Gallipolis, O.

Francis Warriner, Greenwood, N. Y.

OBITUARY.

The Rev. Edwin Warriner, author of this " History of the Warriner Family," died August 29, 1898, — a few days only after the completion of his manuscript, — and now lies buried beside his two little boys in the beautiful cemetery at Huntington, Long Island.

He was born in Ellisburg, Jefferson county, N. Y., January 19, 1839. His father, Solomon J. Warriner, was a farmer in a small way, and also a local preacher of the Methodist denomination. His mother was a child of Irish Roman Catholic parents — John Gillen, a British soldier, and Margaret Paterson, his wife, a lady of high birth. They are said to have been clandestinely married, and to have fled to Canada, and from thence to the United States. One of their children — afterwards the mother of Edwin Warriner — was adopted by an excellent Protestant family, and was named Mary Ann Clark. She was one of the saints of the earth, greatly respected for her talents, and especially as a writer of pious odes. Like the ancient prophetess, the mother of Samuel, she dedicated her son Edwin at his birth to the Christian ministry. This he deemed his first " call." His mother's longing and hope, thus expressed, became in his own breast a passionate aspiration. While yet a child he manifested great interest in theological books, and at the age of seven years, in connection with the Sunday school he attended, he began to write and speak on religious subjects. At fifteen, in accordance with a vote of his class, he received a written license to exhort, signed by his pastor, Rev. Ebenezer Arnold, and the next day he was called to lead a meeting in a school house. Thereafter many school houses, camp grounds and churches became the scenes of his ministrations as " The Boy Preacher."

In his fifteenth year he began teaching in public schools, and in this way, and by the unsolicited aid of a wealthy friend, he was enabled to acquire a classical education, after which he pursued a theological course of study at the Biblical Institute at Concord, New Hampshire — graduating therefrom in 1861. Immediately thereafter he began preaching at South Meriden, afterwards called Hanover.

When the Civil War began there were encamped there for some time a battery and a regiment of cavalry, and many of the soldiers attended the services of the young pastor. So attracted were they by what they called the " dashing style " of his oratory, they presented a petition to Governor Buckingham, earnestly requesting him to appoint Mr. Warriner chaplain of their regiment. This was readily granted and accepted, and in a few days thereafter the young chaplain was off with the troopers to the seat of war.

For three years he served in this capacity amid the exciting scenes of the war, endearing himself to the soldiers with ever increasing affection and respect by his faithful ministrations, when suddenly he was prostrated by the incurable malady which became the bane of his life all through the remaining years of his long ministry. Yet, despite his physical infirmity, — which seems to have deepened his devotions and increased his zeal — few in his calling have accomplished so great and useful a work.

He was a man of far more than ordinary intellectual abilities, spiritual intuitions and sympathies — albeit his discourses were exceedingly plain and practical. His literary tastes and abilities were also of an exceptionally high order. His book entitled " Old Sand Street Church " (Brooklyn, N. Y.), is a work of great merit and of special local and denominational interest. The " Zion's Herald " pronounced it to be unequaled in fullness and interest by any local church history in Methodism — excepting only the history of " City Road Chapel " of London, England. Besides the History of the Warriner Family he left behind several manuscripts of great value.

E. A. WARRINER.

St. Paul's Church Rectory, Montrose, Pa.

INDEX OF WARRINERS.

[The figures refer to the Genealogical Numbers. The larger type denotes a biographical or descriptive sketch of the person bearing the number.]

A.

G.

H.

M.

T.

U.

V.

W.

Z.

II. INDEX OF NAMES OTHER THAN WARRINER.

(Figures refer to the pages.)

284

III. INDEX TO APPENDIX.